★

MORAL VICTORIES

Moral Victories

HOW ACTIVISTS PROVOKE MULTILATERAL ACTION

Susan Burgerman

CORNELL UNIVERSITY PRESS

ITHACA AND LONDON

First published 2001 by Cornell University Press

Printed in the United States of America

Library of Congress Cataloging-in-Publication Data

Burgerman, Susan, 1956-
    Moral victories : how activists provoke multilateral action / Susan Burgerman.
        p. cm.
    Includes bibliographical references and index.
    ISBN 0-8014-3860-8 (cloth : alk. paper)
    1. Human rights—Political aspects.   2. Human rights—International cooperation.   3. Human rights workers—Political activity.   4. Pressure groups.   5. Human rights—El Salvador.   6. Human rights—Guatemala. I. Title.
    JC571.B797 2000
    323'.097281—dc21

                                                                    2001000234

Cornell University Press strives to use environmentally responsible suppliers and materials to the fullest extent possible in the publishing of its books. Such materials include vegetable-based, low-VOC inks and acid-free papers that are recycled, totally chlorine-free, or partly composed of nonwood fibers. Books that bear the logo of the FSC (Forest Stewardship Council) use paper taken from forests that have been inspected and certified as meeting the highest standards for environmental and social responsibility. For further information, visit our website at www.cornellpress.cornell.edu.

Cloth printing   10   9   8   7   6   5   4   3   2   1

FSC   FSC Trademark © 1996 Forest Stewardship Council A.C.
SW-COC-098

★

Dedicated to two of the most principled people I know:
Arthur Burgerman
and
Marilyn Purdy Burgerman

CONTENTS

ACKNOWLEDGMENTS

This project has unfolded over a great deal of time—in many ways, over most of my life. I thank Douglas Chalmers and Hendrik Spruyt for their guidance and patience in helping me shape it into a coherent whole. Thanks to several other readers who took the time to read all or part and give valuable comments: John Ruggie, Margaret Crahan, Stephen Marks, David Holiday, Kathy Sikkink, Michael Barnett, and David Stoll.

I am deeply indebted to the Social Science Research Council's International Predissertation Fellowship Program, the Ford Foundation, and the American Council for Learned Societies for funding my field research. Columbia University's Graduate School of Arts and Sciences provided support while I was writing the first draft, and Columbia's Institute of Latin American Studies has been my institutional home in later stages. The original manuscript was shrunk, tightened, and focused by Roger Haydon, a most persistent (and nearly infallible) editor. As I haven't had the benefit of clerical or research assistance with this book, there is no one but myself to blame for any errors, omissions, misinterpreted events, misspellings, misattributions, and other horrors.

Many thanks to the staff of the National Security Archive, and especially Kate Doyle and Peter Kornbluh, for having made themselves, their expertise, and their hard-won documents available to the scholarly community. I also want to express my gratitude to the Washington Office on Latin America for the steady pipeline of information, and to the many people who granted me time and information in interviews. I thank Miklos Pinther and the attentive staff members at the United Nations Cartographic Section for having made ONUSAL and MINUGUA deployment maps available for use in this publication, and Denise Cook of the United Nations Department of Political Affairs for providing valuable comments and information on the Guatemalan negotiations. Finally, I am indebted to Ambassador Alvaro de Soto for being so very generous with his time and insight.

My field research was aided immeasurably by the advice of Gabriel Aguilera Peralta, Reed Brody, David Holiday, Frank LaRue, Luis Alberto Padilla and the staff of the Guatemalan Institute for International Relations and Peace Research (IRIPAZ), Mario Sandoval, Roger Plant, Paul Wee, the compañeros in ONUSAL and MINUGUA, Gladys Calderón, and the staff of *Inforpress* (among many others). The companionable sharing of information with several other foreign researchers, notably Geraldine McDonald, Stephen Baranyi, Emma Paterson of the BBC, and David Stoll, made life in the field considerably more pleasant. I also owe a great deal to the generous hospitality of Francisco and Herlinda Martínez. Back in New York, Katie Hite, J. Sammy Barkin, and Kate O'Neill gave ongoing encouragement and feedback.

On a more personal level, my lasting and most heartfelt thanks go to Colin Elman and Miriam Fendius Elman for having maintained life-support systems of all kinds while I was out of the country; to my parents, Marilyn and Arthur, for their bemused but unquestioning support; to my sister, Lauren Bergman, for her wicked sense of humor and relentless sense of priorities; to my friend Warren Bush, for helping me get to the finish line with sanity intact; and to my traveling companions Arjuna and Karna, for their unconditional love, often sorely tested.

★

MORAL VICTORIES

Why Do States Cooperate to Promote Human Rights?

Governments do not . . . commit themselves to a collaborative effort to promote the universal enjoyment of human rights if they adhere to the belief that every state has the sovereign right to treat its citizens as arbitrarily as it pleases.

—Inis Claude, *Swords Into Plowshares*

Large numbers of people in all regions of the world raise their voices in public outcry when they are presented with examples of official cruelty. They are not motivated to do so out of private interest or rational concerns. They are not always certain that their actions will accomplish the desired effect. They are aware that, despite a rapid growth in declarations and conventions, international human rights law contains all too few provisions on enforcement. Reference to human rights in official government pronouncements very often does not amount to a policy of observing those rights. For most of the twentieth century, states rarely cooperated to enforce moral values. Individuals who persist in campaigning against human rights violations do so because of deeply held, principled convictions that their pressure is morally necessary, whether or not it directly hinders or changes egregious behavior.

For its first fifty years, the United Nations human rights system was— and in many ways still is—inconsistent, weak, and politically motivated. The Universal Declaration of Human Rights was signed in December 1948, but the signatory states were free to apply or ignore its principles at will. The system lacked viable procedures for enforcement, and states had no substantial incentives to cooperate. Very occasionally, governments did collaborate to implement human rights law, applying sanctions or diplomatic pressure against violator states, but they did so only when it was in their strategic interest or because human rights "fit" with their founding myths or national identity.

Since 1989, however, the United Nations has undertaken several uncharacteristically effective activities that have linked international peace and security with the promotion of human rights. These efforts achieved considerable success in Namibia, El Salvador, and Guatemala, and some success in Cambodia and Haiti. UN-mediated negotiations to end civil wars in El Salvador and Guatemala led to the deployment of human rights missions in which international observers operated freely on national territory over a period of several years. These UN missions established or strengthened institutions that undergird the rule of law. They drafted reforms of judicial and security institutions and oversaw their implementation, to ensure long-term conformity with international standards on human rights. In these countries, as a result, respect for the rights of the person is now becoming a normal part of state-society relations.

How did the UN system evolve from nonbinding statements of opprobrium to intrusive "armies" of human rights observers? During the formative years, human rights principles were invariably subordinated to the principle of state sovereignty. In the mid-1970s, the U.S. Congress began to impose human rights conditions on foreign assistance. Since that time, most members of the international community have come to recognize that human rights are a legitimate political issue. The nearly universal accession of states to core international rights conventions indicates this increasing acceptance of human rights in world politics. And the recent evidence tells us that decision makers consider multilateral human rights *intervention* to be within the realm of actions that can appropriately be taken by international agents, at least under certain conditions.

The trend toward multilateral protection of human rights relies on the work of individuals who are motivated by and who organize around their moral convictions. Pressure from advocates has given states an incentive to intervene where otherwise they might have confined themselves to quiet diplomacy. A growing network of advocates, acting within and beyond their home countries, has been critical in bringing warring parties to the negotiating table, in placing human rights at the top of negotiating agendas, and in monitoring compliance with peace accords. Domestic activists in all parts of the world have publicized their cases before international forums, in particular the UN Commission on Human Rights, its regional analogues, and the U.S. Congress. Foreign nongovernmental and, occasionally, governmental actors have installed themselves as quasi-members of national political systems, providing some level of protection to vulnerable populations when their own state becomes a predator. These intersecting levels of advocacy form a transnational human rights network—a network that has gained access to global institutional channels and to regional judicial bodies in the European and inter-American systems.

We will see how the human rights regime has evolved to become more effective in the recent history of two countries, El Salvador and Guatemala. El Salvador and Guatemala provide excellent laboratories for studying the effects of human rights mobilization. Both states were denounced by international organizations. Other states pressured the governments and militaries of both countries to curtail their abusive activities, and in the early 1980s, both nations were placed under the scrutiny of special rapporteurs from the UN Human Rights Commission. None of these efforts succeeded perceptibly before the UN-mediated negotiations that produced multidimensional peacekeeping and human rights operations—the UN Observer Mission in El Salvador (ONUSAL), in July 1991–April 1995, and the UN Mission in Guatemala (MINUGUA), from November 1994.

Recent Cambodian history corroborates the notion that there is an evolutionary aspect to UN human rights protection. The international community maintained a deafening silence in response to the atrocities of the mid-1970s. With the end of the cold war, however, came a peace accord negotiated under the auspices of the five permanent members of the Security Council, which also established a civilian peacekeeping operation known as the UN Transitional Authority in Cambodia (UNTAC, 1991–1993). UNTAC's political reforms proved a failure, and the coalition government it left behind quickly degenerated. Despite these failures, the Cambodian example shows that by 1991, human rights monitoring and education were considered appropriate components of peacekeeping and necessary components of a lasting peace. What appeared revolutionary in El Salvador, and politically risky in Cambodia, would look like common sense by the time international attention focused on Bosnia and East Timor.

Before the new generation of "peacebuilding" operations, no part of the United Nations' human rights bureaucracy had had the capacity to enforce conventions or to impose binding sanctions on violating states. But something very suggestive of human rights enforcement did take place in the 1990s, in El Salvador, Guatemala, Namibia, Haiti, and Cambodia. I do not claim that because ethical concerns have gained greater legitimacy in international politics, the system will necessarily intervene where needed. In truly hard cases, the enforcement of human rights principles will not be politically or militarily feasible. But under certain circumstances the international community can now enforce human rights. My aim in this book is to explain what those circumstances are.

A FRAMEWORK FOR COMPLIANCE WITH THE HUMAN RIGHTS REGIME

In the chapters to follow I view the historical narratives of international enforcement of human rights through the interpretive lens of transnational network activism. This framework is interpretive; it supplies an alternative means of organizing the historical data. I believe that changes in the normative context of international relations have, at different stages, generated sanctioning mechanisms of varying degrees of coerciveness to protect citizens from their own governments. These mechanisms can be deployed under certain enabling conditions in international politics and in the violator state's ruling coalition, *and* if a network of transnational advocates mobilizes around the issue.[1] These are necessary but not sufficient conditions; the absence of one or more can explain non-compliance with human rights law, but no single condition can alone explain either compliance or noncompliance. Here are the propositions, formulated as an interacting set of necessary conditions in both international and domestic contexts.

Proposition I: Changes in global norms, resulting from the evolution of international human rights institutions, caused human rights to be incorporated over time as a legitimate concern in international politics.

Proposition II: If a major power maintains overriding security or economic interests in the target state, it can inhibit the enforcement of human rights principles and agreements.

Proposition III: Activism on the part of the transnational human rights network provides states with incentives to promote human rights norms by exerting pressure and thus raising the target state's costs of repression.

Proposition IV: A violator state will comply with human rights norms only if a key element of its domestic political elite, one capable of exerting its authority over armed elements, perceives itself to be vulnerable to human rights condemnation or has concern for its country's international reputation as a violator state.

Proposition V: Organized local members of the human rights network are necessary to keep their issues on the international agenda and to provide information to international allies.

Outcome: The interplay of the above conditions will determine the extent to which the international community responds to violations by employing sanctioning mechanisms of the international human rights regime. The consistency and intrusiveness of the mechanism(s) employed will in turn determine the degree of a state's compliance in response to pressure.

I. The International Human Rights Regime and the Moral Incentive

The first condition is the transformation that has taken place since the end of World War II in the normative domain of international politics. The past fifty years has witnessed an evolutionary trend to institutionalize human rights norms in international law and politics. This in turn has resulted in a growing recognition of the "appropriateness" of outside intervention to enforce compliance. I view this process as evolutionary because the direction and pace of change have been channeled by historical events such as the Nuremburg trials and the 1973 military coup in Chile, and by the sea change in U.S. foreign policy following Watergate.

The concept of an international regime is a useful way to approach this process.[2] By *international human rights regime,* I am referring to the system of human rights declarations, covenants, conventions, and protocols under the United Nations and regional international organizations, and the institutions established to promote them. Cooperation among states participating in this regime rests on such intangible benefits as mutual adherence to the norms of an international community, whereas the compliance of target states rests on incentives that are both tangible (such as linkage by cooperating states to economic assistance) and intangible (such as domestic and international legitimacy). The premise guiding this book is that states cooperate with a regime that is based on moral or ethical principles—such as the human rights regime—when decision makers begin to incorporate the regime's norms into their conceptions of national identity or interest.[3] This perceptual shift is brought about through the mobilizing efforts of a transnational network of activists.

Otherwise, states have no obvious incentives to cooperate with the institutions of the human rights regime. Violations take place within the offender's domestic jurisdiction. Except in more extreme circumstances, where violations result in massive migration, the problem does not cross borders, and response by other states is, in public discourse, motivated by some version of moral outrage rather than by material interest. Further, the offending party is not a private party such as a slave trader, counterfeiter, or drug trafficker but rather is the government itself.[4] In cases of pollution caused by state industries, or unfair trading practices of state-owned enterprises, other states may be motivated to sanction the offender to protect their own interests. However, where the offending party is a state and the negative consequences to other states are negligible, there is no clear motive for states to cooperate in sanctions.

The key to understanding the motivation to participate in a human rights regime is that national interests change and are measured not only in terms of security and economic interests. Human rights concerns have emerged in states' calculations of interests when the perception of national identity changes to incorporate them as important values. The British government's active promotion of the abolition of the slave trade in the nineteenth century is often cited as the first example of a state incorporating moral principles into a calculation of its national interest.[5] Since the end of World War II, the foreign policies of most major industrialized states have to a greater or lesser degree incorporated such principles in their projections of the national interest, although ordinarily they subordinate moral to material interests when the two sets of values come into direct competition.

Cooperation with a regime based on moral principles depends on the willingness of cooperative states—those states that consider such principles to be important values and in their national interest—to sanction abusive states through linkages to other issues. Such linkages are not always readily available, however. Where there are clear linkages to be made, for example with preferential trade status, lending, or foreign assistance, they often entail competing values, leaving the state's policymakers to decide between an intangible interest such as moral principle, and material benefits such as expanding foreign markets. In a more extreme case, the conflict could be between moral outrage and a reluctance to expend human and material resources because neither the general public nor decision makers are convinced that the lives of the victims are worth the expense. In Rwanda in 1994, the massacre of more than half a million people went unchecked by the international community, which for more than a month was treated to broadcast images of atrocities that might have been prevented had competing values not gotten in the way.

The U.S. State Department's Bureau of Human Rights and Humanitarian Affairs found itself caught in a less severe but equally obdurate dilemma of competing values in 1979. Bureau staff were attempting to use human rights provisions in Export-Import Bank legislation to pressure the Argentine government to permit an Inter-American Commission on-site inspection of clandestine prisons. In recommending that an Eximbank loan for hydroplant construction be denied, they were met by equal and opposite pressure from U.S. contractors who stood to profit from the project.[6] On that occasion, as on many others, human rights lost and commerce won.

The reality of the human rights regime is that implementation has historically been weak and inconsistent because it is voluntary. Presidents and prime ministers are more than willing to endorse a declaratory regime that entails little or no cost. Strengthening the regime to include even monitoring instruments has been an arduous process, as any advocate who has been involved can attest. Given the difficulties of overcoming states' reluctance to be criticized or to criticize each other publicly, it would seem that a regime's chances of developing mechanisms for enforcement are slim. Very few human rights "laws" include mandatory sanctioning mechanisms, and these refer to judgments by regional human rights courts.

With all this in mind, how can we discuss enforcement of international human rights agreements? The human rights regime originated in the shared values and beliefs of those who designed the cooperative institutions of the postwar system. Although the principal architects of the UN system as a whole were government representatives, the human rights regime owes its existence to a lobby comprising religious, labor, and peace activists. Next, state decision makers have an interest in maintaining the regime because these shared values constitute a "moral interdependence" among states interested in upholding the orderly system characterized as an international community.[7] Although human rights institutions have no power to enforce sanctions, they are influential because ultimately most decision makers are sensitive to the adverse effects of violation—to the costs of a damaged reputation. The bad publicity generated by human rights activists can destabilize trade and diplomatic relations and, moreover, does damage to the violating state's prestige.

While not exactly based on moral values, such concerns for reputation have both normative and material motivation—a mixture of the need for approval and acceptance in a community of states bound by shared values and the material influence that more powerful states can bring to bear on the offender. Massive public outcry will precipitate or combine with assertive action on the part of cooperating states to delegitimize violators both domestically and diplomatically, creating an environment difficult for offenders to ignore. In this respect, values and interests are not dichotomous; reputational concerns lead to change in a violator state's behavior when linked to tangible political or economic sanctions. In this manner, the boycotts imposed on apartheid South Africa reflected the weight of international public opinion, as mobilized by activists, and the perceived existence of an international society whose principles it is risky to violate.

On a definitional note, when discussing international human rights principles, I am limiting the scope to those principles embodied in international treaties.[8] I have further narrowed the scope to those rights variously referred to as "rights of the person," "political and civil rights," "priority rights," "first-generation rights," or, because they prohibit the state from committing certain acts, "negative rights." In this book, I directly address the economic, social, cultural, or communal rights also found in international instruments only where they appear in negotiations or peace accords. I justify taking this narrow approach first, because the historical context of the cases is that of extreme repression, political violence, and civil war. Second, because the nature of state responsibility is different with respect to violations of political/civil rights and rights of the person, which have to do with acts committed, and of economic, social, and cultural rights, which are sins of omission and not amenable to the kind of international pressure under examination.[9] Third, because a primary focus of this book is the evolution of UN human rights missions, whose ability to promote social, economic, and cultural rights depends on the nature of accords struck by negotiators and is limited by time. The process of achieving socioeconomic justice can begin under international observation, but a human rights mission is not a long-term solution for socioeconomic or communal rights.

II. State Power and Human Rights Enforcement

The second element is whether or not a dominant state has an interest in inhibiting cooperation with and enforcement of human rights norms. If a major power continues to support a violator state or opposes international enforcement, the target government can remain impervious to pressure indefinitely. The international political position and relative strength of both participating and target states are important factors in determining whether multilateral action can be mobilized. Action taken to enforce human rights can be effectively blocked, for example, by a permanent member of the UN Security Council, as when in mid-1996 China vetoed the extension of the UN mission in Haiti to protest the Haitian government's recognition of Taiwan and, later, threatened to do the same for the UN mission in Guatemala. Similarly, the Carter administration's support for sanctions against the Argentine military dictatorship foundered on its need to gain Argentina's cooperation with the Soviet grain embargo. In recent years, a concerted international effort to pressure the Colombian military to improve its human rights record has been confounded to an extent by the increasing levels of U.S. lethal aid officially intended for counternarcotics operations.

Furthermore, the target state's position in international politics—its alliances, size, and relative power—partly determines its vulnerability to pressure from other states. In the simplest scenario, a large and powerful state will be capable of resisting pressure, provided that no important elements in its domestic ruling coalition develop a concern for the costs of continued repression to the state's international prestige. China is an obvious example: it is a nuclear state, resource-wealthy, a regional hegemon with a vast potential domestic market and veto power in the Security Council. Despite sporadic attempts by the United States to use preferential trade status as leverage, China has resisted such efforts, which invariably collapse under pressure from U.S. business interests. Even in the case of China, there are indications that sustained pressure can produce rhetorical or limited change, as when the government agreed to ratify the International Covenants and to permit monitors from the International Committee of the Red Cross access to prisons, in exchange for a U.S. agreement not to press for a condemnatory resolution at the 1997 UN Human Rights Commission meeting.[10] The People's Republic of China campaigned hard and unsuccessfully for several years to avoid UN condemnation, demonstrating that even a permanent member of the Security Council considers widespread diplomatic criticism to be meaningful. But the Chinese government continues nevertheless to imprison political prisoners without an open trial, in breach of its obligations under the International Covenant for Civil and Political Rights, because it can do so with impunity. There is not much other states can do in such a case, except to recognize that the threat of UN condemnation produces greater results than unilateral, and especially noncredible, threats.

III. The Transnational Human Rights Network and the Mobilization of Shame

The third piece of this story is the level of continuous pressure from a network of activists who provide governments with both the material and the intangible incentives to cooperate in a regime based on moral principles. The measure of human rights activism during a given period, its decibel level so to speak, is indicated by a range of activities including publicity campaigns, lobbying, petitions before international bodies, and public protest. Without pressure from organized and concerned individuals, government decision makers have little motivation to sanction violators, and without the cooperation of at least some states who are engaged in commercial or security relations with the target state, the threat to its reputation will hold little weight. In effect, human rights activists are the "carriers" of the principles embodied by international law.

To recognize the centrality of nonstate actors in mobilizing an international response to human rights violations is certainly not to dismiss the state's role. States are the accountable parties in cases of such violations, and positive change in violator behavior rarely occurs absent serious, consistent pressure from cooperating states. Nonetheless, highlighting the role of nonstate actors allows us to examine how advocates both within and outside of the political system, mobilized around moral issues, can influence policy. The "transnational moral entrepreneurs" of the human rights network are able to motivate governments to cooperate with the international regime's sanctioning mechanisms. They do so by strategically appealing to mass audiences and identifying available points of leverage.[11]

The Latin America human rights network originated with the 1973 military coup in Chile. Global reaction to General Pinochet's brutality produced a unique moment of tacit cooperation between the United States and the Soviet Union. This enabled the UN Commission on

Human Rights to overcome the internal political machinations that had in the past (and would in the future) prevent it from criticizing violators. An ad hoc working group was assigned to investigate allegations of abuse, an investigation that included an on-site visit, thus establishing a precedent for future special rapporteurs. During this period, church-based and political-activist organizations in the United States and Europe lobbied their governments and international organizations on behalf of Chilean, then Uruguayan, political prisoners, Bolivian and Brazilian peasants, and the relatives of disappeared Argentines. Human rights organizations, for the most part of recent vintage, were able to direct their efforts through a number of new or newly vitalized institutional channels: US State Department foreign assistance legislation, more aggressive reporting by the Inter-American Commission on Human Rights, and UN reporting and investigation mechanisms.

It was in response to conditions typified by Chile under the military regime that U.S. and European human rights organizations developed a hierarchy of rights that quickly became the consensus approach. Dictated by the emergency conditions under severely repressive regimes, "rights of the person"— freedom from torture, arbitrary detention, disappearance, and extrajudicial killing, freedom of expression, association, and movement—became the "priority rights" now referred to in the mandates of UN human rights missions.[12] This category of rights protecting the individual's personal security were, under the circumstances, logically prior to economic, social, and community rights. They were also more amenable to dramatic presentation for mobilization purposes, and for appealing to governmental and intergovernmental agencies for support. Much later, the initial focus on liberal individual rights of the person, driven as it was by strategic necessity and the historical context, was increasingly challenged once the problem of widespread state terror had dissipated.

Church-affiliated organizations took the lead during the early period, lending the prestige of their respective institutions to efforts on behalf of human rights.[13] The U.S. Catholic Conference (USCC) and National Council of Churches (NCC) collected information provided to them by missionaries and by local organizations, for example in Chile by the Vicaría de Solidaridad. They developed this information into individual case dossiers, which were submitted to the Inter-American Commission on Human Rights and to the UN Human Rights Commission. In 1974, another group of primarily Protestant churches, perceiving the need for a formal organization to lobby U.S. foreign policymakers after the

Pinochet coup, formed the Washington Office on Latin America (WOLA).[14] Organized church activists were joined by attorneys in 1978, when the International League for Human Rights and the Council of New York Law Associates jointly created the Lawyers' Committee for Human Rights (LCHR).

The galvanizing moment of the Chilean coup converged in Washington with another benchmark, the arrival of the post-Watergate generation in Congress. Cutting military assistance to Latin American dictators in order to improve an international reputation gravely tarnished by the war in Vietnam became a pressing issue for the new congressional activists. To achieve this objective, members of Congress had to rely on nongovernmental organizations for expertise and for information on individual countries. WOLA staff members drafted the Harkin Amendment (Section 116a of the Foreign Assistance Act), which places restrictions on US economic assistance to gross and consistent violators of human rights. WOLA staff were involved in every congressional initiative involving human rights in the mid- to late-1970s, including Section 660 of the Foreign Assistance Act, which banned all support for prisons, police, or other law enforcement forces outside of the United States.

The State Department's Bureau of Human Rights and Humanitarian Affairs was created as one of these legislative initiatives. In November 1976, the head of the bureau was elevated from coordinator to assistant secretary of state; under the Carter administration, the bureau's profile rose considerably and, with it, that of the network of human rights activists in Washington. As one former House staffer noted, "There was a sense that a small group of people, given that particular moment in history—after the Church Commission [on covert operations] and especially after Vietnam—and given a friendly President and Congress, could accomplish a lot."[15]

Several Latin American opposition groups kept representatives or even offices in Washington and became integral units of the transnational network. For example, Guatemalan labor attorney Frank LaRue, who was forced into exile in 1981 and took up residence in Washington, worked closely with WOLA and the Congressional Commission on U.S.–Central American Relations through the 1980s. In 1982, he and other political exiles formed the Representation of the Guatemalan Opposition (RUOG) to lobby the UN General Assembly to pass a resolution condemning the contemporary wave of massacres. From 1982 until 1986, RUOG attended every annual meeting of the UN Human Rights Commission, the Subcommission on the Prevention of Discrimination, and the General Assembly, managing to obtain a resolution from each body at every meeting. Intensive networking continued through the 1980s; in 1989, LaRue established the Center for Legal Action and Human Rights (CALDH), originally to file cases with the Inter-American Commission. CALDH operated out of Washington, as part of a working group of human rights organizations utilizing the Inter-American protection system, meeting regularly with Americas Watch, LCHR, the Center for Justice and International Law (CEJIL), and the International Human Rights Law Group.[16]

The international human rights network naturally included organizations within Latin America. Local human rights or victims' groups supplied the majority of the network's information, which was then used to lobby Congress or the UN Commission, or to present cases before the Inter-American Commission. The principal Latin American institutions of the network were established in the mid-to late-1970s: the Vicaría de Solidaridad (Chile), the Centro de Estudios Legales y Sociales (CELS, in Argentina, whose membership included the Mothers of the Plaza de Mayo), the Servicio de Paz y Justicia (SERPAJ), and the Federación de Familiares de Desaparecidos y Detenidos por Razones Políticas (FEDE-FAM, which integrated organizations for the disappeared in several Latin American countries). Finally, the Inter-American Institute of Human Rights (IIDH), founded in 1980 and located in San José, Costa Rica, has operated as clearinghouse for human rights organizations interacting with the Organization of American States (OAS).

The strategic focus of many international human rights organizations working on Central America was on U.S. congressional policy. The United States was the major benefactor of Central American governments (or, in the case of Sandinista Nicaragua, of their armed opposition), and congressional appropriations therefore represented the most obvious leverage point for pressuring these governments. This strategy was not unanimous; as mentioned previously, several organizations lobbied OAS and the United Nations. Amnesty International and the Lawyers' Committee had permanent UN observer status and maintained ongoing relations with UN human rights agencies and experts. In general terms, nongovernmental organizations located in Washington (WOLA and the Central America Working Group, for example) focused on US government policy as a formal part of their mandate; those in New York and Europe looked as much or more toward the UN Commission and treaty bodies, as well as other multilateral agencies, according to tactical needs. Because of the seeming parochialism of Washington-based NGOs, some advocacy groups preferred not to open an office in the capital.

Despite the evident weakness of UN human rights mechanisms, Michael Posner, director of the Lawyers' Committee, views efforts to lobby the United Nations as important, especially in light of the previous disjuncture between human rights debates in the United States and those in Europe and the rest of the world. He notes that the human rights discussions that took place within UN organizations and agencies led eventually to the participation of other countries in efforts to negotiate peace agreements for Central America:

> The Spanish government, some of the other Latin American governments—Venezuela, Colombia, Mexico—were more influenced by the UN debate, because that's where they had a role to play. They had no role to play when the US Congress was fighting with itself and fighting with the administration. . . . So you need to multilateralize the human rights discussion. And once you decide that, you sort of plod along even if the results aren't spectacular.[17]

Especially with regard to El Salvador, the human rights network relied heavily on the leverage provided by the polarization of U.S. foreign policy during the Reagan years, and on the pressure points furnished by the administration's requests for military appropriations. Threats by Congress to cut off military aid helped mobilize human rights groups and also had an effect on the Salvadoran military, albeit a limited and almost entirely superficial one in most instances. At the very least, the Central Intelligence Agency considered activists' exposure of human rights violations to be an effective tool for influencing policy. In a 1985 analysis of Salvadoran death squad operations, the Directorate of Intelligence noted:

> Some extreme rightists probably concluded that . . . at least a temporary stand-down in terrorist activities would be required to direct the attention of the US administration away from the issue of human rights. Almost certainly, in our view, the US Congressional focus on political violence in El Salvador and the need for continued US military and economic aid provided extreme rightists additional incentives to curtail terrorist operations.[18]

Nonstate actors will use whatever leverage points and powerful allies they can access. Given the United States' historical role as regional hegemon, and given the Nicaraguan contras' and Salvadoran military's dependence U.S. material aid and training, most of the leverage available for human rights activists working on Central America was to be found among sympathetic members of the US Congress. It was therefore predictable that activists should turn to Congress for support.[19]

The Salvadoran and Guatemalan peace processes developed against this background of a burgeoning transnational network, which mobilized shame and applied pressure at available leverage points, siphoned information out of target states, and furnished moral and material support—and, at times, physical protection—to their local counterparts. All this was possible because the transnational network had linkages varying in type and strength, with dense communication among them. I hope that members of the Central America human rights network will recognize at least a part of their history in this anecdotal account. Understandably, what hindsight reveals to have been an organized and purposive endeavor was perceived at the time to be a series of ad hoc reactions to immediate needs. Nevertheless, this brief background sketch reveals that, in the aggregate, what appeared then as an assemblage of individuals with varying interests, constituencies, strategies, and resources, not only shared an overriding goal and set of principles but also possessed the characteristics of and behaved like a transnational network.

IV. International Reputation and Domestic Elites

The fourth element is the members of a target government's ruling elite that are both concerned with improving the government's international reputation as an egregious violator of human rights and are capable of controlling the state's coercive forces. The effectiveness of international and nongovernmental organizations in promoting human rights is largely based on political and economic elites' sensitivity to the delegitimizing effects of a damaged international image, and the belief that a bad reputation may somehow result in sanctioning by other states and in a weakened position at home.

The threat of international isolation is less compelling where the state is already isolated, particularly if the leadership prefers economic and military autarky to cooperation. A poor and peripheral state with an entrenched, "anti-social" leadership (such as North Korea) could prove less vulnerable to network pressure than one with a more central position in international politics and a more pragmatic leadership, which would be more likely to make tactical concessions in the face of pressure.[20] Take, for example, the current Burmese military government, the Guatemalan military government of the late 1970s through mid-1980s, and the leaders of the military coup that ousted Haitian president Jean-Bertrand Aristide. In each instance, the governing elites remained intransigent and withstood intense international pressure to reform human rights practices—despite severe economic damage, in the case of Haiti. Even civilian elites concerned about reputation will be powerless to implement reforms if they lack the ability to control the military. In the case of Guatemala, a government sensitive to human rights could only begin to cooperate once the military high command had developed fears that its international image might be damaged.

These examples indicate that a state's vulnerability to network pressure has as much to do with decision makers' perceptions of the value for diplomatic and domestic legitimacy of its international reputation, as with the objective availability of points of leverage. The seventeen-year-long economic boycott of South Africa is proof that a state can resist international pressure for a very long time, as long as the ruling coalition does not consider its pariah status to be prohibitively costly. Therefore, if human rights pressure is to succeed, powerful decision makers within the target-state apparatus must have some concern for international reputation, whether for normative or material reasons.

V. The Importance of Organized Local Activists

The fifth proposition refers to local human rights activists who must be in place to relay information to their international allies and be sufficiently vocal to make their concerns part of the international agenda.[21] Domestic organizations are essential because, first, given the volume of claims competing for the international community's attention, more organized voices stand a greater chance of being heard. Second, international organizations require local information, which only on-site monitors can provide. Third, domestic organizations provide their transnational counterparts with a channel into the national political arena, a justification (invitation) for meddling in national affairs, and in many cases a base of operations. Although not legitimately a human rights organization, the Mexican Zapatista Liberation Army (EZLN) is the paramount example of a domestic opposition with very effective marketing skills. The EZLN's leadership excels at making use of the international media and of new technologies, such as the World Wide Web, to place its demands before an international audience.

The size of a domestic network does not necessarily determine its importance, though in certain cases sheer numbers may lend a movement greater legitimacy in international public opinion. The Chinese government has effectively silenced all but a few advocates for democracy. These few are nevertheless articulate and highly visible, and they have an inversely large and correspondingly vocal network of international support. Still, the example of China's democracy movement demonstrates that ultimately, however vocal and organized the domestic human rights community, a violator state can remain obdurate in the face of international moral pressure for a long time in the absence of a key faction in the ruling elite with an overriding concern for international reputation.

In the case of the 1975–76 Khmer Rouge massacres, the inaction and apathy of international organizations and other states is partly explained by the absence of domestic human rights organizations. Because no activists were in place who could raise the alarm and provide evidence of atrocities, the torture, assassination, enslavement, and starvation of what scholars now estimate to have been close to two million Cambodians went largely unheralded by international media. The United Nations did not officially comment on the situation until March 1978. At that time, the Human Rights Commission discussed the case at its annual meeting, with the sole result that the commission requested the Subcommission on the Prevention of Discrimination and Protection of Minorities to consider the problem. Under ECOSOC Resolution 1503 (1970) procedures, the subcommission debates an issue and forwards its recommendations to a five-member working group of the commission for vetting. The commission then decides whether to dismiss the case, consider it further at its next session, study the situation, or (given the target state's consent) establish an ad hoc investigative committee of independent experts.[22] During 1978, governmental and nongovernmental organizations managed to submit information to the subcommission, which then, in what can only be described as a world-class case of far too little and far too late, moved to continue its investigation. The commission itself issued no condemnation. It finally received a formal report of violations in January 1979, after the Vietnamese invasion and after the Khmer Rouge government had been overthrown.

An Amnesty International report attributes the United Nations' inaction to a lack of timely information and the length of time it took for details of the killings to leak out of the country.[23] It also cites the lack of impartial investigations by multilateral or nongovernmental agencies. Hence, the human rights network was not able to obtain and disseminate information, to interview survivors and refugees, or to mobilize international pressure. Without domestic organizations, international networkers had no contacts. Without the information, publicity, and pressure that activists could have generated, the gears of the human rights regime could not turn in a timely fashion, and the situation went unchecked.

Whether the commission could have intervened to the extent of issuing a condemnation or assigning a rapporteur, or whether any such initiative would have been quashed by allied states, specifically by China, is another question. The UN Commission on Human Rights, the bureaucratic center of the global regime, was incapable of generating a timely response of any sort. Although condemnation would probably not have altered the course of events, that the international community was incapable of producing even a minimal response (in addition to leaving a large black mark on the United Nations' human rights record) exemplifies how vital are these networks of nonstate actors.

Mechanisms for Ensuring Compliance

Taken together, the five conditions will interact to produce (a) action of some sort by the international community in response to systematic violations of human rights; (b) some degree of target-state compliance. One could conceive of a scale of coerciveness that extends from publication of government reports to condemnatory resolutions by intergovernmental bodies, voluntary international boycotts, and annual on-site investigative missions from UN representatives, with "enforcement action" at the most coercive end of the scale. A multilateral peacebuilding mission with a mandate to verify human rights conditions and reform state practices is the most recently developed and, to date, the most effective point on that scale.

The evolution of international laws on human rights relied to a great extent on a diplomatic distinction between enforcement and implementation or recommendation. Here, I use the term *enforcement* more broadly than in its accepted legal sense.[24] With respect to international law, enforcement action only refers to the UN Charter's Chapter VII (on forcible, possibly military, intervention to restore international peace and security) operations. In this book, the term *human rights enforcement* may connote highly intrusive action that is technically short of enforcement or intervention but is a great deal more forcible than other available remedies, such as investigatory missions. Enforcement is distinct from other degrees of pressure in that it involves binding international decisions and either military or nonmilitary coercion. For my proposed scale of coerciveness, other forms of sanctioning, such as bilateral trade restrictions, are neither binding nor interventionary.

At lower levels on the coerciveness scale, activists have been successful in placing human rights issues on the international agenda, in generating publicity about violations, and in defining issues so as to maximize the capacity to mobilize support. They lobby decision makers to pressure target governments, identify points of leverage, and help draft legislative reforms designed to align states more closely with the human rights regime, and continually hold political leaders accountable.

It is widely assumed that bilateral pressure from a dominant state is the most effective means of bringing about compliance with human rights law (or, at the least, that nothing happens unless the United States intervenes). However, little empirical evidence supports that assumption. Nor should human rights promotion have to rely on the whims of individual states, first and foremost because the notion of coercive enforcement of human rights by a hegemonic state, acting as a global police force, has dangerous implications. Furthermore, an individual state's human rights policy will vary, depending on whether the administration or executive in power is genuinely committed to human rights principles. Bilateral pressure will also be applied inconsistently, according to whether the pressuring state has competing interests in the target state. For example, the United States has responded to the repression of civil and political rights in Cuba with punishing economic sanctions, to genocide in Rwanda with inaction, and to the arbitrary arrest and imprisonment of political dissenters in China with sporadic outbursts of scolding—which, however inconsistent, the Chinese government nevertheless finds highly offensive.

Stronger multilateral instruments would make it possible to depoliticize enforcement of human rights laws and to make enforcement more consistent.[25] U.S. State Department officials arrived at a similar conclusion in supporting the formation of the UN Working Group on Disappearances in 1980. According to one Bureau of Human Rights and Humanitarian Affairs staffer, the State Department wanted a UN mechanism to handle the problem of disappearances, first because target governments are more likely to cooperate with a multilateral organization of which they are members, rather than appear to submit to bilateral pressure. Second, because it was unlikely that future U.S. administrations would want to "invest the same amount of political capital" on human rights issues as had the Carter government.[26]

United Nations or regional investigative missions are at an intermediate stage of the continuum of enforcement. Under ECOSOC resolution 1503 procedures (described earlier in this chapter), the UN Commission may deploy special rapporteurs, special representatives, or independent experts to countries judged to be consistent and grievous offenders.[27] These are fact-finding missions, tasked to investigate, produce reports, and give opinions and recommendations. Since 1978, UN experts have been sent to an array of states including Afghanistan, Bolivia, Cambodia, Chile, Cuba, El Salvador, Guatemala, Haiti, Iran, Iraq, Myanmar, and Zaire. Similarly, the Inter-American Commission on Human Rights investigates and establishes the receivability of individual petitions sent to the Inter-American Court of Human Rights. Election monitoring missions, whether representing international organizations, governments, or private institutions, are also included in this category.

Representatives of other states or intergovernmental bodies enter a country for a short period of time, often on an annual basis, have reasonably broad access to government installations and to private citizens, but exercise no binding authority. The pressure to accept visits by UN experts increases the visibility of the violator state and highlights its accountability to the relevant human rights agreements. A UN representative is more likely to gain access to military bases and prisons than are NGOs (with the exception of the International Committee of the Red Cross). However, this form of pressure is not consistently effective. Governments are expected but not bound to give serious attention to the experts' findings. Specific recommendations may be complied with: in July 1995, Guatemala's president announced that he was terminating the notoriously abusive institution of military commissioners, at the strong recommendation of the UN Special Expert. Or they may be ignored, without fear of sanctions. Further, the stringency of an expert's report will depend on that individual's perspective and willingness to criticize a host government.[28]

Over the past decade and in an ad hoc manner, the UN human rights system has developed a new channel for multilateral action that can be used where gross and systematic violations coincide with armed civil conflict (which is often the case). This is the "new generation" of peacekeeping or peacebuilding operations that have a human rights division at their core.[29] In addition to more traditional activities involving disarmament and demobilization, they monitor and protect civilians for the duration of the mission and assist in the implementation of institutional reforms to help ensure continued human rights protection after their mandate ends.

The phenomenon is, indeed, new: a multilateral operation on national territory, with a mandate to verify and enforce compliance with human rights agreements, and staffed overwhelmingly by members of the transnational human rights network. Verification personnel are often recruited directly from nongovernmental organizations, and have a record of human rights activism. According to the director of the Human Rights Division of the UN Observer Mission in El Salvador, the majority of division staffers came from human rights NGOs, including the Andean Commission of Jurists and the International Committee of the Red Cross. With the exception of former UN High Commission on Refugees personnel, no staffers were UN careerists.[30]

Returning to the continuum of sanctioning mechanisms, a multilateral human rights and peacebuilding operation certainly raises the volume to its highest level yet. A full-time force of observers is able to "see" more than a special envoy. For even active and ambitious rapporteurs, the hit-and-run nature of inspection visits permits the state to simply direct rapporteurs away from incriminating evidence and to control the worse excesses for the duration of the visit. By contrast, observer missions develop relations over time with members of the local community, including, significantly, those on local military bases.

This stage of human rights promotion differs in several key respects from previous efforts. First, the scope of these operations is relatively vast, in terms of access, mandate, and resources. Especially in a rural environment, an operation can take on the appearance of an invading army—uniformed personnel toting walkie-talkies, with a fleet of four-wheel-drive vehicles and a centrally located communications center. An international presence of this size is certainly felt throughout the country. Second, the level of authority mandated to a UN operation is clearly greater than that exercised at any previous stage of human rights promotion. Governments agree to comply with operation mandates that have the potential to expand, while sanctions for noncompliance are built into implementation agreements.

In sum, the emergence of peacebuilding operations centered on a human rights component represents the latest, most interventionist stage in the implementation of human rights norms. Earlier stages include nearly three decades of network conferencing, lobbying, public condemnation, bilateral pressure, and multilateral resolutions. Placing these various activities on a single continuum of forcefulness by no means implies a necessary or linear movement from one stage to the next. Naturally, different situations call for more or less interventionary mechanisms. Nor are the same set of actors involved in each category of activity. The United Nations is a very different institutional actor, with different political and organizational concerns from a government ministry or a nonprofit organization. However, the individuals involved at each stage of the human rights continuum, whether a UN observer, a State Department official, or an NGO activist, will be motivated by common goals and moral concerns, often sharing in the exchange of information that typifies the network. At different times, the same individual may be found working within any one of these institutions performing activities appropriate to the various levels of forcefulness on the continuum.

Measuring State Compliance

Again, the outcome of the framework's five interacting conditions has two aspects. The second is change in the behavior of the target state, initiated explicitly in response to pressure. Relevant indicators may be either changes of actual practice (for example, restructuring the judicial system to guarantee observance of such legal rights as habeas corpus, demilitarizing internal security forces, ceasing to support paramilitary death squads, or permitting open and competitive elections), or changes in the rhetoric by which state leaders communicate their priorities to their societies and to the international community. Even a self-serving, purely rhetorical change in government discourse from that of national security to that of human rights is an indication that policymaking elites perceive international condemnation to be costly, even if not sufficiently costly to warrant a change in actual practices.

To trace the effects of mechanisms for implementing human rights on government policy and practice, I relied on interviews with many of the relevant actors, as well as on UN mission reports, the evaluations of other scholars and analysts, and the self-critical analyses of mission directors. The problem of how to measure government compliance presented itself frequently over the course of my research. I did not define compliance in terms of a raw measure of behavior, such as a statistical decrease in violations, because a quantitative indicator of increase or decrease in violations is inherently problematic, for two reasons.[31] First, because the numbers themselves may be difficult to verify, especially under conditions of armed conflict. Second, because trends are unsteady and can shift in response to often unrelated or indirectly related impulses—a change in military tactics or strategy, the electoral cycle, different forms of abusive activity, or different targets. I chose instead to measure compliance in terms of long-term change in the institutions and patterns of behavior governing state-society relations in the area of human rights. I believe this to be a more meaningful, albeit more subjective, yardstick than quantitative changes in body counts.

FINAL NOTE: ON THE POLITICIZATION OF HUMAN RIGHTS ACTIVISM

The following histories are of countries that have experienced very long periods of open, armed civil conflict. Although these countries are dissimilar in other respects, their regional context is markedly like that of Southeast Asia during the 1960s, a region whose historical development was also overshadowed and subsumed by the geostrategic perceptions of the cold war. These small countries' civil wars became metaphors for a global struggle that would have been tangential to their internal conflicts, had it not been for the intervention of outside actors.

That these cases of human rights activism and eventual enforcement are also cases of the negotiated settlement of civil wars is therefore not surprising, nor does it make them less relevant. Civil conflict and human rights coexist in a nexus formed by the state's responsibility to respect and protect the rights of its citizens. This responsibility encompasses the treatment of those citizens who oppose state policies or contest its authority. Violations of the most fundamental nature—to the integrity of the person—are in many cases closely associated with conditions of armed domestic conflict. Therefore, it is reasonable to expect that the most highly charged, heavily publicized, intensely politicized instances of gross human rights violations occur in countries experiencing civil wars. Hence the linkage between human rights law, international humanitarian law, conflict resolution, and the politicization of human rights reportage.

Significantly, human rights activism did not engage international humanitarian law (i.e., the Geneva Conventions, which apply to all combatants on both sides of the conflict) until Americas Watch began working closely with the International Committee of the Red Cross in monitoring violations by the Salvadoran guerrilla opposition (FMLN) in

1983–84. Prior to this decision, human rights monitoring was concerned only with violations committed by government forces. This tendency was due largely to the network's history, developed out of the Southern Cone's experience of state repression targeting unarmed civilians, for which the laws of war were not relevant. The Central American civil conflicts were in this respect an unfamiliar context for activists, one that required new tools. Verifying violations of international humanitarian law is a difficult and dangerous task. It entails working in zones of conflict, obtaining security assurances from all belligerents, and endangering the lives of monitors. However, a failure to do so can undermine the credibility of human rights organizations. Much of the accusations (and appearance) of bias in international human rights reporting reflected the network's failure to monitor compliance with the laws of war—a strategy that, ironically, had negative repercussions for Amnesty International's efforts to pursue contra violations in Nicaragua.[32]

The victims of state repression or state terror are often individuals who have no direct political affiliation. One need only refer to the chronicles of the Argentine *guerra sucia*, or to the lists of villages destroyed by the scorched-earth tactics used in counterinsurgent offensives. Nonetheless, the rationale for targeting civilians is that the victims are members of the state's political opposition. One of the most sensitive subjects in dealing with human rights monitoring is the (alleged or actual) affiliation between the monitors and the political opposition. Although the legal or humanitarian nature of the subject matter should impose objectivity in reporting violations, especially on the part of non-nationals, human rights under repressive regimes inevitably becomes politicized. This fact in and of itself is a source of personal danger for anyone involved in human rights work. Further, it is a tool used to great effect by governments and their allies to discredit the entire human rights community, and an ideological blinder that tends to skew otherwise meritorious efforts at honest reporting.

The more reputable of the international human rights organizations in the United States and Europe recognized the need to be careful in selecting local groups in Central America with whom they could be associated and whose information they could consider reliable. This was necessary because of the politicization of human rights issues during the 1980s, the continuing efforts by Reagan administration and embassy officials to discredit their sources, and especially the de facto affiliation of many local groups with insurgent forces.

In this regard, several advocates I interviewed made the distinction between solidarity organizations like the Committee in Solidarity with the People of El Salvador (CISPES), which were blatantly political (CISPES was closely connected to the FMLN), and "nonpartisan" human rights organizations. The tacit assumption was that solidarity groups were more confrontational in approach, less tractable as coalition partners, and slightly tainted by their political affiliations, whereas human rights advocates were more pragmatic and professional (naturally enough, as so many were attorneys). The latter group also had closer ties to the network's "powerful allies" in governments and international organizations, whereas the solidarity sector was more akin to a grassroots-based social movement.

Americas Watch was very selective about its local affiliates, reflecting its concern to maintain the credibility of the human rights community as a whole.[33] WOLA was often required by its relations with Congress to defend human rights reporting, and staff members needed to know that they were fighting on solid ground. This consideration became even more critical toward the end of the 1980s, with the proliferation in El Salvador of groups, both local and international, referring to themselves as human rights organizations but having widely recognized affiliations to FMLN organizations. In the words of WOLA's current director, "NGOs had to be very certain of data because they knew it'd be challenged as coming from an FMLN front."[34] On the other side of the coin, the Salvadoran armed forces office of civil affairs—the military's human rights office—sent monthly reports denouncing FMLN violations to its roster of international agencies.

The legacy of wartime alliances between human rights and political organizations may create obstacles for domestic NGOs after the conflict is over and they are seeking to reorient their work to meet the needs of a post-conflict society. Under the polarizing circumstances of civil war, popular and human rights organizations often develop clandestinely, are necessarily hierarchical and secretive, and are primarily composed of individuals who have lost relatives and friends to government forces. Their awareness as political actors developed in an environment lacking legal, institutional channels for dissent or the possibility for bringing their grievances before an independent justice system. These are conditions that shape behavior in and expectations of the political arena in profoundly undemocratic ways. Furthermore, their status—as victims, survivors, widows, and orphans whose dead are transformed into martyrs of repression—confers on them a special type of international legitimacy, in what David Stoll refers to as a symbolic economy of victimhood.[35]

For these reasons, the context of civil war does present a special case for human rights protection, a context of extreme societal polarization and widespread violence. This book delves into that nexus of human rights and armed civil conflict. Although armed conflict differs from "ordinary repression" in the sheer numbers of atrocities and degree of the distortions on both sides, the principles of human dignity and personal integrity are just as essential, and often just as vulnerable, in peacetime. This is particularly important to bear in mind as the international community moves toward including widespread or systematic attacks on civilian populations during *peacetime* in the legal definition of crimes against humanity.[36] The examples set by international human rights intervention in El Salvador and Guatemala will, I hope, speak loudly and clearly to other cases of systematic violation, even where those cases are not associated with civil war and negotiated peace.

★

PART ONE

Mobilization of Shame in the 1980s

CHAPTER ONE

El Salvador, 1980-1989:
EL MOZOTE TO POLITICAL OPENING

There was a lot of formalism in defense of human rights. What you heard from the United States government was a way of excusing the Salvadoran government's support for human rights violations, always it was "poor Duarte, caught between two extremes who go on killing each other, and he has nothing to do with it. . . ." Duarte didn't have to be sensitive to any pressure, because it was to his benefit that they believed this was a democracy. Things changed after 1989. You can't speak of improvements in human rights during a counterinsurgent war; all you can have are changes in the message, the discourse.

—Héctor Dada

Repression of the powerless is not a recent phenomenon in Salvadoran history. The most massive peasant massacre of the twentieth century in El Salvador took place in 1932, sixteen years before the Universal Declaration of Human Rights gave currency to human rights. It was another twenty-five years before there was any hope for international protection. Human rights abuses in El Salvador did not begin in the 1980s, but the story of transnational human rights activism in El Salvador began in the context of the civil war.

During the 1980s the United States consistently supported the Salvadoran military despite growing evidence that human rights were being systematically violated. In doing so, the United States defected from its responsibility to support the human rights regime. This pulled the sting out of the transnational human rights network's most useful weapon—the mobilization of shame—as the Salvadoran government did not stand to lose its key supporter because of a tarnished international reputation.

The international human rights apparatus, having undergone a period of expansion and institutionalization in the 1970s, exerted its most powerful tools short of an economic boycott in attempting to bring the government of El Salvador into compliance. Annual special rapporteur reports detailing local conditions were submitted to the UN Commission on Human Rights and to the General Assembly, and both bodies issued resolutions condemning egregious practices and calling for compliance. The Inter-American Commission for Human Rights investigated and published its findings on human rights. Although the government privately expressed strong objections to being condemned in international organization reports, condemnation did not cause any change in government behavior during the 1980s. After 1989, however, changes in domestic political conditions (the emergence of an elite with the authority to subordinate the military and a concern for the Salvadoran state's international reputation) combined with a permissive international context (the post–cold war withdrawal of US military support) to produce the conditions for a UN-mediated settlement to the civil war, which resulted in a human rights-based peacekeeping operation.

In this chapter I introduce the key actors in the conflict—the U.S. government, the Salvadoran government, the armed forces of El Salvador, and the armed insurgency—and discuss how international strategic interests affected key domestic political actors. Next, I discuss transnational human rights mobilization, examining the regime mechanisms engaged during this period: bilateral pressure through U.S. foreign assistance legislation and international scrutiny through the UN Commission on Human Rights' Special Representative. Finally, I explain how changes in the domestic elite following El Salvador's "democratic transition" affected human rights compliance and the resolution of civil conflict.

The Background of Human Rights in El Salvador

The Regional Context

For at least the first half of the decade, members of the U.S. Congress sympathetic to human rights concerns engaged in an ongoing debate with the executive branch over U.S. policy in El Salvador. They used the human rights provisions of State Department foreign assistance legislation as leverage against President Ronald Reagan's military appropriations requests. During the 1980s the Reagan administration's ideological stance polarized the issue of human rights protection, as it did all policy discussion concerning Central America. What had, under President Carter, been a limited bipartisan cooperation on Central America policy devolved into open warfare between the executive branch and the human rights community, with members of Congress sympathetic to both sides in the middle. Wavering before a determined White House, the majority in Congress forged a bipartisan policy consensus following the election of Christian Democrat José Napoleón Duarte in 1984.

Ironically, the association of the Salvadoran conflict with cold war geostrategic interests was initially established during the Carter administration. The Carter State Department's fledgling human rights policy came up against overriding cold war concerns after the July 1979 Sandinista victory in Nicaragua and was subordinated to a policy of maintaining government stability in the region. U.S. military assistance had been preemptively rejected by the government of El Salvador two years earlier, in protest over the criticism of its human rights record implied by congressional hearings on the subject. A low level ($5.7 million) of nonlethal military assistance was reinstated in March 1980 (one week after Archbishop Oscar Romero's assassination), and restrictions were lifted in June of that year, in response to the perceived security threat after the Nicaraguan regime fell.[1] Under the Reagan presidency, this strategic posture took on the proportions of a crusade.

Even after the transition from Ronald Reagan's administration to that of George Bush, the government of the United States initially remained reluctant to support a negotiated settlement of the civil war. Despite the thawing of the cold war and the generally lower profile given to Latin America in Bush administration appointments, prior to the guerrilla urban offensive of November 1989, the White House maintained that the Salvadoran government was a democracy under threat, and that the Salvadoran armed forces were winning the war.[2]

However, the military capabilities demonstrated by the FMLN in their November 1989 offensive, combined with the armed forces' poor performance, convinced U.S. military decision makers that the war had been fought to a stalemate. Concurrently, the murder of six Jesuit scholars and two witnesses caused an unprecedented degree of moral outrage in Congress. This was intensified with the May 1990 release of an interim report on the case by a commission headed by Representative Joe Moakley (D-Mass.), which implicated the military. Within a year, the Bush administration declared its support for a peaceful settlement. U.S. military assistance was cut by 50 percent under a bill proposed by Senators Christopher Dodd (D-Ct.) and Patrick Leahy (D-Vt.), which conditioned the remainder on the requirement that both the government and the FMLN negotiate in good faith.[3]

Domestic Political Alignments

The government of El Salvador changed hands several times during this period. A cadre of reformist young officers staged a coup in October 1979, overthrowing a repressive and corrupt military government; the ensuing five-member junta was reshuffled four times. Two interim presidents were appointed—José Napoleón Duarte (December 1980–March 1982) and Alvaro Magaña (March 1982–June 1984). Two presidents, Duarte (1984–89) and Alfredo Cristiani (1989–1994), were elected in what were declared by international observers to be fair and free contests. All three presidents, whether elected or appointed, were civilians.

Both Duarte and Magaña were at least rhetorically concerned for their country's human rights record. Neither was capable of exerting executive authority to modify the military's behavior, given the autonomy that U.S. assistance afforded the military, and given the exigencies of prosecuting a civil war. The few instances of weak cooperation with human rights pressure indicate that the Salvadoran government was at least nervous about any mobilization of the human rights network. The most notable such instance was the (albeit in most cases temporary) purge of a short list of notorious officers provided by Vice President Bush in December 1983. Overall, however, the ebbs and flows in the level of violations throughout the civil war responded to tactical shifts on the parts of the two opposing military organizations and various right-wing paramilitary groups, rather than to the government's intention to comply with the human rights regime.

A necessary factor for human rights pressure to be effective is the existence of a key faction in the ruling coalition for whom international prestige is a major interest—and one did emerge in the late 1980s. Leadership of the militant National Republican Alliance (ARENA) party was captured by its moderate wing, whose leader, Alfredo Cristiani, was elected president in 1989. This indicated an important division within the political right. Cristiani represented a neoliberal, pragmatic force within the economic elite whose principal concern was to salvage the economy from a decade of civil war.[4] To achieve this end, Cristiani vowed in his inaugural speech to promote a structural adjustment program and to initiate peace talks with the armed opposition. By the end of 1989, both parties to the conflict had requested the UN Secretary-General to increase his involvement in the peace process. The following April, the Salvadoran negotiations had formally commenced under UN mediation, a process that led eventually to the deployment of a human rights mission.

State Coercive Forces

The Salvadoran military was almost entirely dependent on external sources of funding for the duration of the civil war. In the early to mid-1980s, the massive increase in U.S. financial, matériel, and training support caused the military to turn away from a traditional dependence on agrarian elites and to affiliate itself more closely with backers in the United States. Whereas officers had formerly sought to advance their careers through ties to the oligarchy, overtly supporting U.S. policies— propping up a weak centrist presidency, promoting a compromised agrarian reform—became the key to personal and institutional enhancement in the 1980s. This inevitably led to a weakening of the military-oligarchy alliance.[5] Just how weak that alliance had become was evident after the 1985 assembly elections, in which the Christian Democratic Party (PDC) received an absolute majority; ARENA, the party representing the oligarchy, challenged the results. Rather than support the agrarian and industrial elites who had formerly provided its patronage, the military tacitly supported the PDC and that party's patron, the Reagan administration.[6]

The alliance between the armed forces and the political-economic elite remained tenuous and often unstable through the civil war years. Economic elites required the military to conduct the war and to keep popular organizations under control but consistently thwarted land-reform efforts that moderate officers considered necessary to stabilize the country and, especially, to retain U.S. support. Factional divisions formed between hardline officers who supported ARENA and participated in paramilitary operations, and more pragmatic members of the high command who feared the loss of U.S. assistance, if they were perceived to be uncooperative on land reform and the rule of law.

This alignment changed radically at the end of 1989: re-evaluation of geostrategic priorities, combined with the U.S. Defense Department's perception of a military stalemate and the discovery of military complicity in the murders of six Jesuit priests, caused the U.S. government to withdraw its unconditional support. Cristiani's faction then gained the upper hand in its power struggle with the military by means of a negotiated agreement to restructure the armed forces, which removed internal policing from its control and cut force levels nearly in half.

Interposed between traditional economic elites and the institutional armed forces were several paramilitary organizations commonly referred to as death squads. The core of this shadow army grew out of *la matanza* (the massacre) of 1932. To prevent further outbreaks of peasant dissent, landowners at that time organized private security forces, or *guardias civiles*. In the mid-1960s these private rural forces were consolidated under a national structure as the Democratic Nationalist Organization (ORDEN), a peasant intelligence-gathering operation under government sponsorship. After the October 1979 coup, one of the governing junta's first acts was to officially disband ORDEN. However, the paramilitary structures remained intact, and continued to operate under members of the security forces opposed to the junta and allied with the ultraright wing of the oligarchy.

The person most often associated with death squad leadership after the coup is Major Roberto D'Aubuisson, who was removed from duty and exiled to Guatemala in May 1980 for plotting against the junta. When he was arrested, the government uncovered a cache of documents linking officials of the armed forces to civilian paramilitary operations.[7] In exile, D'Aubuisson organized a clandestine political organization with the intention of overthrowing the junta, which became the ARENA party on his return to El Salvador in the fall of 1981. A CIA intelligence assessment directly ties D'Aubuisson, ARENA, rural landowners, and several military officers into an internal terrorist network of organizations such as the Secret Anti-Communist Army (ESA) and the Maximiliano Hernández Martínez Anti-Communist Brigade.[8] A variety of terrorist groups were organized under ARENA, some operating directly out of state security offices, others civilian-based. At the height of death squad operations in 1983, an average of eight hundred murders per month were attributed to these shadow organizations.

For a powerful sector of society to conduct its politics through death squads and terror raises an issue of methodological as well as political significance for human rights protection: how to assign responsibility for crimes committed by paramilitary forces. Violations can be directly attributed to state agencies, can involve combatants on either side who endanger civilians, can be committed by paramilitary units with established links to state security forces, or by death squads contracted, financed, and organized entirely by civilians. In any of these cases, the government is responsible for protecting the rights of its citizens and is accountable for preventing or prosecuting terrorist attacks upon its political opponents, even where no direct affiliation between the attacker and state agents can be established.

Nonetheless, for the purpose of continuing and increasing military aid, both the Salvadoran government and the Reagan administration insisted on making a sharp distinction between state and nonstate violators. Death squads were characterized as "right-wing terrorists" to deflect responsibility from the Salvadoran military and security apparatus. The Salvadoran government was depicted as fighting for its very survival, under fire from guerrillas on the left and civilian terrorists on the right. In November 1983, when murders by death squads had reached their peak, U.S. Ambassador Thomas Pickering warned the Salvadoran business elite that the United States could no longer ignore "terrorism of the right" in determining financial assistance. He stated clearly that Congress had voted to reduce military spending by $22 million and to place conditions on what remained, owing to the protest over death squad activities.[9] His warning evidently hit its target: that same month, Defense Minister Vides Casanova declared that the high command was determined to combat terrorist organizations "regardless of their political persuasion."[10]

These statements were made one month after a classified CIA briefing paper documented the paramilitary activities of, among others, Ltc. Rene Emilio Ponce, director of the National Guard Police Department.[11] Reagan administration officials clearly must have been aware of the involvement of Salvadoran security forces in death squad operations. To justify continued military assistance, however, the U.S. administration insisted that the problem was not a lack of political will to reform the security forces but that neither the government of El Salvador nor the armed forces' high command were capable of controlling an autonomous civilian right wing.

The Armed Opposition

Beginning in 1980, what had been sporadic insurgent activity against the military-dominated government exploded into civil war, pitting the armed forces against a unified guerrilla army organized as the Farabundo Martí National Liberation Front (FMLN). The FMLN was established in November 1980 as the military wing of the Democratic Revolutionary

Front (FDR), a left political coalition incorporating centrist political parties, trade unions, churches, students, small business and professional associations, and academics from the two major universities.[12] The political (FDR) and military (FMLN) branches were linked by their joint Political Diplomatic Commission, headquartered in Mexico.

The FMLN-FDR's popular base consisted of rural Christian base communities and popular organizations, particularly labor activists. Peasant sympathizers provided food, storage facilities, communications services and information on troop movements, and recruits. Urban support took the form of neighborhood committees that stockpiled arms, ammunition, and supplies, and provided logistical support during urban offensives.[13] The FMLN was significantly less dependent on international material support than were the Salvadoran armed forces. To an extent, the FMLN retained its independence from outside sources by developing its own munitions industry to produce combat weapons and land mines. The guerrillas did receive some financing from private solidarity organizations in Europe and the United States. The Sandinista government in Nicaragua smuggled arms across the border, although the quantity was always much less than that claimed by the U.S. government and had nearly ceased altogether by the mid-1980s. Cuba supplied capital, explosives, and training during the 1980s,[14] although the Cuban government assured the United Nations in 1990 that it was not providing military assistance to the FMLN.[15] As late as 1989, the FMLN was purchasing inexpensive unused arms from traders among the Nicaraguan Contras.[16] Somewhat inconclusive reports claimed that Soviet bloc countries (particularly Bulgaria) passed large shipments of weapons to the FMLN via Nicaragua, but the Soviet Union did not directly provide material support.[17]

The FMLN's first major general offensive was launched in January 1981. They maintained a strong offensive strategy of territorial occupation through 1984, during which time roughly 30 percent of the country came under guerrilla control.[18] The tide began to turn in 1984. A concerted effort to professionalize the armed forces imposed by U.S. Military Group advisers— tightened command and control, more effective deployment of rapid reaction battalions, and a tactical shift from ground sweeps to aerial attacks—put the guerrillas fully on the defensive.[19] After 1985, the FMLN had shifted to operating in small mobile units dispersed throughout the countryside.[20] What ensued was a prolonged war of attrition, emphasizing economic sabotage and tit-for-tat retaliatory attacks that targeted the families of military officers.

Relative to other Latin American guerrilla movements, the FMLN-FDR was remarkably successful both in its military operations and in its international diplomatic relations. The political leadership operated in exile from Mexico City and had a permanent representative at UN headquarters in New York—marking the first time the United Nations maintained official relations with an insurgent movement. Recognition by the United Nations and by the Non-Aligned Movement countries was granted following the Franco-Mexican declaration of August 28, 1981, that officially recognized the FMLN as a representative political force. An FDR leader observed that, by the middle of the decade, "the government was more isolated than we [FMLN-FDR] were internationally."[21] The FMLN had representatives throughout Europe: in Spain, France, Italy, Germany, Greece, Switzerland, Sweden, Austria, Holland, Denmark, and Norway. In Africa, they were in Angola and Mozambique. In the Americas, they had offices in Washington, Canada, Mexico, and in most Latin American countries. Undoubtedly, the FMLN's diplomatic efforts and exceptional public relations were a factor in the Secretary-General's decision to mediate negotiations and in the great generosity displayed by the international community in reconstructing El Salvador.

TRANSNATIONAL HUMAN RIGHTS MOBILIZATION IN THE 1980s

Network activism continued throughout the civil war, producing limited but nonetheless important results in mobilizing powerful allies, in raising public awareness, and in helping to protect the lives of Salvadoran human rights activists. Agents of international organizations and human rights sympathizers in the U.S. Congress responded to focused pressure campaigns of the transnational human rights network. In Washington, London, Geneva, Mexico City, and New York, nongovernmental organizations were meeting formally and informally, obtaining information and channeling it to policymakers, exchanging information among themselves and with their Salvadoran counterparts, providing testimony to congressional hearings, OAS investigators, and sessions of the UN Commission on Human Rights. Amnesty International published several reports on El Salvador during the decade. Americas Watch released frequent updates of their reports on El Salvador.[22] The Lawyers' Committee for Human Rights, in addition to issuing several reports on judicial reform and on particular cases, co-authored with Human Rights Watch an annual critique of the U.S. State Department

Country Reports on El Salvador. In El Salvador, human rights groups staged public protests, investigated denunciations and sites of massacres where possible, gained access to prisons, endured persecution, and attracted international concern and media attention.[23]

The Human Rights Network and U.S. Foreign Policy

The earliest instances of U.S. congressional pressure to bring the government of El Salvador into compliance with human rights standards took place in 1977. In March, Representatives Robert Drinan (D-Mass.) and Tom Harkin (D-Iowa), and Senator Edward Kennedy (D-Mass.) held hearings on the political repression of popular organizers following a fraudulent election. In July of that year, the House Committee on Foreign Relations' Subcommittee on International Organizations produced an inquiry into the persecution of Jesuit priests.[24] Congressional findings determined that the Salvadoran government was a gross and consistent violator of human rights, and that the State Department should have been prohibited from dispensing military and security-related aid, according to the requirements of the Foreign Assistance Act, Sections 116 and 502(b).[25] However, the military regime in San Salvador, offended by the inquiries, rejected U.S. military assistance to avoid the embarrassment of having it cut off and, in so doing, deprived Congress of what human rights leverage it had at the time.[26]

By 1981 the picture had changed dramatically. The Sandinistas' victory brought Central American internal conflicts into the global arena. The Salvadoran armed opposition appeared to be a genuine threat to an unstable, *anti-communist* interim government. And several cases of egregious abuse by state or paramilitary agents had taken place, among them the murder of U.S. nationals.

These cases of abuse stand out even against a backdrop of ongoing violence for a variety of reasons, and they took on tremendous symbolic value for human rights mobilization. The first case carried perhaps the greatest force for international mobilization. On March 24, 1980, Archbishop Oscar Arnulfo Romero was assassinated while delivering a funeral mass. The Salvadoran government made some quickly discredited attempts to accuse the opposition, while death threats and assassination attempts prevented those charged with investigating the crime from conducting any serious investigation. The Archbishop's human rights office, Socorro Jurídico (later reorganized as Tutela Legal), uncovered evidence of military complicity, which was confiscated by security forces during a raid in July 1980. Other evidence linking ARENA leader Roberto D'Aubuisson, civilians associated with the right wing, and certain military officers to the crime was not considered until a governmental investigation commission had been established in 1987, by which time many witnesses were dead or in exile.[27]

The next highly charged violation took place two months later. Army and security forces, on a ground sweep through the northern part of Chalatenango province, massacred approximately six hundred peasants on the banks of the Rio Sumpul on May 14, 1980. The government denied responsibility for the massacre, which became an international incident because of the involvement of the Honduran armed forces. The Honduran Catholic Church published a condemnation that brought support from U.S. church organizations. An investigation of the incident was then opened by the Inter-American Commission on Human Rights.[28]

On November 27, 1980, the FDR leadership was meeting in a Jesuit high school near the U.S. embassy (which also housed the offices of Socorro Jurídico), preparing for a press conference. The meeting was interrupted when approximately two hundred uniformed and plainclothes police and soldiers surrounded the building. Twenty-five police not in uniform entered the building and kidnapped six key leaders. Found the next day, their bodies revealed that they had been tortured and executed. The undisguised involvement of state agents in these political assassinations led to an international outcry and curtailed any further movement toward negotiations to head off the impending civil war.[29]

Less than one week later, on December 2, three U.S. nuns—Ita Ford, Maura Clarke, and Dorothy Kazel—and a Catholic lay worker, Jean Donovan, were arbitrarily detained by national guardsmen as they were leaving the airport. They were taken to an isolated location, where they were raped and murdered. This case generated a tremendous outrage among the U.S. public and by far the greatest degree of interest in Congress. State Department officials were pressured to personally investigate the situation and to maintain supervision of the military's investigation.[30] It was one of the two cases included in legislation that conditioned military aid on a presidential certification of progress toward reform. It is also one of the few human rights cases for which the material, albeit not the intellectual, perpetrators have been prosecuted. The complicity of senior military officers in prearranging the assassinations and later in blocking the investigation was finally exposed in 1993.[31]

Another case involving the murder of U.S. citizens, which also found its way into the congressional certification process, took place one month later on January 3, 1981. Two labor advisers from the American Institute for Free Labor Development (AIFLD), Mark Pearlman and Michael Hammer, were shot at the Sheraton Hotel in San Salvador while dining with Rodolfo Viera, director of El Salvador's institute for agrarian reform. The Sheraton case resulted in the conviction of the hired gunmen and in mostly unsuccessful efforts by the embassy to prosecute the three officers and one right-wing civilian known to have given the order.[32]

Finally, in December 1981, a U.S.-trained rapid-reaction battalion on a ground sweep entered several villages in the north of Morazán province, the largest of which was El Mozote. They proceeded over a week and a half to rape, torture, and slaughter the inhabitants, including the children. The full body count from the El Mozote campaign varies from more than five hundred (according to the Truth Commission) to close to one thousand (according to Americas Watch), making the massacre the largest in a single incident of the twelve-year war.[33]

The civil war was reaching uncontrollable heights in rural El Salvador, and death squad-style assassinations were a common sight on the streets of the capital by the end of 1981. Congress responded to the public outcry that human rights activists had mobilized by voting to impose conditions on further military aid appropriations. In December 1981, the House and Senate approved legislation requiring that the White House biannually certify that the government of El Salvador was making a genuine effort to comply with international human rights standards and bring its armed forces under control (HR 4042). Certification requirements included progress toward prosecution in the murders of the U.S. churchwomen and AIFLD workers.

This measure held the president accountable for the actions of the Salvadoran government and armed forces in return for the assistance it requested. Predictably, every six months, from January 1982 through January 1984, the U.S. government gave the El Salvador government its stamp of approval. The first certification—approved the same week that Alma Guillermoprieto of the *Washington Post* and Raymond Bonner of the *New York Times* published reports of the El Mozote massacre, and the ACLU and Americas Watch published their seminal report on human rights in El Salvador—was met with severe criticism from the media and from human rights organizations.[34]

The certification process became part of the human rights mobilization calendar, for its duration. Every six months, the State Department and the intelligence community prepared reports, and human rights organizations provided information linking the Salvadoran government and military to human rights violations. The reports, unrealistically mild at first, finally growing more critical at the end of the period, invariably found that the government was doing its best under the circumstances. Presidential certification was based on vague requirements of "progress toward" general goals of political and military reform. These goals were given some definition, however, by including the requirement that progress be made in the prosecution of specific cases of violations against U.S. citizens. While apparently toothless, the certification requirement provided at least a minimal check on the Reagan administration's support for the Salvadoran government. It also caused the State Department to exert itself more seriously in pressing the Salvadoran government for action on human rights abuses. After two years of this, President Reagan terminated the certification bill by pocket veto in November 1983.

Vice President George Bush visited San Salvador on December 11, 1983, to underscore the administration's concern that the human rights situation was seriously undermining prospects for continued military aid. Bush's visit indicates that the White House was not impervious to the growing influence of human rights activists and perceived the need to give at least rhetorical support to the institutions of the human rights regime. The visit occurred less than a month after Thomas Pickering's unsubtle warning in his Chamber of Commerce speech. Bush clearly stated that his mission was critical to administration policy, that he spoke for the president. He provided a non-negotiable deadline for reforms—January 10, the date when Congress would reconvene. The visit was precipitated by the government's incapacity to stem paramilitary activity, by CIA findings linking military and security forces to the death squads, and by growing evidence that Salvadorans living in Miami were funding death squad operations.[35]

Bush met first with acting president Alvaro Magaña and later in a restricted session with the top three military commanders (Defense Minister General Vides Casanova, Sub-Secretary for Defense General Rafael Flores Lima, and Chief of Staff Colonel Onecifero Blandón). Major Oliver North, of the U.S. Marine Corps, also attended the restricted session, as did Ambassador Pickering. After forty minutes, the military session was expanded to include the full high command. Bush was characteristically straightforward in stating the problem to the high command:

I must tell you frankly that it has not been easy for us either. Providing assistance to you is not a popular cause in the United States. Publicity about death squads, great inequalities of income, the killing of American citizens and military setbacks make it a very unpopular proposition in my country. President Reagan has supported you at considerable political cost, because we know it is the right thing . . .

. . . Without actions in these areas there is no point in trying to obtain additional funds for El Salvador, and to be honest, we will not even make the effort, because it would be fruitless.[36]

The "action" required of the military in order to ensure continued U.S. support was that Eduardo Avila, an officer indicted in the AIFLD worker case, be arrested; that other officers involved in death squad activities be arrested and prosecuted; that government investigations should be conducted for a series of rural massacres; that the military lend support to land-reform efforts and the upcoming elections; and that a number of specific military practices be reformed. Most sensationally, Bush handed the military commanders a "short list" of officers and civilians (rumored at around thirty) linked to death squad activities, who would have to be assigned abroad by January 10, 1984. Civilians who chose not to leave the country for an extended period would face intensive investigation and prosecution in El Salvador.[37] General Vides Casanova protested, correctly, that the military had no constitutional authority to order civilians into exile, regarding which Thomas Pickering later observed, "Vides is a stickler in finding legal problems in things he finds difficult to do or does not want to do, but not quite so scrupulous when it comes to legal requirements to carry out actions such as dealing with the death squads."[38]

Bush's visit was a heavily qualified success. Avila was detained on lesser charges, but with the help of an uncle on the Supreme Court, he managed to avoid prosecution.[39] The names on the list of officers to be sacrificed have remained confidential (and General Vides made this a condition for compliance). Shortly following the visit, however, Ltc. Aristides Marquez of the National Police Intelligence Department was reassigned to Spain, Major José Ricardo Pozo of the Treasury Police was sent to Paraguay (but brought back and promoted in January 1986),[40] and Dr. Hector Regalado, ARENA's death squad director and chief of security for the National Assembly, was told to leave the country.[41] According to the CIA, Marquez and Pozo were immediately replaced with "ultrarightist officers, one of whom is a [excised] leader of a police death squad."[42] Further, several officers closely associated with D'Aubuisson (most of whom were rumored to be on the Bush list) were reassigned to prestigious posts, including Ltc. Denis Morán, considered one of those responsible for ordering the murder of the AIFLD workers. Overall, the CIA's conclusion regarding the reforms that followed George Bush's ultimatum was that:

> efforts by the civilian government and military high command to crack down on rightwing violence have made little progress and have been aimed almost exclusively at placating Washington. . . . Defense Minister Vides—whose room to maneuver is limited—appears both personally disinclined and professionally unable to effect a major cleanup within the armed forces any time soon.[43]

The number of death squad victims did appreciably decrease during 1984, only to re-escalate in 1987–88.[44] The visit coincided with an intense effort on the part of the U.S. Military Group to professionalize the Salvadoran army by promoting a national plan (along the lines of winning hearts and minds) and providing troops with seminars on human rights.[45] However, despite the emphasis placed in Bush's "required steps" on reforming military combat and public-security practices, combat-related violations continued, as did abuses by security forces.[46] Moreover, statistical analysis suggests that, as the numbers of death squad killings fell after the Bush visit, there was a compensating significant increase in military attacks on civilians.[47]

The Sanctioning Mechanisms of the United Nations

Human rights activists focused their campaigns on the government of the United States, as the major benefactor of the Salvadoran government and therefore the actor with the greatest leverage. But many network members also sought support from, and worked in conjunction with the UN Commission on Human Rights. On November 27, 1980, barely a week before the rape and murder of the four U.S. churchwomen and, ironically, the very day on which the six FDR leaders were kidnapped, Cuba introduced a resolution to the UN General Assembly that condemned human rights violations in El Salvador.[48] The resolution called upon member states to refrain from supplying arms or military assistance to the Salvadoran government and requested that the commission examine the situation. U.S. Secretary of State Edmund Muskie opposed the resolution and urged U.S. allies to vote against it. He argued that the sponsor of the resolution, Cuba, was supplying illegal arms to the guerrillas, and that the resolution would "seriously undercut U.S. policy in El Salvador."[49] From the start, positions on UN involvement in El Salvador to promote human rights were clearly delineated in cold-war alliance terms.

On December 15 the resolution passed, 70 to 12, with 55 abstentions. The following March, the commission appointed a Spanish professor of law, José Antonio Pastor Ridruejo, as its special representative to El Salvador. His mandate was to investigate allegations of human rights violations and to make recommendations to the government. From September 1981 until he was thanked for his services and relieved of his responsibilities in March 1992, Pastor Ridruejo submitted annual reports to the UN Commission and the General Assembly. The commission decided in its 1992 session that developments in El Salvador—the signing of the peace accord and deployment of ONUSAL—justified moving the case from the category of violator state requiring systematic inquiry to that of advisory services/technical assistance. At this time, Pedro Nikken, a Venezuelan human rights expert who was largely responsible for elaborating the terms of the Salvadoran human rights accord, was appointed independent expert, a role he carried out until 1995.

The reports submitted by Pastor Ridruejo were based on brief annual visits, in late September or early October, during which he interviewed government and military officials, representatives of key sectors (church, business, labor), foreign diplomats, prisoners, members of human rights organizations (in El Salvador and abroad), and members of the opposition (in El Salvador and in Mexico City). He received information and analysis from both Salvadoran and international human rights NGOs, which was evident in the reports. Throughout the period, he received and reported narrative information and numerical data from Socorro Jurídico and Tutela Legal, the Nongovernmental Human Rights Commission, the Human Rights Commission of El Salvador (governmental, established in 1982), Amnesty International, Americas Watch, international church organizations, and U.S. State Department and Council of Europe reports. His conclusions, couched in diplomatic language, consistently found that members of the state apparatus engaged in gross violations of human rights, and that the government made insufficient effort to control its forces and the impunity with which they acted. A balanced effort was made to assess the degree of responsibility for violence against civilians on the part of the FMLN.

The special representative's reports were received by the Salvadoran government (although through 1985 the government extended him an entry visa solely in his personal capacity, not as a representative of the UN Commission), but his recommendations had no direct effect on government or military practice and were often publicly rejected as reflecting antigovernment bias. The greatest effect of the rapporteur system appears to have been in forcing the government to defend itself before other states at commission and sub-commission meetings. An especially important contribution of UN reporting was that Pastor Ridruejo repeatedly confirmed the civilian nature of the targeted population in combat zones. He interpreted Geneva Convention articles on the protection of civilians as extending to all combatants in the Salvadoran civil war, thereby introducing international humanitarian law into the debate.[50]

Final Observations on Human Rights Strategy

International responses to human rights violations usually mobilize around certain especially potent or symbolic cases. In many ways, the use of representative cases by rights groups reflects the need to organize a plethora of information into a manageable narrative that can be packaged for the public. These cases also become indicators of compliance or noncompliance. For example, NGO reports highlight ongoing proceedings in major cases as a device to evaluate conditions of impunity and justice administration. Pressure is more efficient when applied to resolve specific cases rather than to promote vaguely worded general improvements. As noted earlier, a condition of the certification process was that good-faith efforts be made to investigate and bring to justice those responsible for the rape and murder of the four U.S. churchwomen and the death squad shooting of the two U.S. labor organizers.

Members of the human rights network and their "powerful allies" may be brought into the debate on a certain country by their involvement with a particularly significant case. Many church groups became mobilized in protest over the assassination of Archbishop Romero. The Lawyers' Committee on Human Rights became directly involved in El Salvador as legal counsel for the families of the four U.S. churchwomen. Republican senator Arlen Specter, previously reluctant to limit military spending in El Salvador, amended the 1984 appropriations bill in November 1983 to make 30 percent of aid conditional on achieving a verdict in the churchwomen's case.[51]

In a similar vein, the state's response to pressure on individual cases becomes an indicator of its overall compliance with international standards. Thus, when five national guardsmen were finally convicted in the churchwomen's case in May 1984, the State Department was able to point to this fact as evidence of reform. More general activities, for example the initiation of human rights training seminars for military personnel has less weight as evidence of progress first, because the impact is imperceptible or not measurable, and second, because individual cases carry a greater symbolic charge.

Another reason for the focus on representative cases is that it ameliorates the methodological problems of using statistical trends in violations to indicate either compliance or response to pressure.[52] Statistics on human rights increase and decrease unevenly and in waves, making it very difficult to determine the cause of change. The unevenness of trends often indicates shifts in the form of violation. For example, an increase in death squad assassinations may coincide with a decrease in the number of arbitrary detentions and political prisoners.[53] Certain instances of violation may be fewer in number but take on a great deal of symbolic significance due to the identity of the victims, as in the assassination of six FDR leaders in November 1980. Also, an increase or decrease in the numbers of victims may be a response to a temporary policy change rather than an indication of institutional or structural reform. Death squad killings and the use of torture by state agents decreased dramatically following Thomas Pickering's Chamber of Commerce speech and George Bush's December 1983 visit. However, they rose again in 1987–88, indicating that the incentives to conduct politics in this manner had not disappeared.[54] Tracking individual cases therefore furnishes a better indicator of compliance or noncompliance.

Representative cases lend themselves to mobilization efforts because of the nature of the crime and of its victims. Their importance may stem from the victim's moral authority, as with Archbishop Romero and the many targeted religious workers. Or, as in the cases of the two AIFLD advisers referred to in the congressional certification legislation, their importance may stem from nationality. States are responsible for the welfare of their nationals abroad, and focusing on cases of abuse of U.S. citizens holds the U.S. government accountable, thus increasing the likelihood that the issue will be kept on the agenda.

More commonly, the extent of the violation lends itself to mobilization efforts, as was the case for the Rio Sumpul and El Mozote incidents. The massacre in El Mozote in December 1981 achieved international notoriety due to the sheer numbers and senselessness of the killings, despite efforts to squelch the story by the embassy and the U.S. press. A great irony that caused El Mozote to stand out among other massacres, including several of lesser but significant scale in the mid-1980s, also had to do with the nature of the victims. The villagers considered themselves to live under the army's protection and were not at all sympathetic to the guerrilla movement.[55] Such large-scale massacres were routinely justified by the U.S. embassy and the Salvadoran government as combat-related deaths of guerrilla sympathizers; this was particularly illegitimate in the case of the residents of El Mozote.[56]

DEMOCRATIC TRANSITION AND STATE RESPONSE TO INTERNATIONAL PRESSURE

The 1984 election of José Napoleón Duarte has been referred to as a "demonstration" election—engineered by Washington, then proffered as evidence that El Salvador was a representative democracy under threat from a communist insurgency and deserving of military support.[57] The reality in El Salvador was that the country had a corrupt and inefficient government, incapable of promoting its social and economic policies, and faced implacable opposition from the private sector and agrarian elites over its attempts at agrarian reform, nationalization of banks, and electoral recoding.

Duarte's capacity to promote more than rhetorical compliance with human rights standards was very weak.[58] He lacked the political base to control the military during a civil war, and the U.S. embassy failed to lend him the support he would have needed to reform the military. As for moving toward a negotiated settlement of the war, Duarte attempted to initiate talks with the FMLN early in his administration and came up against an obdurate military and the Reagan policy of seeking military victory over insurgents at all costs.

Duarte's election paved the way for the U.S. Congress to release withheld military funds, much of which went into augmenting the air force. This enabled an intensification of the air war, which in turn caused the FMLN, now on the run, to shift to a mobile-unit strategy. Indiscriminate aerial bombing, intended to disrupt the FMLN's supply of provisions and information from rural supporters, caused massive dislocation of the rural population. The U.S. embassy initially supported aerial attacks as consistent with the counterinsurgency aim of depriving the guerrillas of their base of support. The ensuing international media and NGO outcry caused the embassy to retract its claim that civilians living in combat zones were a legitimate target and also led to Duarte's issuing a rules of engagement order in September 1984. The new orders limited air strikes to combat situations or to attacks on guerrilla columns, and required that strike orders be accompanied by statements concerning the location of civilians or International Committee of the Red Cross operations. The rules of engagement order was disregarded by the air force, and aerial attacks on civilians continued.[59]

The process of liberalizing national politics began in 1987–88, as the result of developments at both ends of the spectrum. The terms of the Esquipulas II agreement (a product of the Contadora peace process)[60] included a stipulation insuring the safe return of the opposition leaders Rubén Zamora and Guillermo Ungo from exile. Their return signaled that political space had opened and also led to the formation of the Democratic Convergence (Convergencia Democrática, CD), a coalition of social democratic and Christian left parties, for the 1989 national elections. The political incorporation of the left thus began prior to the end of the war. This factor greatly eased the post–civil war reinsertion of the FMLN into political life and lowered the perceived costs of a ceasefire for the guerrillas.

While important in its own right, the FDR's participation in the Democratic Convergence—and, hence, in the election—highlighted a growing strategic division between the opposition's political and military wings. In January 1989, less than three months before the election, the FMLN submitted a proposal for negotiations that, in effect, dropped their precondition of power sharing, and promised a ceasefire and peaceful cooperation with the electoral process. In return, they demanded that elections be postponed by six months to give the FMLN time to mobilize an election campaign. Duarte rejected the proposal as an unconstitutional postponement of elections. When the archbishop, the State Department, and the CD called on the government to present a counterproposal, Defense Minister Vides Casanova threatened a barracks coup. After weeks of discussion, Duarte finally drew up a compromise, which called for a six-week delay for elections. Fully anticipating a victory, ARENA rejected the Duarte proposal and the FMLN retaliated by calling for an election boycott. In a later interview, the FMLN leader Salvador Samayoa explained that an important reason for the January proposal was to avoid a possible split with the FDR over the issue of the latter's decision to participate in elections in support of the Democratic Convergence.[61]

On the right, meanwhile, the schism in ARENA between the Cristiani faction and traditional militants led by Roberto D'Aubuisson provided an electoral channel for pragmatists who wished to disassociate themselves from ARENA's unsavory image. ARENA's executive committee, acknowledging their founder's international reputation, removed D'Aubuisson from the chairmanship in 1984 and replaced him with the more palatable Cristiani. The party went on to make impressive gains in the 1988 elections, winning nearly 70 percent of mayoral races and gaining an absolute majority in the legislature.[62] The ARENA victory was, perhaps coincidentally, accompanied by another sharp increase in the activities of death squads.

To conclude, the military situation in a civil war largely dictates the conditions for political reform. In the first place, neither side is likely to consider a negotiated ceasefire and participation in ensuing elections if it still believes that a war can be won, or if it perceives continued conflict to be more advantageous than a ceasefire. The costs of conflict are determined by the scope of the war, the international support received by each side, and other military resources, including popular support. The loss of significant resources, such as abandonment by an external patron, increases the costs of conflict. As early as 1984, it had become obvious to many members of the Salvadoran government that the civil war would not be won outright and that to prolong the conflict meant settling into a protracted war of attrition.[63] Despite Duarte's efforts to open a dialogue with the FMLN, the Reagan administration's refusal to consider anything less than military victory kept the costs of continued conflict relatively low for the armed forces. The Democratic Convergence's limited success in the 1988 and 1991 elections demonstrated that the costs of electoral competition had decreased for the opposition. On the other hand, Cristiani's success in the 1988 election increased the militant right's willingness to permit further liberalization, because it proved that free elections would not necessarily mean relinquishing control of the government.[64]

At the end of a decade of civil war, political space began to open. Military stalemate, major changes in the international context that caused an erosion in both sides' military support, and the emergence of a powerful private-sector faction, able to exert its authority over the military and financially sensitive to the damages caused by El Salvador's international pariah status, led the warring parties to sit down at the negotiating table. After a decade of constant and vociferous international attention to the status of human rights in El Salvador, verification of adherence to standards was a central issue in those negotiations.

This was not the result of any single cause. Alfredo Cristiani was able to "go to China" only given permissive and supporting international factors. Had El Salvador's geostrategic significance for the U.S. government not changed with the cooling of the cold war, military support would probably have continued despite the general outcry following the Jesuit murders. The military would have retained its independence, business confidence in El Salvador would have remained low, and Cristiani would have been in a much weaker position to advance a political settlement. By the same token, international intervention is only successful insofar as important elites—after disarmament, specifically the government—are willing and able to cooperate.

Domestic and international conditions changed dramatically after 1989. The domestic factors enabling a political settlement—and, eventually, a human rights verification mission—were, first, a "hurting stalemate" reached by both sides in the civil war, and second, the ascendance of a key faction in the right wing whose interests lay in improving El Salvador's international reputation. The permissive international context in this case entailed an activist period in UN Security Council history (which depended on the generosity of contributing states) and the withdrawal of international military support for both sides of the conflict.

The direction that post conflict peacebuilding would take in El Salvador was shaped in large part by a UN negotiator who was concerned with human rights and who wielded sufficient authority to propose an innovative mandate, and by a member of the UN negotiating team with formidable expertise in human rights. Equally important, transnational human rights mobilization kept the issue on the negotiating agenda and foremost throughout the peace negotiations. Finally, members of the network maintained vigilance over the ensuing mission.

Guatemala, 1980–1993:
INTERNATIONAL PARIAH TO TENTATIVE COMPLIANCE

Our leverage with what we were doing from the beginning with Guatemala was much more limited. We were just getting started then, and we were trying to make our mark by concentrating on the United States Congress and US government as levers for mobilization. Regarding El Salvador, it was easier to find pressure points in Congress. . . . That was not as true in the case of Guatemala. Congress had cut off aid to Guatemala very early, so the main argument for people who didn't want to do anything was "we don't have leverage." Which was true to a certain extent. It's amazing how procedural matters give you the opportunity to work, we depend so much on the creation and existence of fora, the place and time in which you can make your case, if they're not there you have to create them. That's a big difference between Guatemala and El Salvador. . . . Guatemala was a good case for us, because despite the fact that they had elections, we could show that there was no subordination to civil authority and that the army did whatever it wanted in the countryside.

—Juan Méndez

Guatemala has enjoyed a peculiarly notorious status among international violators of human rights. The practice of "disappearing" political opponents or those accused of supporting them was first documented in Guatemala, during the 1960s. Disappearance is an insidious means of obscuring responsibility for state violence, for without a body no proof of guilt, or even of a crime, can be established. By the middle of 1987, approximately thirty-eight thousand forced disappearances had been reported in Guatemala, representing fully 42 percent of all reported disappearances in Latin America.[1] The state achieved international pariah status in the late 1970s and early 1980s. This was merited by both the magnitude of abuse—more than one hundred thousand civilians dead or disappeared between 1978 and 1989, and approximately 1.2 million internally displaced and refugees[2]—and the identity of the victims, the vast majority of whom were indigenous peasants of no particular political affiliation.

As in El Salvador, the transnational human rights network mobilized to pressure the Guatemalan government. International NGOs sent monitors and published reports on conditions throughout the 1980s. Guatemala was subject to scrutiny by the UN Human Rights Commission, although annual reporting began earlier in El Salvador and was more consistent in its criticism of government violations. The Inter-American Commission for Human Rights also investigated and condemned the Guatemalan government. These efforts proved even more futile in Guatemala during the 1980s than they had in El Salvador. The international human rights regime had no mechanisms to enforce compliance, and the human rights network lacked the powerful allies and leverage points to target as in the case of El Salvador. Network activism was further blocked by the paucity of domestic NGOs and human rights institutions capable of providing regular or accurate information.

Conditions began to change in the early 1990s, and a failed executive coup, or autogolpe, in May 1993 provided a major turning point by bringing into alignment the two most powerful forces of the ruling elite. These were officers in the military high command who were convinced that economic development required the legal framework of civilian institutions, and neoliberal pragmatists in the private sector who opposed the antidemocratic and corrupt elements in the military. Both were concerned about the international costs of damaged reputation. The autogolpe also added momentum to an already ongoing resurgence of civil organizations and to the stalled peace talks. Immediately following the failed coup, conditions for human rights enforcement began to evolve through two concurrent developments in domestic politics: the consolidation of civil sectors, and the emergence of a president who, although signally incapable of exerting civilian control over military behavior, was more sensitive to human rights concerns than his predecessors had been.

The Background of Human Rights in Guatemala

The Regional Context

Despite a widespread perception of the Guatemalan government as a puppet of the United States, relations between the Guatemalan and U.S. governments in the 1980s were very different from U.S.-Salvadoran relations. The Salvadoran armed forces' dependence on U.S. financing and training was so great that the threat of losing that aid was a principal factor in their eventual subordination to civilian authority. By contrast, the Guatemalan armed forces had been built up into a modern, well-equipped institution under U.S. tutelage during the 1960s and 1970s, but official military assistance had been cut off under the Carter administration. By the time it was reinstated in 1986, the military had established other arms sources, notably in Taiwan and Israel.

More important, the high command had developed an independent financial profile in banking, real estate, and other industries, and a nationalist foreign policy attitude at the core of which lay the determination not to become, like the Salvadorans, dependent on U.S. assistance. Because of this relative independence, the change in U.S. regional strategy under the Bush administration did not have as determining an effect in Guatemala as in El Salvador. In general, the role of the United States is not as clear or decisive in the case of Guatemala, which suggests that international intervention in the peace process and deployment of a human rights operation had more to do with changing international norms than with U.S. foreign policy.

Finally, an important shift had taken place in the prevailing norms of the Inter-American system with the Santiago Declaration of June 1991, which committed member states to take action in support of threatened democratic governments. This declaration in effect formally elevated support for democracy above the traditional jealous protection of state sovereignty. As a result, the Organization of American States and the U.S. and Mexican governments intervened quickly and decisively in May 1993 on behalf of the Guatemalan civil sectors combating the autogolpe and its hardline supporters in the military.

Domestic Political Alignments

As in El Salvador, the emergence of a dominant element in the Guatemalan ruling coalition concerned for the country's international reputation as a human rights violator was a key factor in bringing about compliance with the human rights regime. In El Salvador, this concern was manifested in the rising fortunes of the pragmatic wing of ARENA, over those of an increasingly embattled army. In Guatemala, neoliberal pragmatists in the powerful Chamber of Agricultural, Commercial, Industrial, and Financial Associations (CACIF) joined forces with liberalizing members of the armed forces against an antidemocratic and notoriously abusive faction of the officer corps. Members of the private sector faulted these military hardliners for having badly mismanaged the economy and for standing in the way of free-trade agreements with the United States (which were threatened by the military's record on human rights). However, the relative capabilities of civilian leaders in the two countries were very different. Only since the beginning of 1996 did Guatemala have a president with Alfredo Cristiani's capacity to confront the military.

Guatemalan governments under both military and civilian administrations failed to comply with the human rights regime. The first UN resolution expressing concern for human rights violations in Guatemala was adopted in March 1980. At the time, General Romeo Lucas García (1978–82) was president. International condemnation continued through the military administrations of General Efraín Ríos Montt (1982–83) and General Oscar Humberto Mejía Víctores (1983–86). It continued beyond the putative transition to democracy through the civilian governments of Marco Vinicio Cerezo Arévalo (1986–91), Jorge Serrano Elías (1991–93), and Ramiro de León Carpio (1993–96).

Normal politics in Guatemala during the 1980s were conducted under an arrangement of regularly held elections with a military-controlled, nonpluralist party system. Because of the way it dominated the political system, the Guatemalan military was able to assert control over the countryside and to circumvent civilian attempts to curtail its authority. Reforms to governmental institutions aimed at human rights protection could not take place under these conditions, and a negotiated resolution of the civil conflict was out of the question. Military control had become institutionalized in the mid-1960s; between 1966 and 1985, Guatemala had a multiparty system in which the candidates of all major parties were either military officers or civilians nominated with military approval. If the official military candidate failed to win in a clean election, either the election would be stolen by fraud or the candidate who won would be permitted to take office only after agreeing to cooperate in the subordination of civilian rule to military authority. Almost any attempt at electoral opposition ended in assassination or exile.

Military organization of the countryside under Ríos Montt and Mejía Víctores effectively destroyed the basis for democratic government at the municipal level. The election of a civilian president in 1985 was engineered by the military in an effort to increase the government's international legitimacy. This was considered necessary to reinstate foreign assistance, to regain private-sector confidence in order to reduce capital flight, in the hopes of limiting social protest by means of a pacted transition. The process was tightly controlled by the exclusion of organizations or parties that sought substantive change or that threatened military power and prerogatives.[3]

Human rights protection under the first two civilian governments improved insofar as the orders for political violence evidently no longer came from the executive office. What did not change was the use of summary execution, torture, disappearance, and other violations of the rights of the person by the military apparatus, particularly the intelligence units, and the climate of impunity within which they were able to operate. Midway through de León Carpio's administration, clear signs of change were perceptible, although human rights violations continued and the civilian president continued to defer to the military on important issues such as the abolition of civil defense patrols. Human rights organizations had offices in the center of the capital and were open and accessible to strangers. Reports of clandestine graveyards being examined by forensic teams appeared in the mainstream national press.

State Coercive Forces

Guatemalan death squads were more overtly linked to the government security apparatus than were those in El Salvador. Although some right-wing civilian paramilitary groups were associated with major landowners or private sector organizations, the vast majority of such operations had direct ties with the military.[4] A variety of state agencies were implicated in death squad operations, including the armed forces intelligence unit (G-2 nationally, S-2 in rural areas), the National Police Technical Investigations Directorate (DIT, renamed in 1986 the Criminal Investigations Directorate, DIC), and the intelligence unit (*Archivo*) of the Presidential General Staff (Estado Mayor Presidencial, EMP). The latter agency operated out of an annex in the presidential palace—directly implicating the executive office in death squad operations.[5]

The administration of General Romeo Lucas García (1978–82), in addition to its notoriously brutal conduct of the civil war, was also remarkable for the degree of corruption at the highest levels of the military.

With an economic crisis brought on by the international recession of the early 1980s, capital flight, and a drop in tourism caused by extreme violence in the countryside, the corruption among high-command officers exacerbated military factionalism. The army was riven by political contests—between officers over fast-diminishing state resources, and between young officers in combat zones and a high command they considered incompetent to defeat the guerrilla. Meanwhile, the small group of senior officers who increasingly monopolized government positions and economic benefits alienated many of the military's civilian allies in the business sector.[6]

In March 1982, two weeks after a presidential election, a junior officers' coup headed by General Efraín Ríos Montt overthrew the outgoing government of Lucas García and annulled the election. The coup was motivated by the perception that the high command was losing the guerrilla war and that the unusually high degree of corruption was threatening the institutional unity of the military.[7] A ruling junta was formed, which dissolved the cabinet and suspended Congress, all political parties, and the Constitution.

The junta decreed a new counterinsurgency strategy, the National Security and Development Plan, into law in April. In this plan, Ríos Montt outlined a four-pronged effort to promote stability and economic development. Political stability, and international and domestic legitimacy, was to be established by returning to a legal constitutional system. Normal politics was to be conducted as a necessary component of the military counterinsurgency effort, with the goal of pacifying the countryside and consolidating an efficient, economically viable national security state.[8] Under Ríos Montt, the level of human rights violations in Guatemala City declined sharply from that of the 1980–81 urban offensives, while scorched-earth warfare intensified and accounted for a marked rise in rural massacres.

The controversial system of Civil Defense Patrols (Patrullas de Autodefensa Civil, PAC) was key to the National Plan. By conscripting the (primarily indigenous) rural male population into local security service, the military was able, first, to control rural communities from within. Second, it obtained on-site intelligence on dissent within the community and on the movements of the guerrilla forces. Third, PACs provided the military with a convenient scapegoat when atrocities were committed. Although they unquestionably acted on orders from local military authorities, PACs were formally autonomous and nominally voluntary, thereby affording the local military base commanders deniability.

When the system was put into practice in mid-1982, 25,000 peasants were drafted into service; by the end of the year the numbers had grown to 500,000.[9] During Ríos Montt's first month in office, members of the local patrol in Rio Negro, Baja Verapaz raped, tortured, and murdered close to 150 women and children and dumped the bodies in a clandestine mass grave.[10] During 1982 and 1983, PACs were used widely in sweeps to round up the internally displaced and bring them under military control in "development poles," a resettlement system along the lines of the strategic hamlets used in Vietnam. These were located in regions depopulated during scorched-earth attacks, which the army then resettled under its command.

Ríos Montt dismissed the other members of the junta in late June and on July 1 declared a national state of siege. Press censorship was imposed, and special military tribunals were formed to try civilians accused of subversion. (The tribunals became the subject of an Inter-American Court advisory opinion.) These actions were followed by a series of rural massacres. The state of siege was extended in February 1983. Reacting to pressure from an urban middle class and small business sectors angered by rations on foreign exchange and gasoline, Defense Minister Méjia Víctores removed Ríos Montt in August 1983, declared himself chief of state, lifted the state of siege, and in response to pressure from the Inter-American Commission, abolished the special tribunals.[11]

Four more massacres took place in the highlands between August and November of that year, and more than eleven thousand people were arrested during sweeps in urban areas in the first months of the new government. Then, with rural areas coming under control, military strategy began to shift from large-scale indiscriminate attacks to targeted disappearances and assassinations. Bodies that showed evidence of death squad-style executions (not a tactic commonly employed during the Ríos Montt government) began to reappear in the streets.

Mejía Víctores began the process of demilitarizing government and preparing to hand the administration over to civilians. The military would retain reserve domains of authority over all areas of public policy, but in the public eye, civilian elected officials would be formally responsible. Military control of the countryside was ensured through the PACs and the Inter-Institutional Coordination system, which organized all state functions and all development programs under the local military authorities. By these means, the bases for effective civilian government at the municipal level were obliterated. When Mejía Víctores orchestrated the transition to civilian government in 1985, the military enjoyed effective control over Guatemalan politics and stood to lose little by relinquishing the presidency.

The Armed Opposition

The Guatemalan National Revolutionary Unity (Unidad Revolucionaria Nacional Guatemalteca, URNG) was formed on January 25, 1982, as a coalition force of four previously existing armed movements.[12] The URNG did not enjoy even the relatively low level of international material support provided to the FMLN. The FMLN itself supplied some military assistance, and the URNG received direct support from Cuba in the late 1970s.[13] However, even at their strongest, in 1980–81, the estimated twelve thousand guerrilla combatants were clearly at a disadvantage against the heavily armed and professionally trained Guatemalan armed forces. By the end of 1982, the military had driven the guerrillas out of the capital, and after an intensification of scorched-earth warfare in the countryside under Ríos Montt, they were reduced to an almost negligible force operating primarily from remote strongholds.

As a military force, the URNG fared far worse than the FMLN partly because Guatemala had a better-disciplined army. Guerrilla leadership were clearly unprepared for the intensity of the military response in the highlands, badly miscalculated their popular support, and were incapable of defending the rural population from army reprisals. Their ties to labor and peasant organizations were weaker and less structured than were those of the FMLN. After 1983, there remained only a rump force in relatively inaccessible regions, without the capacity to organize an urban uprising. The URNG remained on the defensive through much of the decade; a sizeable percentage of the field command of all four organizations had been lost. A resurgence of guerrilla activity in 1987 resulted in a major aerial counteroffensive from September 1987 through March 1988. The URNG continued to occupy villages, attack army bases, and sabotage civilian infrastructure until a conditional cessation of hostilities was called in March 1996; however, it never revived as a significant military force after the early 1980s.

All but defeated militarily, the URNG was also much less successful in gaining international political support than was the FMLN during this period. Like the FMLN, the Guatemalan guerrilla maintained a political-diplomatic commission, sent delegates to annual UN Commission on Human Rights meetings in Geneva, and established relations with the United Nations in New York. However, political solidarity organizations sympathetic to the URNG in the United States were fewer in number and also smaller, less well organized, and less politically sophisticated than the network in solidarity with the FMLN.

After 1983, the guerrilla command made an effort to build an international network of political support, capitalizing on the government's image as a human rights violator. But there was nothing resembling the network of representatives the FMLN had in foreign capitals. The URNG's comparative failure to establish diplomatic relations could partly be attributed to its military decimation: a successful opposition is far more likely to receive outside support and publicity. It also reflected the lower priority the URNG placed on developing international relations.[14] However, it was equally due to the URNG's lack of internal organization and consensus. A unity in name only, the leadership was prone to severe factionalism and disagreement over international strategy, particularly regarding relations with Cuba and the USSR.[15]

Transnational Human Rights Mobilization in the 1980s

International human rights organizations and groups of Guatemalans in exile had been active in publicizing government violations since the late 1970s. Elements of the human rights network, especially Americas Watch, the Washington Office on Latin America, Amnesty International, and the Lawyers' Committee for Human Rights, published reports at least annually, provided the UN Commission on Human Rights and the Inter-American Commission with information, and critiqued the annual U.S. State Department country report on Guatemala. They appealed directly to the U.S. Congress to pressure the Guatemala government through its economic assistance programs and control of military sales contracts. They appealed to European foreign ministries to exert diplomatic pressure and to place human rights conditions on aid and arms transfers. And they appealed to international public opinion through their publications.

Amnesty International's 1981 report on Guatemala focused on the Reagan administration's allegation that abuses were caused either by the guerrilla or by anticommunist right-wing terrorists unaffiliated with the government. Amnesty investigators received testimony that the selection of targets took place in the military telecommunications center located in an annex of the National Palace, directly under the president's control. Death lists were then circulated to the regular security forces to conduct death squad operations.[16] Owing to this and subsequent evidence, the state's responsibility for death squad operations was not ambiguous or diffused, as in El Salvador.

Americas Watch, which began publishing monitor reports on Guatemala in November 1982, introduced the issue of international humanitarian law by condemning the URNG for kidnappings and retaliation against informers. Addressing violations committed by insurgents proved necessary to counter accusations of bias and to buttress the reports' credibility. The extreme nature of government repression meant that virtually no human rights organization existed in Guatemala during the first half of the decade to supply the transnational network with information and to keep Guatemala on the international agenda. Americas Watch reported that the absence of local human rights organizations, which could not survive under the military governments, seriously inhibited investigations and data collection. A great deal of evidence during the early 1980s came from refugees in Mexico, and from the Guatemalan Human Rights Commission (CDHG) and the Committee for Justice and Peace, both located in Mexico. Americas Watch also annually called on the Guatemalan government to permit the International Committee of the Red Cross to establish a permanent office in Guatemala that could have monitored both sides' respect for international humanitarian law. The government finally responded to the ICRC's request to enter Guatemala in 1988, but its staff continued to be severely hampered in their operations.[17]

Although international activists exhausted the available options for mobilization, they had even less impact than in El Salvador. The network lacked access to meaningful sanctions that would have given the Guatemalan government material incentives to comply. U.S. foreign assistance legislation as an instrument for pressuring governments was unique at the time. Most European governments had no such bilateral human rights policy: Scandinavian countries often attached conditionality to foreign aid, but as a matter of policy rather than law. Having such conditionality legislated by the U.S. Foreign Assistance Act provided human rights NGOs with direct leverage, but it was only effective in cases where the amount of aid appropriated was significant, and where the political will existed in Congress to seriously scrutinize the case. In the case of Guatemala, overt military aid was minimal, and there were no procedural pressure points comparable to the biannual Salvadoran certification process and appropriations decisions.

Human rights organizations therefore had to focus lobbying efforts on

Western European governments. The foremost example is the British Parliamentary Human Rights Group, which monitored conditions and conducted in-country investigations in October 1984 and November 1986.[18] European NGOs, such as the Minority Rights Group and the Catholic Institute for International Relations in London, and organizations affiliated with the national sections of Amnesty International, appealed to their own governments to apply diplomatic pressure to the Guatemalan government and especially to use their votes in the UN General Assembly and the Human Rights Commission. The European Parliament could and did pass resolutions condemning violations but had no institutional mechanisms for sanctioning violators outside of the European Community.

European Community states were able to cooperate with the international human rights regime to the extent of using their votes and influence in the UN Human Rights Commission and Subcommission, working groups, and treaty bodies to press for increased scrutiny on the Guatemalan situation. They also had occasion to exert pressure through the "quiet diplomacy" of their embassies in Guatemala, many of whom maintained relations with Guatemalan human rights groups after the mid-1980s.[19] European embassy officials, especially the French, provided information and feedback for international NGO monitoring missions.[20] Finally, the Canadian embassy was instrumental in assisting with many asylum cases.[21] These embassy officials interfered in Guatemala's internal affairs in defense of human rights and contravened the customary diplomatic envoy principle of noninterference. They were not tasked to do so by national human rights legislation but rather were motivated by their moral principles and did so on a voluntary basis.

The Inter-American system provided greater institutional recourse, particularly after Guatemala accepted the jurisdiction of the Inter-American Court in 1986, because that court can make a determination of guilt and award damages to the victim if a case is found to be admissible. The Inter-American Commission on Human Rights sent several investigatory missions, and its reports consistently held the Guatemalan government accountable for violating human rights agreements. The first successful verdict against Guatemala was passed in August 1983. Americas Watch and the Lawyers' Committee for Human Rights had filed an amicus curiae brief with the Inter-American Court in July concerning death-penalty sentences issued by Ríos Montt's special tribunals. The court issued an advisory opinion against the government. Although Guatemala had not yet accepted the court's jurisdiction, Mejía Víctores dissolved the tribunals upon taking command in August and referred to this as evidence that his government was committed to the defense of human rights. However, civil courts were subsequently forced to accept the validity of verdicts passed by the secret tribunals prior to September 1. Americas Watch estimated that between two hundred and four hundred political prisoners were awaiting sentencing at the time, but only seventy were referred by the new administration to ordinary courts.[22] This precedent facilitated the use of the Inter-American Court system for future cases, but the petition system worked very slowly, and few cases were eventually referred from the commission to the court for judgment.[23]

As for the UN Commission, its strongest tool was to assign a special rapporteur with the mandate to investigate, evaluate, and make recommendations. The effectiveness of the rapporteur system unfortunately rested on the approach taken by the individual representative and the political will in the commission to maintain scrutiny. As I explain below, these two factors were weak and resulted in reports that failed to hold the government accountable for compliance with international standards or to assign responsibility for violations.

The Human Rights Network and U.S. Foreign Policy

Guatemala never commanded the congressional attention lavished on El Salvador and Nicaragua, but human rights organizations working on Guatemala still expended much of their advocacy efforts on the U.S. government. They did so because the United States was the major economic and military force in the region and had for decades exercised hegemonic authority over the Guatemalan government. They therefore expected that U.S. pressure had considerable influence over military behavior.

U.S. military assistance had been preemptively rejected in 1977 by President Kjell Laugerud to protest the interventionary human rights conditions placed on appropriations. Congress responded by terminating military aid in 1978. In reality, this was only a partial cut-off, as support still in the pipeline continued and many military supplies could be reclassified as nonmilitary. When the Reagan administration requested that Congress reinstate military assistance to Guatemala in 1983, human rights NGOs lobbied the United States and other governments to end military aid and arms sales, as well as all financial assistance, including multilateral loans, except for carefully overseen distribution of basic humanitarian aid. Under Reagan, the U.S. posture toward Guatemala was consistent with its overall Central America strategy, which was to support military counterinsurgency and head off criticism from Democrats in Congress sympathetic to human rights concerns. As in El Salvador, this was accomplished by promoting the election of a civilian government. Once a civilian president was in office, congressional obstacles to military assistance quickly faded.

Which is not to say that military assistance to Guatemala ever provoked the kind of debate in Congress that there had been over El Salvador and Nicaragua. This was partly due to the low intensity of the conflict itself after the surge of massacres in 1981–83. It was also due to the fact that Guatemala solidarity groups in the United States were less well organized and less active than their Salvadoran counterparts.[24] This left Congress without much incentive to hinder the administration's appropriations requests, while having technically cut off military assistance that during the period of widespread massacres enabled representatives to deny responsibility for human rights violations.

Nonetheless, Reagan's requests to renew lethal aid to Guatemala were rejected until elections were held in 1985, because of the publicity over ongoing, egregious violations. When the request was approved, Congress attached conditions to future military aid. These stipulated that the aid must be requested in writing by the civilian president of Guatemala, rather than directly by the military, and that the State Department must certify that human rights conditions had in fact improved. Overall economic assistance to Guatemala increased sharply with the election of a civilian government, and U.S. military personnel became directly involved in combat operations, training, joint exercises, and logistical support.[25]

The State Department's willingness to criticize Guatemala's human rights record increased dramatically under the Bush administration. The language in State Department country reports became much stronger from 1989 on; these reports first criticized the Cerezo government for a lack of will to stem political violence and then the Serrano government for not following through with his stated intention to control the military. For the first time, the reports openly acknowledged that the majority of human rights abuses were committed by security forces and civil patrols, and questioned both the fiction that PACs were voluntary and the government's rationale that victims were guerrilla sympathizers.

Several diplomatic actions over the next few years indicated the rising volume of U.S. pressure. First, in March 1990, U.S. Ambassador Strook was temporarily recalled to Washington to protest a lack of progress in several key human rights cases.[26] Secretary of Defense Richard Cheney visited Guatemala in February 1992, where he delivered an uncharacteristic statement emphasizing the importance of human rights in relations with the United States. Assistant Secretary of State Bernard Aronson pressed the Guatemalan government in October 1992 to investigate the 1990 murder of Myrna Mack, a Guatemalan anthropologist and human rights activist. The following month Aronson telephoned Serrano to express his deep concern over judicial harassment of indigenous rights organizer, Amílcar Méndez. Evidently in response to U.S. diplomatic pressure, the Cerezo and Serrano governments made several arrests of lower-ranking military and intelligence officials in the major cases specifically indicated in State Department communications (the murders of U.S. citizens Michael Devine and Diana Ortíz, of activists Héctor Oquelí, Myrna Mack, and Refugio Villanueva de Barrera, and the Santiago Atitlán massacre), and Serrano complied with another U.S. request by creating a presidential human rights commission (COPREDEH).

Even after military assistance was reinstated in 1985, the amounts remained relatively minuscule, and threats to suspend aid were irritations rather than incentives to change behavior. Deliveries of lethal aid to Guatemala were temporarily suspended in December 1990, due to evidence that senior military officers were obstructing the investigation of the June 1990 murder of Michael Devine, a U.S. citizen. At this point, direct military assistance totaled approximately $10.2 million, with an additional $3 million appropriated for fiscal 1991. Five conditions were given for reinstatement: prosecution of the murders of Griffith Davis and Nicolas Blake, U.S. citizens who had disappeared in 1985; prosecution of the Michael Devine and Myrna Mack cases; prosecution of the Héctor Oquelí case (a member of the Salvadoran political opposition murdered in Guatemala); unlimited access to refugee settlements for the ICRC; and establishment of a government human rights commission.[27] Congressional appropriations legislation for fiscal 1992 and 1993 prohibited all military assistance, including Economic Support Funds, but permitted commercial arms transfers.[28]

Following the May 1993 autogolpe, the Clinton administration sought to bolster the new government by resuming military and police training and joint military exercises, but direct military assistance remained suspended.[29] Under intense media scrutiny and with the embarrassing presence of U.S. activist Jennifer Harbury conducting a hunger strike in front of the White House, the Clinton administration announced on March 13, 1995, that all remaining military assistance, including officer-training programs, had been terminated.[30] In any event, as a 1996 investigation revealed, covert funding and CIA operations were continuous throughout the period.[31] These revelations raised serious debates within U.S. government circles over intelligence oversight, although they were hardly met with surprise among Guatemalans or in the transnational human rights community.[32]

In addition to pressure from the executive branch and Congress, in rare instances U.S. domestic courts have been used to prosecute violators. Federal courts have jurisdiction over tort cases between foreign nationals in which the offense has been committed on foreign soil, provided that the violator is staying in the United States. By this means, in April 1995 a U.S. federal court judge in Boston awarded Sister Diana Ortiz, a U.S. citizen, and eight Guatemalan plaintiffs $47.5 million in their civil suit against former Defense Minister Héctor Gramajo. Prosecutors were able to bring this case before a U.S. district court because Gramajo was at the time attending Harvard University's Kennedy School of Government. Gramajo dismissed the ruling as a political ploy designed to damage the army's reputation and to undermine his own presidential candidacy. As for the amount of the judgment, he merely claimed that he didn't have $50 million centavos, much less dollars, and had no intention of paying the damages.[33]

In sum, U.S. human rights policy in the 1980s failed to provide even the amount of pressure it had in El Salvador. First, because military assistance deliveries were cut off, and after they were reinstated the amount allocated was too low to be significant in light of the Guatemalan armed forces' material independence. Second, because congressional debate was focused on other issues in the region and the political will among supporters in Congress could not be mustered to exert consistent and strong pressure on the Reagan administration or on the Guatemalan government.

With the shift in geopolitical interests under the Bush government, the State Department increased its scrutiny of military behavior and its pressure on civilian presidents to demonstrate a degree of compliance with the human rights regime. Several attempts were made to bring the material authors of major crimes to trial, particularly during the Serrano administration, but the pressure did not result in any significant change in policy or increase in civilian control over the military prior to the domestic political realignments of the mid-1990s.

UN Sanctions

It must be said that the UN human rights system failed Guatemala during the 1980s. This failure was particularly disheartening because, in the absence of U.S. congressional pressure, the United Nations was the human rights network's most powerful leverage point. The Commission on Human Rights expressed its concern for the situation in Guatemala in 1979, passed condemnatory resolutions beginning in 1980, and requested the appointment of a special rapporteur in March 1982. In December of that year, the chairman appointed a representative from Costa Rica as special rapporteur, but the Guatemalan government vetoed the candidate and requested that the chairman assign an individual who had not served as a country representative.[34] British viscount Colville of Culross, former chairman of the Working Group on Disappearances, was appointed on March 11, 1983.

At this point, the main flaw in the rapporteur system became one of individual inclination rather than of an unresponsive system. Appointment of a special rapporteur under agenda Item 12 (the commission agenda item under Resolution 1235 procedures that considers individual countries found to have a consistent pattern of gross violation) was the strongest measure available to the commission. In addition to the increased level of pressure signified by the presence of a UN investigator on national soil, Item 12 status can be a consideration in decisions concerning bilateral or multilateral assistance. A thorough and unprejudiced rapporteur provides human rights activists, both local and international, greater access to the UN apparatus. Unfortunately, Colville's approach to the military government was one of constructive engagement rather than independent investigation.[35] He did not attempt to establish responsibility for violations, he accepted without comment the military's claims regarding the salutary effects of the development pole program, and he overlooked evidence of abuse.[36]

The commission renewed the special rapporteur's mandate in 1984 and 1985, and Colville continued to hold the position. Largely owing to Colville's uncritical acceptance of the military's assurances and his equation of elections with democracy and rule of law, the commission terminated the special rapporteur's mandate in March 1986. Guatemala was removed from Item 12, and instead the commission requested that the Secretary-General assist with an advisory services program and appoint a special representative.

The UN Advisory Services program had by the mid-1980s developed into the mechanism of choice in dealing with violator states whose governments were democratically elected. It avoided the opprobrium associated with Item 12 status and implied that the state was making progress toward compliance.[37] The NGO community and many governmental delegates had requested continued scrutiny under Item 12, arguing that the civilian government was only one month old and should not be given a blank check.[38] To no avail; Colville was renamed special representative, a role he conceived as being one of information collection with no investigatory or recommendatory powers.

When this position was terminated in March 1987, the commission requested that the Secretary-General name a UN expert to assist with the advisory services program. Héctor Gros Espiell, a Uruguayan attorney, was named in June; his mandate was renewed in 1988 and 1989. As expert, Gros Espiell subordinated his investigatory function to the advisory. He chose not to investigate specific allegations nor did he visit sites of violations, and the majority of his contacts in-country were with civilian government officials.[39]

The UN representative's role was again redefined in March 1990, when the commission requested the Secretary-General to appoint an independent expert. A German jurist, Christian Tomuschat, was named to the position in July 1990, and renewed in 1991 and 1992. With Tomuschat, the UN Commission apparatus began to operate as intended. He extensively interviewed representatives of civil sectors as well as the government and the military, sought and used information from international NGOs, and was straightforward in his criticism of the government. In one incident, while visiting an area of the Ixcán occupied by Communities of Population in Resistance (CPR, internally displaced civilians who had formed self-sufficient communities in remote parts of Guatemala), he happened to arrive immediately following a military aerial bombing of the civilian population. Tomuschat harshly criticized the practice on his return to Guatemala City. Serrano responded with an apology and dismissed the air force commander. The UN expert's public criticism inhibited further systematic use of aerial attacks on the CPRs.[40] Tomuschat's successor, the Argentine jurist Mónica Pinto, appointed in 1993 and acting as independent expert until 1996, was even more stringent in her evaluations and recommendations.

The Resurgence of Guatemalan Nongovernmental Organizations

Until mid-1984, international NGOs had no domestic counterparts in Guatemala on whom to rely for information. Several Guatemalan organizations were working in exile to draw international attention to the situation and to provide the institutions of the human rights regime with documentation and analysis. The United Representation of the Guatemalan Opposition (RUOG) was formed in Geneva in 1982, officially for the purpose of lobbying international human rights forums. Members of the political opposition who had been forced to leave the country organized:

> as a response to the massacres that Ríos Montt was tearing out in this country. My labor confederation where I used to work was busted the 23 of June 1980, and 37 leaders meeting there were abducted and never appeared again. After that we still kept on working, then I left. So I had just arrived a year before in the States, when I was contacted by other Guatemalans, because we were getting messages from other people here, how bad things were. . . . So little by little information began filter out. For the UN General Assembly in 1982 we decided to go as a team of Guatemalans in exile, to lobby for a resolution on a proposal on Guatemala, and we actually got the resolution. After that, the next year we went to the Human Rights Commission in February, then went to the Subcommission in August, then we went back to the General Assembly again at the end of '83. We just began going to the cycle of UN meetings.[41]

In Mexico, the Guatemalan Human Rights Commission (CDHG) was founded by exiles and regularly sent reports documenting violations to the UN human rights apparatus. The Guatemalan Church in Exile (IGE) was active in solidarity campaigns in the United States. Later in the decade, in 1988, the Center for Human Rights Legal Action (CALDH) formed in Washington, D.C., to present Guatemalan human rights cases before the Inter-American Commission and Court.

The first human rights organization to form in Guatemala during the 1980s was the Mutual Support Group (GAM), composed of relatives—mainly women—of the disappeared. GAM was established on June 5, 1984, with 25 Guatemala City residents who had met and formed connections while searching hospitals and morgues for their family members. By the end of the year, membership had grown to more than 350. GAM leaders met with Mejía Víctores four times in late 1984, and began attracting international media and NGO attention, bringing fresh scrutiny to government practices and a credible counterweight to the gloss offered by the U.S. embassy. The organization met with predictable violence. First, GAM spokesperson Héctor Gómez Calito was kidnapped, tortured, and shot on March 30, 1985. Five days later another

GAM leader, Rosario Godoy de Cuevas, was kidnapped with her brother and two-year-old son; all three bodies were found later, with signs of torture. GAM at this point was alone in protesting human rights violations, and these acts of intimidation caused a significant drop in their membership. Acts of violence against GAM members intensified under the civilian government of Vinicio Cerezo.[42]

But the transition to civilian government also saw a resurgence of civil-sector organizing, so that by the end of the decade GAM was surrounded by a growing network of human rights, labor, refugee, and other organizations. The Center for Investigation, Study, and Promotion of Human Rights in Guatemala (CIEPRODH) was founded in 1987 by attorney Factor Méndez Doninelli. In addition to organizing seminars and conferences, and training popular organizations in human rights protection, CIEPRODH developed a database registering individual violations and statistical analyses that have been used by several UN agencies (the Commission on Human Rights, the Working Group on Torture, the Human Rights Centre, and soon after its establishment, by MINUGUA), as well as by the government attorney general's office and the Human Rights Ombudsman.[43] The Council of Ethnic Communities Runuel Junam (CERJ) was organized in El Quiché in 1988 to combat the forced recruitment of indigenous men into the PACs. CERJ quickly became a national organization and extended its mandate to broader issues of human rights protection. The National Coordination of Guatemalan Widows (CONAVIGUA) also formed in 1988, with a focus on indigenous and women's issues, also protesting PAC violations and forced military recruitment.

The Catholic Church had no human rights office prior to 1990. Archbishop Próspero Penados had promised in 1986 to establish an office similar to Chile's Vicaría de Solidaridad or El Salvador's Tutela Legal the following year. However, it was another three years before he considered that conditions were secure enough to risk church personnel. The Archbishop's Office for Human Rights (ODHA) finally opened in January 1990, as a project administered by Catholic Relief Services and co-funded by Caritas Norway.[44] ODHA quickly came to play a role similar to that of Tutela Legal—an autonomous investigative body and provider of the most reliable data on human rights violations for international media and NGOs, backed by the institutional credibility of the Church. Offices remained inside the Metropolitan Cathedral building for security purposes.[45]

International contacts were vital to each of these organizations. GAM was first organized under the protection of Peace Brigades International (PBI), a Canadian-based organization whose purpose is to provide accompaniment to groups or individuals threatened by state repression. GAM was housed in the Peace Brigades headquarters in Guatemala for the first three years of its existence, and PBI provided 24-hour-a-day accompaniment for GAM leaders following the 1985 killings. Peace Brigades later provided the same protection for CERJ members.[46] Regional and international human rights groups made contact with GAM soon after its establishment, first the Latin American Federation of Families of the Disappeared (FEDEFAM), then members of Amnesty International and Americas Watch, who provided material and logistical support in addition to the security of international attention.[47] As these organizations formed, they became members of a wide network of regional organizations that included the Central American Human Rights Commission (CODEHUCA), the Inter-American Institute for Human Rights (IIDH), and the Latin American Association for Human Rights (ALDH).

. Guatemalan human rights activists interviewed for this book universally attached great importance to their contacts with international NGOs, which gave them a modicum of security and brought outside scrutiny to the government and military. This validates one of the principles of human rights mobilization: whether pressure from nonstate actors can directly cause a change in government behavior, international attention—the eyes of the world—benefits individual targets of repression.[48] In the words of two Guatemalan human rights activists:

> If it were not for that international assistance, principally from Americas Watch, Amnesty International, the World Council of Churches, solidarity organizations from democratic countries, Canadian organizations, organizations of Guatemalans working in the US, Canada, or Europe, without the moral and political help of those organizations, I believe that we would have been dead many years ago, the army would not have permitted our organization to develop.[49]
>
> . . . if you don't have the contacts, if the people who are doing the killing know that nobody is going to do anything if you disappear, then you disappear. If you have the contacts and you're doing work that is known outside, that gives you strength. . . . And the people who started the office [ODHA] knew this, that they had to have outside contacts for their own security, for the security of the work they were doing, and the security of those people they were working for. . . . Also for the cases in

their hands, it was important to have contacts so that information could go outside, and people who were in trouble, if they needed to leave the country, they knew they could through the support of this office.[50]

Transnational NGOs have an advantage over intergovernmental or governmental actors in that they are more capable of operating directly on the ground, where a state or organization of states would be hindered by the diplomatic and legal issues entailed in violating state sovereignty. The United Nations does not (yet) impose human rights operations where the state does not grant its consent, but nongovernmental accompaniment or monitoring groups are generally not restricted by the same concerns.[51] Counterbalancing their greater flexibility, NGOs lack the institutional authority of the United Nations or of a diplomatic envoy. Their members enter the country as individuals, often known to be affiliated with a suspect organization, which can mean difficulty in obtaining visas or, worse, vulnerability to attack while working in the target country.

To conclude this examination of transnational human rights mobilization, the network of human rights advocates working on Guatemala applied pressure where they could: on U.S. congressional allies to utilize what little leverage was provided by foreign assistance legislation, on European governments to use quiet diplomacy, and on the United Nations to provide in-country scrutiny and objective reporting. We have seen that governmental and intergovernmental measures were practically ineffective during this period. More effective was the grassroots, immediate relief they offered local organizations, especially in extending a measure of security over the tenuous lives of human rights workers. Transnational nonstate actors intersected the international human rights protection system, providing domestic NGOs access to both bilateral and multilateral resources and attracting international scrutiny to their situation.

DEMOCRATIC TRANSITION AND STATE RESPONSE TO HUMAN RIGHTS PRESSURE

Guatemala's "democratic transition" of 1985 did not produce any real movement toward compliance with human rights standards. Civilian presidents Vinicio Cerezo (1986–91) and Jorge Serrano (1991–93) gave rhetorical support to human rights and made sporadic efforts at an appearance of reform, but the military retained a veto over change by its capacity to overthrow the government, if threatened.

Riding on what appeared to be a clear popular mandate, incoming president Cerezo ordered the National Police Technical Investigations Directorate (DIT) to be raided and disbanded on February 4, 1986. Around six hundred civilian police agents working for the DIT were placed under investigation for human rights abuses and corruption, and were released from service. However, only one was ever charged (with the murder of a fellow agent); the majority were quickly rehired into other state security agencies. The DIT was reorganized into the Criminal Investigations Department (DIC), and a number of the fired DIT agents were incorporated into the new force. No effort was made to reform the military intelligence apparatus.

In fact, the influence of the praetorian guard, the Estado Mayor Presidencial (EMP), grew under civilian presidents, largely by controlling the presidential agenda. The EMP's intelligence unit, the Archivo, was implicated in an array of illegal activities, including the June 1990 murder of anthropologist Myrna Mack. The Army High Command Intelligence Directorate, G-2, continued its extensive mail interception and phone-tapping operations throughout the country and has been linked to death squad activities including the 1989 rape and torture of the Ursuline sister Diana Ortiz, a U.S. citizen.[52]

Human rights monitors agree that there was greater freedom of expression and an overall decrease in the volume of politically motivated violence during the first year of the Cerezo administration, although targeted killings and disappearances did continue. However, this trend was reversed in 1987–88. With an increase in the level of violations came the reappearance of death squad-style killings, indicating that the 1986 decrease had to do with the degree of military control established in the countryside and the absence of popular organizations, rather than to an increase in civilian control of the security apparatus. Bombs exploded at the GAM and PBI offices in August 1989, coinciding with a series of attacks on university students.[53] In late 1989, Guatemala joined Brazil in the practice of using security forces to rid the streets of homeless children.

Popular mandate notwithstanding, Vinicio Cerezo probably never had much of a margin for asserting his authority. For one thing, the Cerezo government was unable to control the ongoing recession or to restructure the economy. And by the time Cerezo left office, his administration was thoroughly discredited by successive scandals and widespread corruption.[54] But most crucial was the simple fact that a faction of the military remained opposed to civilian rule and retained its capacity to overthrow any civilian government that threatened it, whatever the cost in terms of foreign assistance. Attempted coups in May 1988 and again in May 1989, and near coups in August 1988 and August 1989, demonstrated the civilian government's weakness while also highlighting the growing divisions within the military. Human rights violations increased sharply following both attempted coups.

When Cerezo left office, human rights conditions were worse than when the military had handed over the presidency. Targeted violence and the intimidation of popular organization leaders escalated even further under Jorge Serrano. Ramiro de León Carpio, who held the office of Human Rights Ombudsman during the Serrano administration, publicly denounced the military's continued forced recruitment policy and the government's unwillingness to investigate or prosecute human right violators. He accused Serrano of making purely rhetorical promises to exert civilian authority over the military, to end impunity for human rights abuses, and to investigate disappearances.

Serrano became increasingly isolated in office and intolerant of criticism during 1992 and 1993, as the rampant corruption in both the executive and legislature became public and his political coalition foundered. His trade and fiscal policies had led to improved relations with international financial institutions but had also contributed to extreme social dislocation and mass protest over state-imposed rate increases for electricity. It was in the context of uncontrollable student riots that on May 25, 1993, Serrano announced the partial suspension of the constitution, dissolved Congress, the Supreme Court, the Constitutional Court, the Public Ministry, and the attorney general's office.[55] He announced that he would govern by presidential decree pending a new constitution, closed the national news media, and ordered elections of a new Constituent Assembly. The presidents of Congress and the Supreme Court, and the Human Rights Ombudsman were placed under house arrest. (The latter, Ramiro de León Carpio, made a dramatic escape over his back wall.)

A variety of civil sectors reacted immediately in opposition, beginning with an association of political parties, trade unions, attorneys and judicial workers, and CACIF. Two days later, the Catholic Church, popular organizations, academics, and journalists formed their own association and presented Serrano with a petition demanding a return to constitutional government. Representatives of CACIF met with members of the military institutionalist faction, to exchange views of the costs that the country would incur owing to an antidemocratic coup. On May 30, both sides of the opposition movement formed an Association for National Consensus (Instancia Nacional de Consenso).[56]

Figuring large in the private sector's decision to ally with popular organizations was the United States' announcement on May 27 that it would suspend special trade status, freeze credit, and vote against World Bank and International Monetary Fund loans unless democratic rule was re-established. The U.S. Congress immediately suspended most economic aid programs that were channeled through the Guatemalan government and all security assistance, military and police training, and joint military exercises. Similar threats emerged from the European Union, and the Organization of American States acted quickly to support the constitutional system on the basis of the 1991 Santiago Resolution, which requires the OAS to adopt procedures to restore democratic government in the event of a disruption of constitutional rule.

Given the private sector's opposition and the threat of economic isolation, on June 1 the majority of the high command (which had been divided over the executive coup) broke ranks with the defense minister and joined civil sectors in demanding Serrano's resignation. The Constitutional Court declared the presidency and vice presidency vacant on June 4 and ordered Congress to designate a new executive. The Association for National Consensus provided Congress with three approved candidates, and on June 5 Congress elected Ramiro de León Carpio to serve the remainder of Serrano's term.

In the aftermath of the constitutional crisis, three major changes had taken place in the landscape of Guatemalan politics. First, civil sectors had united, if only briefly in the case of cooperation between the business and popular sectors, and further consolidated the nascent arena of civil society. Second, the inability of the military to control the political process during the crisis hastened the diminution of military control over national politics. Finally, it became evident that regional norms had evolved to recognize support for representative government on an equal footing with strict observance of the sovereign authority of the state.

De León began his term in office indicating that he intended to promote security and intelligence reforms in compliance with the recommendations of the UN Independent Expert.[57] Within the first month he had retired two former defense ministers who had supported the autogolpe and sent another hardline general into diplomatic exile. His new defense minister, General Mario René Enriquez Morales, was generally considered to be an institutionalist moderate.[58] However, despite the forthright positions he had taken as Human Rights Ombudsman, de

León lacked the political strength as president to instigate the reforms he had demanded of his predecessors.[59] He had not been popularly elected and had neither a party base nor an electoral mandate. His government was unable to overcome the ongoing economic decline. The intimidation of activists continued; a campaign of violence targeting judges and police investigators in charge of human rights and military-related cases took place in August and September 1994.[60]

Following the putative democratic transition, improvement in human rights conditions came far more gradually in Guatemala than in El Salvador. But there were indications of a degree of compliance on the part of the Guatemalan government by the mid-1990s, in spite of the slow pace of change. Under de León Carpio, there was a marked increase in open dissent from opposition groups and from the national media. Although NGOs continued to sharply criticize the government's human rights record and the president for his volte-face on several issues, working relations were established between the human rights community and the executive office during his administration. In July 1995, the government announced that it would discontinue a particularly abusive paramilitary institution, the "comisionados militares," a reform that had been strongly advised by the independent expert Mónica Pinto in her 1993 and 1994 reports.[61]

This inching toward compliance was caused, first, by the emergence of factions among the military high command and the private sector that strongly preferred civilian constitutional government and were increasingly sensitive to human rights pressure. A second factor was the gradual consolidation of Guatemalan civil society, especially by means of the multisectoral forums and ad hoc umbrella organization formed to combat the autogolpe. Third, de León Carpio's previous work as Human Rights Ombudsman had established him as a member of the human rights network, so that as president he remained a high-profile ally, if an often ineffectual one.

On the international front, UN independent experts' reports had become progressively more pointed, and their advocacy gave the human rights network important access to international attention. The U.S. government's willingness to take a firm stand against the 1993 coup and the embassy's rhetorical support for human rights activists under the Bush and Clinton administrations further emboldened the NGO community. But the most important factor is that the UN-mediated peace process gained momentum after 1993, which generated confidence among civil sectors and established a multilateral human rights observer force in Guatemala.

✩

PART TWO

Multilateral Response in the 1990s

ONUSAL Deployment as of April 1992. Map no. 3825, UN Cartographic Section.

El Salvador, 1989–1996:

NEGOTIATED REVOLUTION TO ONUSAL

I want to say clearly that the work of human rights groups was extremely important, without any doubt it was a very important element of protection. But if the armed conflict had not evolved, these efforts would not have been sufficient. The behavior of the state apparatus and the paramilitary organizations began to be modified, specifically with the signing of the first accord between the government and the guerrilla in San José. The quantity of violations had already begun to decline, but with this accord a much more perceptible change took place. With the signing of the peace accords this tendency increased perceptibly until it arrived at a minimum point of compliance.

—Francisco Díaz (author's translation)

A decade of consistent pressure from the institutions and organizations engaged in human rights work could not cause the government of El Salvador to comply even minimally with standards of international human rights law, as we have seen. The Salvadoran government claimed that gross and consistent violations were necessary to prosecute the civil war. Its chief ally and benefactor, the U.S. government, publicly exhorted the Salvadorans to conform with human rights and humanitarian law but in real terms subordinated those principles to the U.S. geostrategic interest in containing insurgent movements in Central America. Nevertheless, that the Reagan administration was compelled to pay lip service to human rights principles in its dealings with the Salvadoran government reflects the strength of the transnational human rights lobby and the extent to which these principles had become institutionalized as a legitimate concern in international relations by the mid-1980s.

What changed to permit a negotiated resolution of El Salvador's civil war, and how did that process involve government compliance with international human rights pressure? The answer lies first in a changed international context. By the early 1990s, the normative framework for international politics had evolved to a point at which decision makers considered a human rights component to be an appropriate element in multilateral peacekeeping. The Salvadoran government displayed compliance in accepting an interventionary operation, and once deployed, the mission itself became a mechanism to enforce continued compliance. The international political scene was very different after 1989. U.S. strategic interests became less ideological as the cold war cooled. No less important, a relaxation of cold war hostilities also ushered in a period of activism in the UN Security Council.

The second part of the answer has to do with domestic factors. The preferences of political leaders on both the right and the left had changed. A schism had formed among conservatives, from which arose a pragmatic elite seriously concerned with international prestige and therefore more susceptible to human rights pressure. Complementing the changed preferences and power shifts in the ruling elite, the post—Esquipulas II electoral opening to opposition political leaders (detailed in chapter 1) led to a division within the guerrilla movement and the political left over the utility of participating in elections. Domestic political realignments led the two sides to enter into a negotiation process mediated by the Secretary-General's personal representative. The final part of the answer lies in the history of transnational human rights activism in El Salvador throughout the 1980s. The involvement in the peace process of actors allied with the human rights network ensured that the UN verification operation that emerged from the negotiations would be centered on human rights promotion.

These international and domestic factors were mutually reinforcing, in that the civilian leadership's capacity to subordinate the military reflected the change in U.S. interests as much as it did Alfredo Cristiani's internal influence. Not until Congress credibly threatened to withdraw military support after November 1989 was Cristiani able to enter negotiations with the military's endorsement, and even then cooperation among the high command was not absolutely assured. The FMLN's November 1989 urban offensive and its aftershocks definitively shattered the U.S. congressional "bipartisan consensus" on cooperating with the

White House's El Salvador policy. Congress was motivated to draw the line on military assistance by an act that set off a visceral and bipartisan wave of moral condemnation—the assassination of six Jesuit priests and scholars, and two witnesses to the murders. Human rights were therefore central to the Salvadoran peace process from the outset. In retrospect, it seems inevitable that human rights protection would be a cornerstone of the peace process, after a decade of intensive mobilization.

Chapter 1 ended with a description of how international and domestic conditions for enforcement of human rights standards in El Salvador changed following the events of 1989. This chapter examines how the changed conditions enabled international human rights institutions to utilize more intrusive mechanisms to enforce state compliance. The decisions made in establishing the UN operation and in implementing its mandate created precedents for further innovations in peacebuilding. In many respects, the Guatemalan and later East Timorese missions have followed in evolutionary progression from the Salvadoran peace accords.

A Negotiated Revolution

In addition to the above changes in post–cold war geopolitics and domestic politics, other factors specific to the Salvadoran context made it unusually favorable for the successful conclusion of a negotiated peace process. On the domestic front, first, conditions of "ripeness" for a political settlement existed. The conflict had reached a mutually hurting stalemate, so that both sides recognized their interests lay in a political rather than a military resolution.[1] Second, both sides were able to credibly commit their respective forces to abide by agreements; the guerrilla hierarchy remained intact, and the government was able to extract at least rhetorical loyalty from the military. Third, the armed forces, which might have seriously undermined or vetoed the process altogether, were heavily dependent on foreign assistance. The threat of having that assistance withdrawn could be used successfully to subordinate the military to civilian control.

The involvement of military officers from the start in the mediated dialogue was taken as a positive indication of the high command's commitment to support Cristiani in seeking a political settlement.[2] It must be noted, however, that in late 1989, the military was split between a faction committed to total war and a more pragmatic faction willing to discuss a negotiated settlement.[3] The division later widened considerably as the evidence mounted of the high command's involvement in the November 16, 1989, assassinations of six Jesuit scholars, their cook, and her daughter. Junior officers began to express dissent, particularly with the military's efforts to block the investigations.[4]

The ongoing prosecution of the Jesuit case throughout the negotiations had an immeasurable effect in keeping the military on board. Military compliance was primarily explained by the fact that continued U.S. military support, which the armed forces had been able to take for granted for more than a decade, was suddenly insecure. The Dodd-Leahy legislation passed in November 1990 cut military assistance by 50 percent and made the remainder conditional upon good faith in negotiations, acceptance of UN mediation, progress on the Jesuit case, and control of military violence against civilians.[5]

In terms of international politics, several exceptional circumstances assisted the successful outcome in El Salvador. Both parties' foreign military support eroded with the end of the cold war. The collapse of the socialist bloc and the loss of Nicaraguan assistance after the Sandinistas were defeated in the 1990 elections deprived the FMLN of much of its international political support. Attempting to reduce its isolation, Cuba added its voice to the chorus urging the FMLN to cooperate in a negotiated resolution. The U.S. Congress, joined eventually by the Bush administration, exerted unilateral pressure on the Salvadoran government and military. At the same time, the U.S. and Soviet foreign ministries joined in bilateral efforts at diplomatic persuasion. That no major power opposed it was essential to the peace process. Finally, the high-profile nature of El Salvador's civil war drew generous commitments from international agencies and other states to assist in implementation and reconstruction.

Regarding the nature of UN mediation, this was the first instance of direct mediation of an internal conflict by a representative of the Secretary-General. For the office of the Secretary-General, it was an unprecedented diplomatic intervention.[6] The domestic and international circumstances surrounding the Salvadoran peace process were unusually favorable, leading some analysts to argue that the Salvadoran example does not altogether apply to less conducive situations.[7] Although I believe that the Salvadoran situation was not as exceptional as has been claimed, that conditions were so favorable does qualify the lessons to be drawn from it.

Getting to the Table: Intervention by Mediation

Both the Duarte government and the FMLN had made overtures toward negotiating in the mid-1980s[8] but without success; not only were positions on both sides inflexible, but the Reagan administration also opposed a nonmilitary settlement.[9] The beginning of a successful peace process dates from the June 1989 inauguration speech given by incoming president Alfredo Cristiani, in which he identified a negotiated peace as one of his administration's two top priorities. Preliminary talks began in September of 1989, facilitated by the Catholic Church, with UN and OAS representatives present as observers. The fruitless initial period of dialogue terminated when the FMLN formally withdrew from the process after paramilitary forces bombed the National Federation of Salvadoran Union Workers (FENASTRAS) building on October 31. Then came the FMLN urban offensive and the November 16 Jesuit assassinations. Most analysts agree that the November offensive and the Jesuit killings provided a turning point necessary to convince all parties to the conflict that a military victory was infeasible, and that a political solution was unavoidable and urgently needed.[10]

The November offensive demonstrated to the FMLN that, despite its military capabilities, it was not able to incite a general urban insurrection and was therefore not likely to break the existing military stalemate. For the armed forces, the demonstration of FMLN capabilities convinced their supporters in the United States that a military solution was not possible. Testifying before Congress in February 1990, the chief of U.S. Southern Command, General Maxwell Thurman, painted a grim picture concerning the armed forces' chances for victory, concluding that "I think they are ultimately going to have to go to the table and negotiate."[11] Pressure from the U.S. government to cooperate in the peace process also increased as a political consequence of the military's bombing of civilian neighborhoods during the offensive.

FMLN commanders Salvador Samoyoa and Ana Guadalupe Martínez requested a meeting with UN representatives Alvaro de Soto and Francesc Vendrell in late November. They met in Montreal on December 8.[12] Samayoa and Martínez conveyed the message that the FMLN was interested in having the United Nations act as third party broker for the negotiations but was concerned that the Secretary-General's office was too much under Security Council (meaning U.S.) control. In the course of this meeting the idea of a parallel mechanism was first broached, to provide the Secretary-General with a political base independent of the Security Council. This eventually became the "Group of Friends of the Secretary-General," an advisory body composed of the representatives to the United Nations from Venezuela, Colombia, Mexico, and Spain.

By mid-December 1989, both parties had concluded that UN Secretary-General Pérez de Cuéllar would be the logical choice for neutral third-party participant in the dialogue, given the implication of neighboring states and the Catholic Church in the conflict, and formally requested that he exercise his good offices to guarantee the process. It remained for the mediator's role to be defined, with de Soto and the FMLN proposing full mediation and the government holding out for a more limited role. The issue was finally decided in late March 1990, when the parties agreed to an invented category, that of "intermediator," which was in effect the more active role that the FMLN had requested.

In retrospect, it is clear that had de Soto accepted a less active role, had the definition of "good offices" remained ambiguous and open to interpretation, the Secretary-General's credibility would have been risked in a negotiation over which his office had relatively little control. After two months of discussions with the Secretary-General's representative, the government came to accept the stronger role of active intermediation. This was a compromise that significantly determined the tenor of the Salvadoran negotiations and introduced direct mediation as a tool for UN intervention in internal conflict.

Getting to Yes: Human Rights on the Peace Agenda

The UN-mediated peace process began in Geneva on April 4, 1990, with the signing of an agreement to negotiate in good faith. One of the provisions stipulated at Geneva enabled the Secretary-General to release information to interested governments. Pérez de Cuéllar used this as a mechanism to cultivate the Security Council's interest in the Salvadoran process (but without inviting members to interfere with it), to keep the "four friends" involved, and occasionally to enlist the support of the United States, the Soviet Union, and Cuba.

An agenda agreement was signed in Caracas on May 21. The order of items agreed to emphasizes the status that the protection of human rights and the creation of an institutional environment for their long-term promotion had acquired. The order of issues to be negotiated were first, military restructuring; second, human rights; third, the judicial system; fourth, the electoral system; fifth, constitutional reforms; sixth, economic and social reforms; seventh, UN verification of accords.

The UN mediator's role began to evolve almost immediately, with the round of talks held in San José, Costa Rica, on July 20–26. The agenda item for the meeting was purification of the armed forces; the previous meeting had ended without an agreement on this same issue. All involved were concerned by the possibility that the peace process may once again have reached an impasse, and that its momentum and credibility would be lost.

Prior to the San José meeting, on July 16–17, a convocation had been held in Geneva of human rights specialists from Latin America, North America, and Europe. It was headed by the Venezuelan jurist and human rights expert Pedro Nikken, who was at that time legal counsel for the UN delegation, and included Salvadoran legal scholars and human rights advocates. They compiled an outline for a human rights agreement, from which Nikken drafted a UN working paper to be presented when the subject of human rights came up (following the armed forces topic on the negotiating agenda). Three major innovations in human rights enforcement were discussed at this meeting. For the first time, the UN contemplated the possibility of effectively blanketing a country with human rights monitors. Then, this was the first instance in which human rights had been made the focus of a conflict resolution process. And the United Nations, for the first time, approached the idea of including institutional reforms aimed at long-term human rights protection in an accords package.[13]

When it appeared that the San José meeting would end in another stalemate on military restructuring, de Soto decided to advance the agenda to the next topic in order to salvage the credibility of the process. He opened discussions on the issue of human rights, using the experts' document as a basis. The resulting accord, signed on July 26, 1990, was essentially an elaboration of the working paper drawn up in Geneva. The accord committed both parties to respect and guarantee nothing more nor less than "those rights recognized by the Salvadorian legal system, including treaties to which El Salvador is a party, and by the declarations and principles on human rights and humanitarian law adopted by the United Nations and the Organization of American States."[14] The first substantive accord of the peace process required the Salvadoran state to comply with international human rights instruments to which it was already party but which had never previously been enforceable.

The FMLN was likewise obliged to respect international human rights and humanitarian law. Both parties were pledged to cooperate with international observers and to take any recommendations made by the mission into consideration. Although not binding, this latter concession was augmented in July 1993 by a more aggressive interpretation of the observer mission's mandate, which focused on measures the parties were actually taking to achieve compliance.[15]

The original terms of the human rights agreement stipulated that international verification would commence with the cessation of hostilities. However, as soon as the accord was signed, the FMLN delegates came under fire from their civilian sympathizers and field commanders, for having committed themselves to such a degree without having gained anything in return.[16] From the start, the FMLN had insisted that, until the topic of the armed forces had been dealt with, there could be no progress on other issues. Now they appeared to have buckled under pressure and demanded immediate verification to pacify their constituents.[17]

The Salvadoran human rights agreement thus created another UN precedent: ONUSAL was deployed prior to a ceasefire. The subject of early deployment raised very real security concerns for the United Nations. The civil war continued unabated in combat zones; indeed, another (albeit lesser) guerrilla offensive was launched in late fall of 1990, and the FMLN was making effective use of its newly acquired surface-to-air missiles to keep up pressure for a negotiated settlement. The extreme right wing of the ruling ARENA party was vociferous in protesting the violation of national sovereignty that a human rights verification mission would represent. In fact, following deployment mission personnel were subject to death threats and at least one serious attack by Salvadoran nationalists.

Aside from concern for personnel safety, deploying the mission prior to a ceasefire carried political and interagency implications that had to be resolved. It would have required much less in the way of verification had the accord committed the FMLN and the military to respect international humanitarian law *after* hostilities had formally ceased. Deployment under combat conditions entailed making a legal decision on whether the mission would be responsible for verifying the Geneva Conventions, a task that up to this point had always been the responsibility of the International Committee for the Red Cross. The Secretary-General's office decided against tasking the mission to monitor international humanitarian law. A preliminary mission visited El Salvador in March 1991. Its report enabled the Secretary-General's office to determine that the threat to security was at an acceptable level and that combat zones could effectively be placed off limits until a ceasefire was in place. These areas had a low population density, so that the mission could credibly monitor human rights compliance for the majority of the population without entering combat zones.[18] In the end, the Secretary-General relaxed his decision not to duplicate the ICRC's efforts in the field so that the mission could take action in certain cases of severe threat to the civilian population.[19]

Aside from the question of verifying international humanitarian law, the sharpest critique of the decision to deploy the mission prior to a ceasefire refers to a tension produced by the UN's dual mandates of mediating a peace process while monitoring human rights compliance. The necessity to maintain relations with both parties during the negotiations, and with the government after the FMLN disarmed, led many to accuse the United Nations of being overly cautious, even biased, in reporting human rights violations. Accusations of partiality came from both sides; because the mission could only selectively verify the Geneva Conventions, government officials considered the early human rights reports to favor the FMLN.[20] From the other perspective:

> In everything it did in the role of mediator until the accords were signed, the UN acted in a neutral manner. But in everything it did *in situ*, in observation and active verification, it was not neutral. The mission in El Salvador acted as if its presence were the result of a diplomatic agreement, subject to international treaty law. And as if the host agency, its counterpart, were the government. And this is not the case, because the UN's presence in El Salvador is not the result of an accord between the government and the UN, but an accord between the government of El Salvador and a Salvadoran insurgent force, that requested it to come to verify the compliance. . . . ONUSAL for the length of its presence has treated the government with deference, protocol, diplomatic caution. In the compliance with reciprocal obligations, it has been much more demanding of the FMLN than of the government, despite the fact that 90% of the obligations pertain to the government.[21]

The mission's caution was understandable, in that full disclosure of violations or pressure on one party or the other to comply could have destabilized the negotiations. But a failure to report violations engenders public cynicism, especially among the disappointed human rights community, and damages the United Nations' credibility.[22] The Secretary-General attempted to bolster the separation between the diplomatic process and the human rights mission by receiving the reports and passing them on to the Security Council without vetting or editing. This was intended to serve two purposes: to allow uninhibited human rights monitoring, and to distance the mediator from the mission so that, should the monitors report something offensive to either party, it would not jeopardize the negotiations.[23]

The two functions should have been mutually supporting, the presence of monitors on the ground acting to deter violations, to lower the intensity of the conflict, and to build confidence for the negotiations. However, the need to avoid alienating either side by publicizing every offense did have the effect of giving the mission the appearance of subordinating human rights principles to diplomatic expediency. This outcome may be inevitable where one of the parties has committed 90 percent of all reported abuses and where that party is in a position to exercise "operational blackmail" over the mission. In this regard, a UN mission director explained that "we have an agreement that basically relies on the Salvadoran government to allow us to do our work. With the costs and complexities of ensuring full respect for human rights, it's easier at times not to deal with things."[24]

ONUSAL originated as a human rights mission, with a mandate limited to verifying the San José agreement. A previously unthinkable advance in international human rights protection, it reflected the historical context and policy trends within the Secretary-General's office. Once the paralysis of the cold war was lifted, the United Nations found itself in a position to resolve an unprecedented number of conflicts, in a flurry of experimental activity. Drawing on the precedent of the transitional authority in Namibia, de Soto proposed a verification operation under civilian rather than military administration, which would report directly to the Secretary-General and to the Security Council. The operation's complete design was developed over a period of months after the human rights accord was signed. The original agreement calls for a UN human rights verification mission but does not specify the mission's relationship to overall verification of peace accords. The idea of deploying the mission as part of an integrated multidimensional operation was proposed partly for administrative/budgetary purposes but principally for the tactical advantage of placing it squarely under the Security Council's authority and oversight.[25] Members of the advocacy network continued to be involved in the design process. Human rights experts met with the negotiating team on four occasions following the San José accord for consultation on such topics as judicial reform.[26]

One issue stalling progress toward a military accord over the following months was the question of impunity for past violations. To overcome this obstacle, the UN team began to formulate a mechanism to research and publish findings on selected outstanding cases of human rights violations; this would become the Commission on the Truth for El Salvador. The Truth Commission's terms were developed quietly by the United Nations over the next several months. When the topic of constitutional reform came up in April 1991, de Soto recognized this as the auspicious moment to insert the Truth Commission into the accords. It met with no serious opposition from among the delegations at the time, although military officers quickly voiced their discontent once the agreement was signed.

The April 1991 round marked another turning point in the peace process. Following an impasse of many months, again over the problem of military restructuring, the parties decided to focus on the topic of constitutional reforms. The current legislative assembly term would end on April 30, and had they missed this deadline, constitutional reforms would have been delayed for three years. The accord signed in Mexico on the night of April 27, and approved by an extraordinary session of the outgoing legislative assembly in the early hours of April 30, entailed amending 35 of the 274 articles of the 1983 Constitution. The reform package included the restructuring of security forces, which brought public security under a civilian ministry and created a new civilian police force. It also included modifications to the justice and electoral systems, and the creation of the Truth Commission. In this way, the United Nations committed itself to intervene in the constitutional affairs of an intact member state.

Another milestone agreement was signed in New York on September 25, 1991. This accord created a National Commission for the Consolidation of the Peace (COPAZ), a representative body charged with overseeing the implementation of all political accords, and an Ad Hoc Commission to vet and purify the military of human rights abusers. It set the framework for reductions to the armed forces, reforms to doctrine and training, and outlined the enlistment and training of a new civilian police force. Finally, the agreement addressed the issue of land tenure and created the Social and Economic Forum. A secret annex to the New York agreement detailed the formula for incorporating the FMLN into the civilian police. In exchange for equal access to the police force, the FMLN withdrew the demand that its combatants be integrated into the government armed forces.[27]

The final act of the Salvadoran peace process ended with an appropriately dramatic flourish. With only three days remaining of Javier Pérez de Cuéllar's term as Secretary-General, and amid rumors of an impending coup intended to prevent him from signing the military reform agreement, Cristiani returned to New York on December 28 at the urgent request of the "four friends" and the U.S. government. At the very last minute of Pérez de Cuéllar's term—midnight December 31, 1991—the two parties signed the Act of New York, the final step in El Salvador's long journey toward an end to civil war.

Getting to Peace and Staying There: Lessons from El Salvador's
Peace Process

The degree of interest the international community displayed in the Salvadoran peace process is unusual. Much of the international support for the peace process had to do with Pérez de Cuéllar's personal interest in resolving the Central American conflicts. He had so committed himself to the process that the Secretary-General's credibility as a peacemaker was at stake, which increased the pressure to achieve a final accord. More generally, the civil conflict in El Salvador had come to symbolize global ideological and geostrategic divisions, and the severity of human rights abuses invited international attention from other sources.

Pressure to arrive quickly at a final peace accord came from all directions, both domestic and international. This served as a double-edged sword. It produced an end to the armed conflict in a relatively short time but at the cost of inclusiveness of the process and breadth of the resulting accords. Socioeconomic reforms—issue number six on the negotiating agenda—were severely limited because of the diplomatic pressure to produce a final peace accord in as short a time as possible and the FMLN's strategic need to ensure the safe reintegration of its combatants. Land reform was addressed only in the context of reintegrating former combatants and refugees and is the part of the accords package that has met with the greatest degree of resistance during implementation.[28] The Social and Economic Forum created under the New York agreement was delayed and underfunded, mandated only to discuss critical issues such as labor relations, and was rendered ineffective because the government and business sector were able to block any of the labor organizations' initiatives.[29]

The lack of civil societal participation in the Salvadoran peace process is considered to have been an important omission, one that was largely due to the closed nature of the negotiations. The FMLN initially attempted to install a parallel negotiating table system similar to that developed later in Guatemala, with civil sectors convening separately from the armed parties. This scheme was repeatedly rejected by the government. Members of the FMLN delegation held official meetings with labor leaders, political parties, church representatives, and human rights organizations before every round of talks, in order to receive their recommendations and to inform them of the results of previous rounds.[30] Ambassador de Soto likewise recognized the need to "build a constituency" for the negotiation process, to give members of society the sense of being involved without actually interfering with "running as tight a ship as possible in the negotiations."[31] He attempted to balance these two competing values—the mediator's need for control and the desirability of civil participation—by meeting with sectoral representatives. In the end, however, issues vital to popular sectors, especially labor rights and land reform, were sacrificed to the strategic interests of the parties.

Arguably, this negotiation was intended to end an armed conflict, not to establish a social pact among civil sectors or to reform the economic system. Further, increased transparency and the participation of societal actors can hamper the process by increasing the level of contentiousness. But both opposing parties claimed legitimacy based on the assertion that they represented sectors of civil society. Retaining the discussion within the immediate circle of negotiators facilitated the Salvadoran process but, as is always the case of pacts among elites, at the expense of marginalizing organized civil sectors and leaving open the possibility of renewed conflict. Popular involvement in peace talks ensures that substantive proposals from relevant sectors are seriously considered. Ignoring organized members of civil society during negotiations risks their apathy or downright obstructionism during implementation. This is one lesson that was carried from the Salvadoran peace process to Guatemala (and hence to Colombia).

The most significant aspect of the peace process was that it generated a powerful instrument for the promotion of human rights principles. The active role of UN mediation was a major determinant; the proposal drafted by Pedro Nikken and the group of human rights experts in Geneva outlined a radical departure in international verification. The Salvadoran government's consent to host an interventionary operation on national territory indicates that, under particular circumstances, the competing international norms of state sovereignty and human rights protection have become better balanced. The leadership of both parties effectively ceded a great deal of control to the United Nations, first by requesting third-party mediation and then by acquiescing to an open-ended commitment to cooperate with an "invading army" of human rights observers.

The UN Observer Mission in El Salvador (ONUSAL) was designed to integrate Human Rights, Military, and Police Divisions, plus an Electoral Division to assist with registration and polling for the 1994 national elections. The following overview of ONUSAL's major functions is concerned with human rights protection and promotion.[32] I focus on the verification and institutional strengthening components of the Human Rights Division, discuss some of the difficulties they encountered, the means by which they were overcome, and the mission's overall success in promoting human rights.

International and domestic factors related to the conditions discussed above influenced the mission's successful deployment. First, it was in both parties' interest to have observers in the country during negotiations. The government was under pressure from the U.S. Congress as a result of the Jesuit killings. Human rights verification could both contribute to improving its international reputation and convince the United States that it was serious about human rights, while also placing the FMLN under international scrutiny. The FMLN could appease its social bases by placing government forces under observation. Finally, generous international assistance provided both with needed incentives to comply in implementing the accords. Financial commitments from bilateral donors between 1992 and 1995 came to nearly $700 million, and multilateral agencies during the same period committed more than $900 million toward demobilization, reconstruction, and implementation projects.[33]

Conducive factors certainly did not obliterate the political obstacles to implementation. The process was contentious, and the parties frequently displayed a lack of political will to cooperate. At times, the mission's leadership found itself isolated, with neither party willing to support the implementation effort, and with the local human rights community complaining that the mission had failed to go far enough. The phased disarmament had to be rescheduled several times during 1992, the year of the "armed peace." The government stalled at every step of demobilizing former security forces and deploying the new civilian police. Despite pressure from ONUSAL, criticism from the Secretary-General, and threats to curtail further funding from international donors, many reforms to the electoral and judicial systems have yet to be passed into law, owing to the divisiveness of Salvadoran politics.[34]

The intervention of the United Nations in El Salvador involved the organization in domestic political struggles, a role for which there was no precedent and no simple solution. It goes without saying that political actors have incentives to cheat on agreements to promote short term interests. Mission leadership propelled the implementation process by developing and maintaining permanent, dynamic relationships with the parties' leaderships, relying on their political interests in keeping the process on track. While in several cases the United Nations found itself unable to overcome the parties' incentives to cheat, on at least one occasion, by holding firm, ONUSAL was able to pressure the parties into backing away from a side agreement that threatened to corrupt the civilian police force. Similarly, the mission's efforts to purify the judiciary were characterized by alternating public pressure with diplomacy. Throughout the process, the mission had to tread a careful line between disrupting its relations with the host government, while at the same time taking an expansive approach to its mandate.

The Human Rights Division: "Active Verification"

ONUSAL was deployed on July 26, 1991, exactly one year after the San José accord was signed, with ample human and material resources and a broad mandate that greatly contributed to its success in the field. During its first year, the mission received and investigated complaints, while developing extensive contacts with justice officials, the defense ministry, the government human rights commission, FMLN representatives, and, to a lesser extent, with human rights NGOs. Accusations of human rights violations continued at a high level during this period. Despite a perceptible deterrent effect stemming from the sheer size of the mission and its ability to conduct investigations unannounced, violations persisted well after the ceasefire.[35]

In October 1992, with the arrival of its third director, Diego García-Sayán, the Human Rights Division was reorganized into two work units. A verification unit handled casework and reporting, and an administration of justice and institution-building unit lent technical assistance to the judicial system, the civilian police, and the National Counsel for Human Rights. After having operated for a year without methodological guidelines, a manual for human rights verification was created that standardized the categories of offense, the criteria for admissibility, and gave guidelines for follow-up investigations and for initiating investigations ex officio. García-Sayán developed a more aggressive approach to the work, which he labeled "active verification," intended to be a systematic investigation process aimed at gathering information, initiating specific corrective measures, and promoting activities to strengthen institutions.[36]

ONUSAL's human rights verification was criticized for weaknesses in three areas: methodological problems in reporting and technical deficiencies in personnel training; limitations in the interpretation of its mandate; and the failure to establish solid relations with Salvadoran nongovernmental organizations and with the general population. The methodological problems were resolved when the verification manual was created in fall 1992. A version of this manual was adapted for the UN human rights mission in Guatemala (MINUGUA). Personnel recruitment, orientation, and training continued to be a weakness for the duration of the mission.[37] The second category of criticism stems from the mission's initial focus on casework, to the detriment of institutional strengthening. The doctrinal shift under García-Sayán was an attempt to redress this problem. Finally, the mission has been roundly criticized for not having properly educated the public regarding its presence in the country or established close working relations with local human rights NGOs. The San José agreement tasks the mission to carry out an information campaign on human rights and on the mission's function. Community outreach unfortunately received little attention upon deployment, and public ignorance is seen to have contributed to the "unrealistically high expectations on the part of many Salvadorans."[38]

ONUSAL's relations with Salvadoran NGOs were perhaps its greatest weakness.[39] Communications broke down early into the mission. Relations were promising for a brief period at the beginning, partly because of the local organizations' role in lobbying for ONUSAL's early deployment, and partly because the mission staff was heavily drawn from the human rights network, especially from the Southern Cone NGOs. But relations quickly worsened due to a number of factors. First, the language of UN reporting is diplomatic, at times ambiguous, reticent of the kind of finger-pointing in which human rights NGOs typically engage.[40] It was also caused by the (often accurate) perception that Salvadoran NGOs were highly politicized and organically affiliated with the FMLN, so that very close relations could have jeopardized the mission's appearance of neutrality.[41]

The mission's poor relations with the NGO community also partly reflected the overall tension between its dual political-diplomatic and monitoring aspects, discussed earlier. In this regard, relations were tense within the mission, between the human rights professional staff (largely of NGO background), the political directorship (who were viewed, perhaps unfairly, as having a bureaucratic bias), and the uniformed personnel, naturally considered to be antagonistic to human rights concerns. It also had to do with simple resentment; Salvadoran human rights workers had always been severely restricted in their work by the lack of resources, whereas ONUSAL observers had vehicles and communications equipment that enabled them to conduct investigations in remote areas of the country and enjoyed a degree of access unthinkable for national NGOs. Generally, the mission's early focus on casework rather than on strengthening local institutions meant that personnel had little support or resources for developing relations with the NGO community.

Salvadoran human rights activists were not consulted, nor were they kept apprised of mission activities. Only toward the end of ONUSAL's tenure, in 1994, was there a serious effort to rectify the problem. As part of the institution-building program, ONUSAL and the nongovernmental Human Rights Commission (CDH) cooperated on a series of seminars in verification and investigative techniques, and in human rights law. Reed Brody, the last director of the Human Rights Division, placed special emphasis on improving relations with the NGO community. Carrying the lesson to Guatemala, Brody was also instrumental in coordinating meetings between UN officials and the Guatemalan human rights community in preparation for MINUGUA's establishment.

Administration of Justice and Institution-building

In conjunction with human rights verification, ONUSAL oversaw the implementation of significant reforms to the country's political institutions, the majority of which were mandated by the Mexico agreement of April 1991 on constitutional reforms. The Office of the National Counsel for the Defense of Human Rights (Procuraduría de Derechos Humanos, PDH) was the principal institution the accord established to promote long-term respect for human rights. The PDH's purpose during the transition period was to identify and eradicate groups engaging in systematic violations. This included the authority to close down jails or detention centers. Although the office of the Procuraduría officially opened in February 1992, it was greatly delayed in opening auxiliary regional offices; the budget the government had allocated was insufficient.[42] The Procurador was reduced to requesting startup funds from the UN Development Programme, to cover office expenses and salaries.[43] Mission personnel worked closely with PDH staff, accompanying and providing technical assistance and training to the investigative teams. Several mission members complained in interviews of the lack of experience or training in human rights law among PDH staff, of the overly legalistic, procedural approach taken by the office, and of its lack of initiative. Salvadoran human rights NGOs were even less flattering or optimistic. The office was strengthened considerably with the election of a more committed director in March 1995, but its effectiveness continues to ebb and flow with the abilities of the incumbent.

The judicial reforms mandated under the accords overall sought to increase the judiciary's independence from political influence and to enhance legal safeguards for civil and political rights. The National Council of the Judiciary was restructured to make it independent of other government bodies and political parties. A Judicial Training School was created under the National Council of the Judiciary. ONUSAL organized training courses in human rights and due process for justices and magistrates in conjunction with the council. The mission also assisted in the process of evaluating justices and developing lists of judges found to be involved in corrupt or unprofessional conduct, who were then recommended for purgation by the Supreme Court. Like the Procuraduría, the council was weak and ineffective for most of the mission's duration, but its institutional capabilities increased with time.[44]

The Mexico agreement altered the selection process for Supreme Court justices, with the intent to make the Supreme Court a nonpartisan body. By the terms of the reform, justices are elected by a two-thirds majority for staggered terms, rather than as a bloc elected by a simple majority. A new, more independent and professional Supreme Court was elected in July 1994 under these rules. Constitutional reforms aimed at decentralizing the Supreme Court's authority within the judicial branch met with less success. The Truth Commission recommended devolving certain administrative functions, especially oversight of lower court judges, from the Supreme Court to the more independent Judiciary Council. This recommendation, although binding under the terms of the Mexico agreement, was not ratified.[45]

Other Truth Commission recommendations were complied with, including acceptance of Inter-American Court jurisdiction and accession to a number of international human rights instruments. The latter reforms are examples of the United Nation's carrot-and-stick incentive provision. Just prior to ONUSAL's official termination in April 1995, the Secretary-General linked further international aid to compliance on these outstanding issues. Alvaro de Soto visited the country to verify the implementation of remaining accords in June 1996. He negotiated an agreement among parties in the heavily factionalized legislature, with the result that they ratified several constitutional amendments, including habeas corpus guarantees, reductions in the length of time permissible for administrative detention, and gave legislators, rather than the Supreme Court, the authority to remove members of the Judiciary Council.[46]

Public Security and the National Civilian Police

Civilian oversight of military and intelligence agencies and the creation of a civilian police force were the most detailed areas of institutional reform introduced by ONUSAL.[47] The accords outlined a plan for removing public security from the military by replacing the existing National Police, National Guard, Treasury and Customs Police—all of them military units—with a single National Civil Police (PNC). The new force was to operate under the Ministry of the Interior and Public Security, newly restructured from the old Interior Ministry, rather than under Defense. A new security doctrine emphasizing the rule of law and human rights standards was developed, to be thoroughly instilled during the police academy training program. A national police academy was established and staffed by international experts to ensure that all force members would be trained uniformly. The National Guard and Treasury Police were abolished, their members to be incorporated into the regular army. The remaining National Police were to operate under international supervision during the transition period and be replaced by the new police force according to a graduated timetable.

The transition to the new civilian police force was marred by considerable irregularities and unfortunate incidents. The new force was finally fully deployed, after many delays, in September 1994; the former National Police was officially dissolved on December 31, 1994. Although the transition to civilian police was completed, there continue to be worrisome signs that the new security doctrine does not guide police action.[48]

As for military institutional reform, the armed forces were substantially downsized and restructured, and the officer corps was, after a great deal of delay and international pressure, purged of those members cited by the Ad Hoc Commission. As a result of the commission's recommendations, the Defense Minister was replaced and eight other high-ranking offenders were dismissed; in July 1994 the remainder of those recommended for dismissal were simply permitted to retire with full honors. The existing national intelligence agency was abolished under the accords and replaced by a new state intelligence agency under civilian leadership directly responsible to the president. The scope of the new agency's authority was limited, and its activities regulated by law.

Overall, ONUSAL's peacebuilding was a success, albeit a qualified one. Deficiencies were caused largely by a lack of political will on the part of domestic actors, rather than by problems with the mission's mandate or performance.[49] The ceasefire was accomplished without a single reported violation, although after several reschedulings. Former combatants were demobilized and returned to civilian life; however, there were numerous, severe problems with reintegration programs, particularly with regard to the indemnification of demobilized civil patrols.[50] The professionalization of the judiciary is still proceeding, although impunity remains a major obstacle to national reconciliation. The new civilian police force was fully deployed by the end of 1994. Former militarized and paramilitary security forces were disbanded, but ongoing reports of police violence indicate that civilian security norms have not yet been properly inculcated as of this time. Certain of the constitutional reforms—most notably an article that would invalidate extrajudicial confession and strengthen the right to defense—were delayed by several years. An inter-agency commission of ONUSAL and UN Development Programme officials was established in October 1994 to continue administering post-mission technical assistance to the institutional strengthening and reinsertion programs, electoral reform, and assistance to demobilized former combatants.[51]

ONUSAL's work on behalf of institutional reform provided a precedent for later peacebuilding efforts. For example, the second item of Guatemala's Comprehensive Accord on Human Rights deals with strengthening national institutions that promote and protect human rights. Institutional reform by a multinational operation is also likely to prove controversial, as it more clearly intervenes in states' internal political affairs than did ceasefire monitoring or other traditional peacekeeping activities. Nonetheless, protecting human rights during the tenure of an operation and implementing structural and institutional reforms that will promote human rights after the mission has departed are equally essential to post-conflict peacebuilding. The two efforts are related but not identical. Human rights components monitor compliance and can inhibit violations only for the duration of the mission. After UN observers have left the country, the situation can revert unless precautions have been taken to implement protective reforms, demilitarize security forces, and strengthen the political and judicial systems with respect to international human rights standards.

The international human rights regime turned a corner with El Salvador. It represents one of a handful of UN peace operations that had a fully developed human rights component. In addition, El Salvador set important precedents for the United Nations. It was the first (and to date least problematic) example of UN mediation of an internal conflict, and it was the first example of an integrated peacekeeping operation centered on a human rights division. There was nothing inevitable or predetermined about the nature of the outcome. The mission in El Salvador was designed by individuals, many of whom shared the human rights network's principles and goals. These developments were the sometimes unintended outcome of decisions made during a negotiation process, which have left an undeniable legacy for the future of human rights protection.

The United Nations has only a limited ability to prevent domestic actors from cheating on or outright refusing to comply with agreements, or to sanction them when they do. For example, in October 1992, with the timed disarmament threatening to break down and the international community expressing its impatience, President Cristiani promised to remove the officers cited by the Ad Hoc Commission in order to ensure ongoing international support. He failed to fulfil that promise and even sidestepped the United Nations to cut a separate deal with the FMLN, who let up their insistence on the military purge in exchange for special benefits for their field commanders.[52]

UN officials may express frustrated resignation in the face of political actors who "simply welsh" on their agreements, but a mission is not necessarily hamstrung by limitations on its authority. If no domestic actors had an incentive to cheat on agreements, there would be no need for an agreement in the first place. International regimes are formed in part to overcome the problem of cheating. In isolated instances, a human rights mission can do little to prevent domestic actors from cheating or to sanction them when they do. However, over time the mission's presence becomes an institution in and of itself. Relations between mission personnel and local actors are iterative and dynamic, creating parallel incentives to comply in order to ensure that the process will not break down, that the United Nations will not pull out, and that international donors will not impose sanctions.

Ultimately, El Salvador's road from civil war to negotiated peace, and the two-year peace process that got it there, were by no means as uncomplicated and preordained as perhaps they appear in retrospect. The process could have broken down, and at times did break down, along the way. It is a testament to the Salvadoran people's desire for peace with reconciliation, and to the United Nations' willingness to intervene in the affairs of a sovereign state in order to promote human rights, that the majority of the accords have been implemented and political repression (if not criminal violence) is a thing of the past in El Salvador.

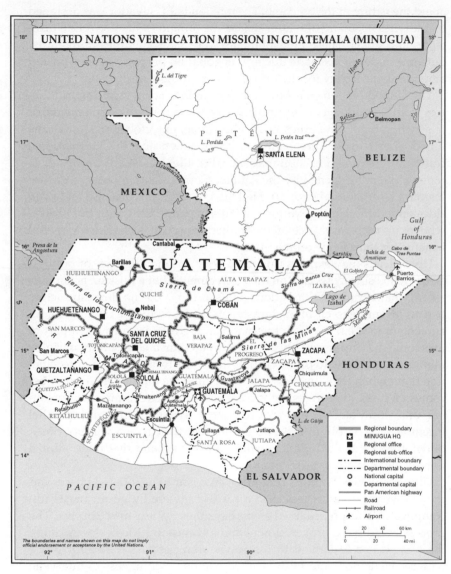

UN Verification Mission in Guatemala (MINUGUA). Map no. 3839, UN
Cartographic Section.

CHAPTER FOUR

Guatemala, 1989–1996

NATIONAL DIALOGUE TO MINUGUA

MINUGUA's existence has roots not only in the Guatemalan peace process, but also in a significant, recent evolution in international thinking and practice about the causes and solutions of conflict. In the newly emerging framework, human rights and peace have been inextricably linked.

The United Nations has been a key innovator in this regard, incorporating human rights as an indispensable component to the pursuit, maintenance and consolidation of peace. Nowhere within the activities of the organization is this trend more evident than in the growing importance of human rights functions in UN peace-keeping operations.

—Leonardo Franco, *Human Rights Verification in the Context of Peace*

In the aftermath of Guatemala's May 1993 executive coup, the presidential palace was occupied by a newly appointed president who had been elevated from the position of national human rights ombudsman. He proceeded both to jumpstart the peace process and to back away from the very policy changes he had previously advocated. Government compliance with international human rights principles grew gradually during the early to mid-1990s. The level of fear diminished palpably, and there were even a few concrete instances of compliance. The improvement in Guatemala's human rights situation was most clearly influenced by the irreversible momentum of the peace process and the intrusive presence of UN observers throughout the country, once MINUGUA was deployed in November 1994.

The historical setting for internationally mediated negotiations in Guatemala differed in many respects from that in El Salvador.[1] The withdrawal of U.S. support was a determining factor in the Salvadoran armed forces' decision to seek a political solution. U.S. military support for counterinsurgency in Guatemala was of nowhere near the same magnitude and therefore had less direct leverage over military or state decision making. After 1989, the shift in the U.S. posture was noticeable primarily in the State Department's willingness to denounce human rights abuses. It was also visible in the Clinton administration's forceful action during the May 1993 executive coup. Nonetheless, this post–cold war geostrategic change did not determine the military's cooperation with negotiations (which undermines the frequently made assertion that the change in U.S. regional policy is sufficient to explain the successful Central American peace processes).

Another distinction among the international factors in the two cases was that the UN Secretary-General was more willing to risk the credibility of his office in the Salvadoran negotiations, which took place during a period of Security Council activism following the collapse of the Soviet Union. By the time the Guatemalan process had reached its final, continuous phase in 1994, the Security Council had become more reluctant to intervene in the internal conflicts of member states, partly owing to perceived disasters in other regions and largely because of budgetary pressure imposed by the U.S. government. In the end, this did not impede a human rights operation, which indicates that the trend toward human rights enforcement was not limited to a brief period in UN history.

There were also important differences in domestic factors. Whereas a mutually acknowledged military stalemate had been essential in the Salvadoran case, the conflict in Guatemala had by no means reached a hurting stalemate. The URNG, whose membership at the time varied from 1,300 to 1,500 mostly poorly trained indigenous peasants, was not going to fight the armed forces' 46,000 heavily armed and disciplined soldiers (plus approximately 530,000 armed civil militias) to a draw.[2] A hurting stalemate would have entailed both parties' recognition that the conflict had arrived at a no-win situation, with gradually increasing costs for both sides. The military institutionalist faction had come to desire an improved international reputation as a means for ensuring economic stability and foreign aid. Nonetheless, the armed forces did not consider that the costs of gaining a military victory were too high to continue. The

URNG's position was that, although the military situation was clearly unbalanced, the ongoing economic crisis would erode the government's legitimacy so that over the long term, the URNG could improve its position by playing for time. Neither side was convinced that it had no alternative but to cooperate in a political solution. Each considered that its strategic position would improve with time.[3]

From its position of strength, the military high command could and did refuse to recognize the URNG as a legitimate opposition force and an equal partner in negotiations, insisting that it was nothing more than an irritating band of terrorists—a position the government maintained until 1996. This posture contributed to the exaggerated length of the negotiations, which dragged on—with long pauses between rounds—from 1990 to December 1996. In the end, however, it did not preclude government consent to UN mediation, nor did it prevent the United Nations from deploying a human rights operation.

In agreeing to negotiate in the first place (a tenuous agreement, and not easily or quickly obtained), the Guatemalan military was assured that it would not be required to make large concessions and was motivated by a dual interest in enhancing its international image and its financial portfolio. By the end of the process, a civilian president, Alvaro Arzú, had demonstrated an unprecedented (although by no means complete) degree of authority over the military, by purging corrupt and hardline officers and extracting significant concessions from the armed forces.[4] In place of a hurting stalemate and the withdrawal of foreign support, both the Guatemalan government and the URNG were prompted to take their places at the table and to negotiate in good faith by sets of incentives that included pressure from foreign allies, from human rights organizations, and from organized sectors of Guatemalan civil society.

First Phase: The Gathering of Civil Sectors

Catholic Church leadership brought organized civil society into the peace process during its earliest phase, which began in 1989. Bishop Rodolfo Quezada Toruño convened a National Dialogue in March of that year, in compliance with the Esquipulas II injunction to promote national reconciliation. This forum was composed of delegates from forty-seven organizations, who represented all civil sectors with the exception of the private sector's peak association (CACIF), and all political parties except those of the military and the extreme right. The ultimate goal of the National Dialogue was to outline the agenda for direct negotiations between the URNG and the government.[5] Although the Dialogue appeared to have run out of steam by the end of 1989, it created an arena in which, for the first time in recent history, diverse members of Guatemalan society met as equals for the purpose of discussion and reconciliation. Progress stalled over the controversial question of human rights reforms and because popular-sector delegates were under continual harassment from security forces and paramilitary organizations. The initiation of the first serious phase of negotiations, in Oslo on March 30, 1990, came as the result of Quezada's efforts to resuscitate the Dialogue.

International allies of both sides to the conflict and of the Guatemalan human rights community began to press President Cerezo for progress toward a political solution. Aside from humanitarian incentives, concern about the regionalization of the Guatemalan conflict motivated external pressure. The Mexican government had been a promoter of the Contadora peace process and had a national interest of its own in resolving the situation. Nearly 150,000 Guatemalan refugees were living in the southern states of Mexico; the URNG used Mexican territory for base camps and the border region as a supply corridor, and the Guatemalan army conducted illegal incursions across the border into Chiapas.[6] Other governments became involved; according to one observer, "The Norwegians, who had been playing peacemaker around the world, thought that this was a great opportunity to begin the process in Guatemala and they knew that they were on the right track, this was something that the Guatemalan population wanted and that the international community wanted."[7] A participant in the dialogue noted that international nongovernmental organizations played a major role in the preliminary stages: "Suffice it to say that the Guatemalan peace process is very unusual, since it was not begun at the initiative of the parties, but rather at the urging of the Lutheran World Federation, and the World Council of Churches, with the support of the Vatican. They initiated the contacts to try to see if there could be a meeting."[8]

The Lutheran World Federation's International Affairs and Human Rights office in Geneva took the initiative. Relying on its credibility from conciliation and refugee work in African countries and in El Salvador, the LWF arranged with the Vatican to send a delegation to what it proposed as a senior-level meeting between the parties and then contacted Defense Minister Gramajo and URNG representatives in Europe. Cerezo agreed to send representatives from the National Commission for Reconciliation to informal talks. The LWF then arranged with the Norwegian government to sponsor the meeting and to provide security for participants. Talks were held outside of Oslo on March 26–30, 1990.[9]

UN involvement in the Guatemalan negotiations began at the Oslo talks. The agreement drawn up at Oslo included a request from both parties that the Secretary-General assign an observer to the talks.[10] The UN representative continued in the role of observer, with markedly less initiating authority than in El Salvador, for the next three and a half years. Talks continued for the remainder of 1990 and through 1991, either between the parties or between one party and the UN observer. The Bush administration expressed its approval of the peace process in May 1990. A week later, the OAS issued a resolution granting its strong support for the dialogue and requesting that the UN Secretary-General continue to offer his full assistance.[11]

The Oslo accord also established a series of five meetings to take place over the following months at which the URNG was to meet with the organized sectors of Guatemalan society, with Quezada officiating and the Secretary-General's representative, Francesc Vendrell, observing. At one of these, in Ottawa on August 31–September 1, the URNG met with nine high-level representatives of CACIF. No joint agreement was signed at this round, although both sides issued separate declarations voicing their respective commitments to peace and prosperity.[12]

Second Phase: Direct Negotiations under a "Conciliator"

Jorge Serrano was the only candidate to openly advocate a negotiated settlement during the 1990 presidential campaign. After his election, he often stated that his support for the peace process had won him the presidency. He had been a member of the delegation to Oslo and was thus in a favorable position to promote peace talks. Serrano's former association with the military (he had served as head of the Council of State in the Ríos Montt administration) gave him an advantage over Cerezo in persuading the high command to cooperate in negotiations. Because he was considered sympathetic, he was able to ensure the armed forces that their prerogatives were not at risk, and that he would push for a short negotiation period and agreements that would not require deep concessions on their part.[13]

The initial direct contact between a high-level government delegation and the URNG took place April 24–26, 1991, in Mexico. The government delegation included five ranking military officers, three of whom were closely identified with the institutionalist faction.[14] Again, Bishop

Quezada presided as conciliator, and Francesc Vendrell was present in the role of observer. The resulting agreement established the procedural mechanisms for the peace process. Notably, by the time the Mexico Accord was signed, UN verification of accords was not controversial. Owing to the precedents set by the Esquipulas verification agreements, the UN operation in Nicaragua, and the preliminary deployment of ONUSAL, complex peacebuilding missions were perceived as "appropriate" in these circumstances.[15]

The first item on the Mexico Accord agenda was democratization and human rights. A general agreement to strengthen democratic institutions and the rule of law and to subordinate the armed forces to civilian authority was signed in July in Querétaro, Mexico.[16] At this point, however, negotiations arrived at an impasse that lasted more than two years, during which the parties were unable to reach agreement on several issues under the topic of human rights.[17] The subject of civil patrols (PACs) in particular became a point of contention. The stalemate began to loosen somewhat in January 1992, when the government agreed to eliminate forced recruitment and paramilitary groups, and to respect the lives of human rights activists. In February, Quezada announced partial commitments by the government toward a human rights accord.[18] But President Serrano continued to balk at immediate verification, for fear that the URNG would use the United Nations' presence in the country to draw international attention to government violations and thus gain leverage in the negotiations.[19]

These partial commitments provided the working text for what would, two years later, become the Comprehensive Human Rights Accord. The government's willingness to break the impasse reflected increasing pressure from abroad to move forward with the peace process. The European Parliament announced in February 1992 that future trade relations would be conditioned on respect for human rights. (European states, especially Germany, are important markets for Guatemala's agricultural and artisanal exports.) The same month, Secretary of Defense Richard Cheney visited the country to emphasize the important of compliance with human rights standards in relations with the United States. In March 1992, the Consultative Group of the World Bank and donor countries discussed conditioning financial assistance on government progress in social spending, respect for human rights, and the negotiation process.[20] Notwithstanding the heightened international pressure, talks were stalled for the duration of Serrano's presidency as the parties failed to reach agreement on four key points: dissolution of the PACs, creation of a truth commission, application of international humanitarian law, and the timing of UN verification.

The May 1993 autogolpe elevated military institutionalists over hardliners, unified civil sectors temporarily, and demonstrated clearly to Guatemalan elites that the international community would intervene to protect democratic institutions where it could do so effectively (chapter 2). Following the coup attempt, the new president, Ramiro de León Carpio, indicated his intention to achieve a political settlement by repopulating the military high command with officers known to favor the peace process. The peace process remained on hold until de León announced in July that he would resume talks. Despite the apparent political will of the executive and the military high command, negotiations quickly deteriorated over the role the UN representative was to play and the question of including civil sectors at the negotiating table. The debate reached another impasse in early October, at which point de León Carpio presented a "National Plan for Peace," which essentially overturned the agenda agreed to in April 1991. No direct meetings were held for the rest of 1993.

Third Phase: UN-mediated Negotiations

In early January 1994, officials from the UN Department of Political Affairs called a direct meeting of the parties to reformulate the negotiating format and expedite agreements. This time the round ended with a new framework accord, and the representative of the Secretary-General (a position that had been held since July 1992 by Ambassador Jean Arnault) was solicited to act as moderator. The role of the six "friends of the Guatemalan peace process"—Colombia, Spain, the United States, Mexico, Norway, and Venezuela—was also clarified, as lending support to the UN moderator and providing confidence in the accords. The increased direct participation of these other states was partly a continuation of the support each had provided throughout the regional process. To an important degree it also reflected concern that the Guatemalan conflict would exacerbate regional instability, coming a week after the Zapatista uprising in neighboring Chiapas.[21]

The accord also created a new institution, the Assembly of Civil Society (ASC), consisting of all legitimate, representative, and legal nongovernmental sectors of Guatemalan society. The ASC was to produce recommendations for submission to the negotiating table on the substantive topics yet to be addressed by the parties and evaluate the accords signed on substantive topics to facilitate their implementation. The assembly was not given veto power over accords, nor was there any guarantee that those at the table would seriously consider the consensus documents submitted by the civil sectors. Nonetheless, the assured participation of these sectors in the peace process meant that the government and the URNG would be held accountable to their social bases. Once it was formally established, on May 17, 1994, the ASC produced proposals on the resettlement of displaced populations, indigenous rights, the socioeconomic and agrarian situation, civil-military relations, and constitutional and electoral reforms. CACIF was the only major civil-sector organization to refuse membership in the assembly. The absence of the private sector's peak association primarily served to weaken the assembly's proposal on socioeconomic and agrarian issues, for which CACIF offered its own proposal.

The parties signed a Comprehensive Accord on Human Rights on March 29, in which they invited the Secretary-General to establish a human rights verification mission in the shortest time possible. The final obstacle to signing the human rights agreement was overcome when the thorny question of establishing a formal truth commission was removed from the accord and an agreement reached to address the issue within two months. This was a major concession for the URNG; a truth and justice commission had been a fundamental demand of the popular movement since the beginning of the peace process. The URNG balked until persuaded by pressure from the "friendly nations" and from the United Nations to sign the accord as it stood.[22]

The accord's principal innovation was a section on strengthening the state and nongovernmental institutions protecting human rights. From the government's perspective, this had the advantage of ameliorating the scrutinizing nature of verification, making it appear more as a technical assistance mission and less as an invasion by international auditors.[23] For the human rights community, a mandate to strengthen judicial and public prosecutorial agencies gave international experts access to and channeled UN resources into reforming the institutions most responsible for the impunity enjoyed by human rights violators. The language for this section was recommended to the negotiating teams by a delegation of UN advisers who had participated in ONUSAL's development. Thus, the United Nations was able to carry from its experience in El Salvador an understanding of the necessity to address institutional strengthening at the outset. In the words of a government adviser, "the design for MINUGUA was found in the analysis of what was good and what was lacking in ONUSAL."[24]

The Comprehensive Accord was the culmination of several years of pressure from Guatemalan and international human rights advocates. The terms of the accord reflect clearly institutional learning on the part of the United Nations, primarily drawn from its experience with ONUSAL. MINUGUA was given the same powers as ONUSAL's Human Rights Division, including direct reporting to the Secretary-General and the obligation to make recommendations based on its findings. As in El Salvador, UN officials expected that reporting directly to the Secretary-General would alleviate the problem of conflicting interests or tension between the United Nations' diplomatic and verification functions. The accord also emphasized working relations with both governmental and nongovernmental human rights agencies. In this way, the mission would not be likely to repeat ONUSAL's mistake of neglecting local NGOs. Further, the Guatemalan mission was specifically tasked to work closely with state judicial and investigatory institutions. This would enable it to avoid the mistake that ONUSAL's administration made by its initial exclusive focus on casework. And it was hoped that the overall emphasis on strengthening local institutions would serve to relieve concerns that the UN mission would come to replace Guatemalan institutions in the minds of the population, a danger that critics frequently cited in El Salvador.

Although their acceptance of the agreement was tempered by skepticism regarding the viability of separate talks on a truth and justice commission, civil sectors were generally pleased with it. The following accord, signed June 17, 1994 in Oslo, on the resettlement of displaced and refugee populations, was similarly well received.[25] Churches, human rights organizations, and the military held public debates on the issue of a truth and justice commission during the months following the signing of the accord. The military's public position was that it was conditionally willing to consider such a proposition, provided that it did not become a channel for vengeance, and that no individual member of the armed forces would be asked to put his neck in a noose. The church's position was that justice required that a commission be formed but that its objective should be national reconciliation (as opposed to individual reprisals). The position of human rights NGOs was that justice required that parties guilty of human rights violations be judged in a court of law and punished, and that failure to do so could only perpetuate impunity. President de León Carpio's position, stated at a press conference in San José on May 11, was that a truth commission would polarize society, open new wounds, prolong the conflict, and do more damage than good.[26]

The government was dislodged from this rigid position through the intervention of other governments, most notably in Norway and Sweden. An accord was signed in Oslo on June 23, 1994, which outlined a three-member commission, to be headed by Jean Arnault (Christian Tomuschat ultimately became the commission's international member), who was to appoint two Guatemalan members. Investigations were to begin once the final accord was signed, and the commission was projected to cover the period of conflict beginning in 1960 in six months, with a possible six-month extension. The report was not to name individuals responsible for violations, merely indicating which institution had committed the crime. The commission had no authority to recommend sanctions, and its findings were to have no judicial import whatsoever.[27]

Response from the human rights NGOs was measured at first, but by early July had become a storm of dissent, and lost the URNG much of its credibility as the popular organizations' interlocutor at the negotiating table. The popular sectors, in particular victims' groups, felt betrayed by the prohibition against naming names and the lack of judicial recourse. The military had to contend with hardliners' displeasure with the concession to permit such a commission in any form. Arnault himself temporarily lost credibility as a mediator for having caved in to pressure from the "friendly nations" to sign an accord that the Department of Political Affairs considered weak and reportedly for overstepping his authority in allowing himself to be named to the commission.[28]

The protest over the Commission to Clarify the Past, as it was called, is analogous to the outcry that confronted the FMLN after the signing of the San José Human Rights Accord in July 1990. In that case, the FMLN had returned to the United Nations with a request for early deployment of the verification mission in order to mollify its popular constituency. Here, the URNG found that it had to proceed with extreme caution and to ensure that further accords would enjoy wide acceptance among civil, especially popular, sectors. In a blatantly self-critical internal memo, the URNG command admitted to not having sufficiently communicated its negotiating strategy to civil sectors and regretted the appearance of being more sensitive to international pressure than to the needs of its bases. The General Command committed itself to consult with civil sectors when preparing future proposals, sought to regain its credibility by promising to hold out for a strong accord on indigenous rights, and stated that it would "continue the negotiation process, only if the contents of the accords are directed at achieving structural changes in Guatemala."[29]

An overlong delay in establishing the human rights verification mission also fueled the URNG's reluctance to return to the table after its failure in Oslo. Deployment prior to a ceasefire in Guatemala was not considered a security risk for the United Nations as it had been in El Salvador. The Guatemalan conflict was considerably less intense and the parties had committed themselves in the human rights accord to provide security guarantees for international monitors.[30] A preliminary team of UN officials and expert advisers had visited Guatemala in late April and had submitted a report to the Secretary-General recommending that a preparatory office be opened immediately. Nonetheless, the decision to establish the Guatemalan operation stalled in the Security Council from May through September 1994.

The delay in establishing MINUGUA exemplifies a trend away from an activist Security Council following the initial post–cold war exuberance. The causes of the delay were, first, the U.S. government's objection to a Security Council mission on budgetary grounds. The United States preferred a cheaper General Assembly operation for the human rights component, to be supplemented, not expanded, by a limited Security Council peacekeeping operation to oversee the eventual ceasefire and demobilization. Second, the Mexican and Colombian governments argued that the Security Council should not handle human rights protection, which is properly under the purview of the General Assembly's Economic and Social Council (and further suggested that ONUSAL's human rights division should also have been under the General Assembly). Finally, the Guatemalan government opposed the deployment of a single, integrated operation on the grounds that a Security Council mission could be used as an unconstrained instrument of international pressure.[31]

In the end, Boutros-Ghali recommended that the General Assembly rather than the Security Council authorize the Guatemalan verification mission. Machinations by states interested in preventing the Security Council from authorizing another human rights operation were symptomatic of the backlash against UN interventionism, following the perceived peacekeeping failures in Somalia, the former Yugoslavia, and Rwanda. MINUGUA was deployed despite this context of backlash and U.S. pressure to downsize—a clear demonstration of the widespread international support in principle for human rights enforcement by means of verification missions.

While the URNG withdrew to recover from the Truth Commission talks, the Assembly of Civil Society began to develop its position paper on the next topic, which was identity and rights of indigenous peoples. The two most sensitive social issues in Guatemalan politics have historically been the maldistribution of land and problems with land tenure, and the severe discrimination against indigenous peoples, who actually make up a majority of the population.[32] The divisiveness of the indigenous topic came close to pulling the assembly apart. After days of rancorous debate, Bishop Quezada actually withdrew in disgust at the sectors' inability to compromise, threatening not to return unless they reached a consensus. Most at issue were the Mayan bloc's demands for political autonomy for indigenous communities and the return of land seized by the state and by coffee planters in the nineteenth century. A consensus document was ultimately produced on July 8, 1994, which incorporated the majority of the Mayan sector's proposals.[33]

During this battle, the more intransigent indigenous groups found themselves in confrontation with the human rights organizations. The division between indigenous and human rights groups illuminates how, despite their overlapping membership, tactics, and objectives, real differences will become obvious on policies that affect only one group or one aspect of the greater rights community. This is partly a function of interest-group politics but also has much to do with how the boundaries of the human rights community were initially defined. In this respect, their situation is analogous to the position of women's organizations in the human rights network.[34] When early human rights organizations, particularly Amnesty International, developed the strategy of focusing on individual civil and political rights to the near exclusion of economic, social, and collective rights, they created an effective but ultimately limiting sphere. The result has been that, when push comes to shove, organizations representing "special interests," such as indigenous or women's rights or environmentalists, may find themselves outside the boundaries of mainstream human rights organizing and, in fact, find their demands opposed by the mainstream.[35]

Formal negotiations resumed on March 13, 1995, on the topic of indigenous rights. It appeared again as if domestic political factors would conspire to derail an agreement on this most sensitive of topics. It was an election year, the president was a lame duck, the military was again experiencing internal tensions between hardline and institutionalist factions, and the URNG was determined to sign nothing less than what the civil sectors had proposed. After nearly two weeks of fruitless discussion, the government's chief negotiator, Héctor Rosada, reportedly walked out of negotiations in anger, returning to Guatemala for further instructions. At this juncture, a happy coincidence of events in the international arena apparently produced the catalyst required to conclude the indigenous accord. On March 22, U.S. congressman Robert G. Torricelli (D-N.J.), a member of the House Intelligence Committee, announced that he had sent a letter to President Clinton containing the allegation that Col. Julio Roberto Alpírez, an active duty G-2 officer on the CIA payroll, had ordered the murders of Michael Devine, a U.S. expatriate who had been killed in June 1990, and ORPA commander Efraín Bámaca Velasquez (the husband of U.S. attorney Jennifer Harbury, who was at the time of Torricelli's announcement conducting a hunger strike across the street from the White House).[36] The government's unexpected cooperation at the negotiating table a week later was partly related to its need for damage control in the face of the exploding scandal. An accord on indigenous rights was signed on March 31 in Mexico.[37]

The dynamics of the process had changed following the Accord on a Commission to Clarify the Past. The human rights community's rejection of what most considered to be a bad accord had caused the URNG to become disaffected and overcautious about returning to the table. Their increased caution, although it frayed nerves among international supporters of the peace process, led to an accord on indigenous rights that contained the majority of what civil sectors had proposed. The indigenous accord was almost universally hailed as a document that fairly reflected the pluricultural nature of Guatemalan society.[38] With the indigenous accord, and with the socioeconomic and agrarian situation topic that followed, the URNG wisely appropriated the ASC consensus documents, strategically aligning itself with the civil sectors (minus CACIF), and placing the government in check.[39]

Predictably, negotiations on the socioeconomic and agrarian situation dragged on for nearly a year, despite pressure from international donors on the government and CACIF to cooperate. Talks were also held up by the URNG's decision not to negotiate with the outgoing government. Supporters of the peace process were concerned that the new government might refuse to recognize the accords signed under previous administrations, in light of the very real possibility that a surrogate for General Ríos Montt would win the presidency. To prevent this, an agreement was signed in August 1995 by all major political parties, including Ríos Montt's Frente Republicano Guatemalteco (FRG), declaring that accords should be considered commitments of the state rather than of the government currently in power.

Negotiations regained momentum only after the November 1995 national elections and the accession of the new government in January 1996. Incoming president Alvaro Arzú proved to be a strong supporter of the negotiation process, meeting privately (through the Italian peace organization, San Egidio) with the URNG both prior to the second round of voting and following his election. He appointed a new COPAZ team headed by Gustavo Porras Castejón, a respected political analyst and director of a major economic policy institute, who had been an EGP commander in its early years. On March 21, 1996, the URNG declared a unilateral suspension of military activities. The armed forces made a reciprocal announcement the following day. In this promising context, direct negotiations recommenced on March 27, and an accord on socioeconomic reforms was signed May 6, 1996.[40]

Negotiations on the final substantive accord, concerning the strengthening of civilian authority and the role of the military in a democratic society, were relatively brief and amicable. An agreement was signed on September 19.[41] The army pledged to dissolve the mobile military police force (PMA) within one year, to remove itself from internal security, to reform intelligence agencies, to a troop reduction of 33 percent during 1997, and to reduce the proportion of the GNP allocated to the defense budget by 33 percent by 1999. (The URNG and ASC had proposed 50% cuts.) The agreement mandated the creation of a new National Civil Police (PNC) under the Interior Ministry, with full deployment of at least twenty thousand agents, trained at a new police academy, projected for 1999.[42] The accord committed Congress to dissolve the civil patrols (which process was already underway at the time of signing). Overall, the accord covered most of the key points in the ASC position paper, with the notable exception of requiring that the Minister of Defense be a civilian. The reforms mandated under it, if complied with, represented particularly significant gains for the human rights community.[43]

Negotiations on the final procedural accords were imperiled in October 1996 when an ORPA cadre kidnapped the matriarch of a wealthy family. The incident cast doubt on the URNG high command's ability to credibly commit its forces to the peace process and weakened the URNG's hand going into the remaining talks, on the ceasefire, constitutional reforms, and the reintegration of combatants. Further, as soon as the parties had completed the reintegration agreement, peace spoilers in the FRG-dominated Congress rammed a highly controversial "National Reconciliation Law" through legislature. This bill extended an amnesty to combatants on both sides for all combat-related crimes except those violations for which responsibility cannot be amnestied under international treaties ratified by Guatemala. Guatemalan human rights NGOs had been preparing for such an amnesty bill for several months, holding public debates and seminars on the subject and making frequent public statements on the dangers of impunity and amnesty laws.[44] Although the smooth finish was ruffled in the final hours by the kidnapping case and contention over the National Reconciliation Law, Guatemala's thirty-five years of civil war formally came to an end at a public ceremony held in the National Palace on December 29, 1996.

Gaining Ownership of the Peace: Lessons from Guatemala's
Peace Process

An Agreement on the Implementation, Compliance and Verification Timetable for the Peace Agreements was signed in February 1997, which divided the implementation calendar into three phases: a ninety-day period from January 15 to April 15, 1997, during which all preparation for all long-term goals was to take place, and which also covered the demobilization and reintegration processes. The more visible of the commitments, such as establishing a fund for the resettlement of refugees and the mechanisms to compensate victims of human rights violations, were to be completed during this period as well. Next, all social investment programs, reforms to the state structure and public administration, fiscal reforms, and security reforms were to take place during the period from April 15 through the end of 1997. The third phase was designed to last through 2000; during this time, all legislative, judicial, penal, electoral, and land-tenure reforms were to be completed.[45] The timetable stipulates specific goals to be achieved during each phase, using measures of compliance to be provided by the statistical analyses already available through the World Health Organization, UNESCO, and nongovernmental organizations that work on development issues. It also establishes civil-sector commissions (successors to the ASC) to oversee the implementation of accords.

Demobilization of combatants and refugee repatriation were completed within a reasonable time, and other agreements (especially the government's commitment to increase the tax base) appear to be delayed but not abrogated. Unfortunately, many institutional reforms require constitutional amendments and were sabotaged by a poorly designed popular referendum in May 1999.[46] Even more unfortunately, the brutal assassination on April 27, 1998, of Bishop Juan Gerardi, director of the Catholic Archbishop's human rights office, had a depressing effect on Guatemalans who justifiably believed that politically motivated murder was a thing of the past.

The role of nonstate actors in the long, meandering Guatemalan peace process was truly unique. First, international human rights activists allied themselves with domestic civil sectors to initiate the negotiations. Second, the process of dialogue in and of itself contributed to the development of tolerance and cooperative norms within civil society. The necessity for political, economic, and military elites to cooperate with popular organizations in developing the agreements helped to create to a less polarized environment. Finally, civil sectors directly participated in drafting and later in implementing an accords package that is remarkable in the breadth and substance of the issues addressed. For example, the Socioeconomic and Agrarian Accord emphasizes the state's obligation to guarantee a basic social safety net while pursuing development and sustainable growth. It commits the government to tax reform, education, social security, labor and fair employment, housing, health care, and land tenancy measures. Even if fully implemented in a timely fashion, the accord alone could not be expected to lift the majority from poverty or rectify one of the hemisphere's most infamous maldistributions of resources. Nevertheless, the government and the URNG (now a registered political party) are bound by the terms of the documents they signed to make verifiable efforts toward alleviating Guatemala's social inequities.

For the transnational activist network, Guatemala's experience underscores the importance of being involved from the outset in ensuring that human rights is prominent on a negotiating agenda. It also highlights the need to coordinate the inevitably conflicting interests of diverse, marginalized groups. The human rights network's emphasis on the integrity of the person (see the Introduction) was the most appropriate strategy for mobilizing against violently repressive states and continues to represent a set of values that resonates across cultures. However, the trend toward human rights enforcement will force advocates to weigh competing human rights values. The danger is that some groups will find their rights privileged and others will be further marginalized by the very network of actors that purports to defend them.

Interagency cooperation is critical to any long term peacebuilding effort.[47] From the start, there was a healthy coordination between MINUGUA and other UN agencies, especially the UN Development Programme, on institutional strengthening projects. Representatives from the UNDP, the World Bank, the International Monetary Fund, the Inter-American Development Bank, and the International Labor Organization were involved in developing the terms of the Guatemalan accords. This had reciprocal benefits: the parties received an education concerning international standards on each issue, and the intergovernmental organizations were involved in the reconstruction process from the outset. According to a member of the UN negotiating delegation to the Guatemalan talks, the involvement of other UN agencies and Bretton Woods organizations was "one of the main lessons from El Salvador."[48] Coordination among agencies and donors was especially important in MINUGUA's case, as the mission's budget and staffing levels barely increased when the mandate was expanded in January 1997, and resources from within the UN system had to be tapped for verification of the other agreements.

THE EVOLUTION OF UN HUMAN RIGHTS ENFORCEMENT AND PEACEBUILDING

The UN Mission for the Verification of Human Rights and of Compliance with the Commitments of the Comprehensive Agreement on Human Rights in Guatemala (MINUGUA) was the first fruit of the six-year-long peace process. Formally established on November 21, 1994, MINUGUA was fully deployed by the end of the following February. It was initially a human rights mission, in the same way that ONUSAL was a stand-alone human rights division for its first six months. Just as ONUSAL was expanded to include police and military divisions and verification of the entire accords package, MINUGUA was also expanded after the final accord was signed. In this case, however, verification of the ceasefire and demobilization was conducted by a force of 150 military observers under Security Council authorization, with a fixed three-month mandate beginning March 3, 1997. The military group was directed by MINUGUA's chief of mission but under a separate mandate from the rest of the expanded operation, which remained under the General Assembly's authority. The expanded mission remained under the assembly's regular budget rather than the peacekeeping budget. The regular budget is planned biennially, and continued pressure to resist deficit spending resulted in an operation much smaller than ONUSAL at its full force.

Human Rights Verification

MINUGUA's operations were initially divided between two branches: a verification unit and an institution-building unit. MINUGUA was given the same broad powers that ONUSAL had enjoyed. Monitors were empowered to receive and follow up on complaints, to judge if there had been a violation, to collect any information deemed relevant, to operate freely throughout national territory, to conduct private interviews with any individual or group, to visit state or URNG facilities without prior notice, to make recommendations to the parties, and to report directly to the Secretary-General. The concept of "active verification" (buttressing systematic investigation with recommendations of specific corrective measures), which had been pioneered in El Salvador, was a guiding premise from the outset.[49]

MINUGUA reports were more pointed and critical, and somewhat less diplomatic, than ONUSAL's earlier reports. They criticized both parties' compliance efforts, while noting significant progress in certain areas, especially forced recruitment into the armed forces, freedom of expression, and the willingness (if not ability) of the Interior Ministry and national police to investigate violations. To avoid the problems of inflated expectations and backlash from unmet expectations, the reports emphasized factors out of the mission's control, such as long-term political trends, which could account for a lack of reform despite the United Nations' best efforts.

From the start, MINUGUA officials emphasized publicly their appreciation for the assistance of local human rights organizations in furnishing information on cases, acting as intermediaries between international observers and victims, and providing the observer teams with access to local communities until an independent basis of trust could be formed. Privately, mission observers expressed the same sorts of difficulties with local human rights activists as those encountered in El Salvador, which primarily had to do with a lack of methodological rigor in collecting and categorizing evidence.

The verification teams sought to reinforce local NGOs and the National Counsel for the Defense of Human Rights (Procuraduría de Derechos Humanos, PDH). MINUGUA staff held monthly meetings in the Guatemala City office with representatives from the major human rights organizations, to gain an understanding of their needs and develop the means to meet them. MINUGUA assisted local PDH offices by offering logistical support, especially transportation, and helping staff with their investigatory and educational work. Local human rights workers considered that MINUGUA's presence in the field provided a degree of security, removed their sense of isolation, and led to an observable self-restraint on the part of the armed forces, civil patrols, and police.[50] MINUGUA was also credited with securing the political space for popular organizing that enabled the political opposition to form a coalition party for the 1995 elections. The regional offices' grassroots educational efforts exposed rural communities, often for the first time, to what human rights signify, and what rights are guaranteed in the Guatemalan Constitution and under international treaties. MINUGUA's educational talks helped to legitimate and depoliticize the subject of human rights:

> Even last year when I was giving some courses in November when MINUGUA was starting, I had people from some villages who did not want to take [a copy of] the human rights accord. They would read it and talk about it in the seminar, but they did not want to take it back to the villages because they said that the comisionados militares would look at it as something subversive. . . . The topic of human rights has become legitimate. Now people come out and denounce military officers, that's new.[51]

The progress in human rights promotion was offset by a general deterioration in public security. The rise in violent crime was often associated with corrupt officials and the ongoing impunity for violators. These factors necessarily complicate an objective evaluation of MINUGUA's long term impact on human rights compliance.

Institution-building

Within two months of deployment, MINUGUA's institution-building branch (FORIN) established a joint unit with UNDP, co-supervised by the UNDP resident representative and MINUGUA's director. The purpose was to develop short-, medium-, and long-term projects to strengthen national institutions for human rights protection.[52] The government had everything to gain by this degree of international technical assistance and was generally cooperative with the program. The unit offered consultation and support to the public prosecutor's office. A team of three international penal experts who were familiar with the Guatemalan justice system worked directly with prosecutors, advised on cases and legal procedures, and in conjunction with USAID's justice project, offered technical-training seminars.[53] FORIN drafted a comprehensive project in early 1995 designed to restructure and reform the entire administration of justice system.[54] MINUGUA also worked with the Interior Ministry on police and prison reform. UN police experts, with funding from Venezuela, improved the coordination between police and public prosecutors in criminal investigations.[55] Because MINUGUA's regular budget did not cover institution-building, funding for these projects was coordinated by international donors through a Trust Fund for the Guatemalan Peace Process.[56]

The lack of feedback between the verification and institution-building units was identified as a potential problem early into the mission. To overcome it, MINUGUA installed a reporting system by which the regional and subregional verification offices supplied FORIN with information on certain key local institutions, for example, the public prosecutor's regional office or the local police. This was a step toward better integration of the mission's branches and also provided a mechanism to evaluate the impact of FORIN projects in the field. It is essential that institution-building be evaluated on an ongoing basis. Training programs in the capital are a waste of donor funds if they have no effect on the behavior of state agents further down the chain of command. In fact, in many parts of Guatemala the dysfunction of state agencies was due as much to fear of retaliation or lack of resources as to a lack of training.

The Central American human rights operations are examples of how, at least in this realm and at least some of the time, the United Nations is capable of evaluating feedback from internal sources or from the environment, of reflecting on that information, and of changing its policy in response. MINUGUA's deployment and design owes a great deal to preceding UN missions, especially to ONUSAL. At the planning stage, the recommendations made by the preliminary team reveal a degree of institutional learning from previous operations. The Secretary-General's preliminary mission, which visited Guatemala and Mexico City from April 24 to May 7, 1994, included representatives from ONUSAL's Human Rights Division, UNDP/El Salvador, USAID/El Salvador, and two nongovernmental human rights experts. Given this level of familiarity with both countries, it is hardly surprising that MINUGUA, from its establishment, tried to avoid the problems that had plagued ONUSAL: methodological inconsistencies, an uncomfortable integration of civilian and uniformed personnel, inflated public expectations, and poor community relations.[57]

Where ONUSAL had limited its focus for the first two years to casework, MINUGUA immediately sought to strike a balance between verification and institution-building. Furthermore, there were frequent reminders in the internal documents, public statements, and private comments of mission officials that MINUGUA's purpose was not to become a substitute for national institutions (however inconsequential, corrupt, or repressive these might have been) but rather to assist the Guatemalan people in reforming their own institutions. This was another lesson brought from El Salvador. Learning was also evident in the way mission coordinators set out to build strong relations with local human rights groups.

MINUGUA's presence undoubtedly strengthened the foothold the international human rights regime had established in Guatemala. With a mandate signed by both parties to the conflict, the mission carried more institutional weight than either the UN Commission's special representatives or independent advocacy organizations. Because a UN observer mission projects an image of credibility and neutrality, its judgments tend to be more widely accepted and influential.

The reforms negotiated in Guatemala were more comprehensive overall, but in the cases of the socioeconomic and civil-military agreements less carefully specified than those mandated by the Salvadoran accords. The particular dynamics of the negotiations, stemming from variations in context and in the balance between the actors, produced very different agreements. The elite nature of the Salvadoran process led to an accords package that focused on human rights and on provisions for ex-combatants, military restructuring, and reforms to electoral and judicial institutions, with very little attention given to redistributive reforms. Because the two parties were more equally weighted, an authoritative and at times dominant UN mediator played the part of balancer. A strong civilian president was able to maintain the cooperation of military delegates with a minimum of open dissent.

By contrast, the Guatemalan dynamic was more complex. Until the final year, the process took place under weak civilian presidents, leaving the government delegation (and the government itself) overshadowed by the military. The URNG was very weak, with nothing like the civilian base that the FMLN had been able to claim. The opposition elements in civil society were hardly as hierarchically organized under or organically linked to the URNG. Further, civil sectors organized in order to participate in the negotiations early into the process, under a strong leader who had the moral authority to hold together a fractious assembly. Finally, the UN mediator was in a comparatively weak position and was also inclined to take account of the proposals submitted by the Assembly of Civil Society. The result of this dynamic were substantive accords on issues crucial to societal reconciliation: human rights, refugees and the displaced population, indigenous rights, economic and social policy, and civilian control of the military. These were negotiated and signed prior to the topics relating to demobilization and reintegration of forces.

This comparison yields several conclusions. First, although a major state's active opposition can inhibit human rights or peacebuilding intervention, the hegemon's willingness to cooperate in promoting human rights principles does not by itself account for multilateral action. What happened in Guatemala cannot be explained solely by a change in U.S. strategic interests in the region. Second, international normative support for human rights intervention has reached a stage at which, given the enabling circumstances, such a mission could be deployed even during a period of UN contraction. Third, the international pressure that was brought to bear on the Guatemalan government to negotiate a settlement was more often motivated by Guatemala's status as a pariah state than by military or geostrategic concerns.

Tangible incentives, such as a threat to condition trade relations on human rights compliance, were important. But the sanctioning states and international organizations were motivated by moral incentives, and the violator states were largely motivated by such intangibles as concern for international legitimacy and prestige. After more than a decade of transnational mobilization, the topic of human rights was so fundamental to the Guatemalan peace process that it was placed first on the original eleven-topic negotiating agenda. The centrality of human rights, the elevated role of civil sectors, and the precedent set by ONUSAL combined to produce a human rights mandate that was broader and more inclusive than any that had preceded it.

How Do Human Rights Institutions Matter?

Suffering does not necessarily ennoble or even mobilize—some victims do transform their pain into principled politics, but others become paralyzed, bitter, or even calculating in the face of overwhelming loss. This sad and sobering observation is unexpectedly empowering, because it shows that *ordinary* people can do extraordinary things. Social change does not require heroes; it require some small group of limited human beings to behave courageously on some days—and simply to persist on others.
—Alison Brysk, *The Politics of Human Rights in Argentina*

Born after World War II to protect vulnerable populations from state-sponsored genocide, the regime of human rights institutions later came to be associated with political prisoners and politically motivated state terror under dictatorial governments. During the 1980s, international human rights pressure became an ideologically charged issue in the climate of renewed cold war hostilities. When the simplifying constructs of the cold war faded, the meaning of a human rights regime took on a greater complexity. Genocide is now an almost common occurrence but is conducted by both states and nonstate agents. Human rights intervention became associated during the 1990s with military intervention to control humanitarian crises and mop up the effects of ethnic violence, while still targeting the more "traditional" conditions of political repression such as in China, Myanmar/Burma, or Sudan.

I began this book by asking how it was that the international human rights regime became less toothless following the end of the cold war. One answer, of course, is that it has not in many respects. The evolutionary process I referred to in the Introduction has not been consistent across states or even within a single state. For example, the Chinese people currently enjoy a degree of daily freedom unprecedented in their recent history, unless they demand to exercise the right to free expression. From an initial set of nonbinding instruments and institutions with no sanctioning capacity, the regime evolved in the 1970s into a semi-confidential investigatory and reporting system motivated by the publicity campaigns of nonstate actors. After 1989, the regime further increased its enforcement capabilities through a new generation of multilateral onsite verification and institution-building missions. They were deployed under a mutually dependent set of necessary conditions, which I have modeled as a framework for compliance with the international human rights regime.

The discussion in the previous chapters showed how these conditions worked in El Salvador and Guatemala. Could this sort of enforcement mechanism be used in harder cases, in which both "rational" appeals to material interests and the perceived desirability of recognition and acceptance by other states fail to sway elites? Or where leadership of the ruling coalition is fragmented and no single coalition member is able to credibly commit the other(s) to comply with regime standards? I return to these questions briefly later in this chapter, but they remain to be answered by others working in the relatively uncrowded field of systematic research on the causes and consequences of intervention to promote international standards on human rights.

Based as it is on moral principles rather than on tangible incentives, the human rights regime was born weak and was slow to develop teeth. As a set of institutions, the regime will most likely continue to develop in its current direction unless its progress is intentionally rechanneled. We can therefore predict with some measure of certainty that the advances of the 1990s will not be reversed, and that international human rights institutions will continue to breach the diplomatic fiction of state sovereignty with increasingly intrusive measures when human rights advocates mobilize international public opinion against particular atrocities.

CAMBODIA: KILLING FIELDS TO UNTAC, 1975–1992

Cambodia offers a useful comparison because it is an example both of egregious violations perpetrated by contenders for control of the state and of a UN multidimensional peacebuilding operation. The international human rights regime had reached the same stage in its post–cold war evolution as in the Central American cases, so that rights provisions were considered an appropriate and necessary element in such an operation. The international political context was also similar in that the termination of cold war rivalries led patron states to withdraw support from the Cambodian factions and to pressure their clients to negotiate.

However, important differences in domestic elites' interests and in the scale of transnational mobilization gave human rights a lesser priority on the negotiating agenda and in the resulting peacekeeping operation. Unlike the cases of El Salvador and Guatemala, human rights mobilization was weak for most of the period, primarily because Cambodia had no domestic human rights organizations. Domestic elites were not highly motivated by reputational concerns and only reluctantly consented to the UN mission; moreover the two strongest factions defected altogether after a few months, causing a near failure of the operation. In contrast to the Central American cases, Cambodian elites' commitment to conflict resolution was not credible, and led to only partial compliance with the agreements. Because the topic of human rights was kept peripheral to the negotiating process, the human rights division was much less robust and had a less authoritative mandate.

The case of Cambodia demonstrates clearly how necessary transnational network activism is to international cooperation with human rights law. The network's intensive lobbying and strategic use of available leverage in the cases of El Salvador and Guatemala ensured that sponsor states and intergovernmental organizations maintained human rights as a priority item on the negotiating agenda. In Cambodia, by contrast, the weakness of network mobilization enabled the issue to become buried by the security agenda during negotiations. International human rights organizations had no access to Cambodia before UN observers were in place, and domestic human rights organizations had simply never existed. International NGOs began to disseminate verified reports of violations by all factions toward the end of the 1980s, but members of the human rights network were not involved in the negotiations, as they were in El Salvador and Guatemala, and had little input into the agreements, if any.

Nonetheless, the final agreement included a broad mandate for promoting human rights and included a human rights component in the peacekeeping operation. Thus, by 1991, human rights monitoring and education was considered appropriate to a UN peacekeeping mandate, and necessary to the construction of a firm and lasting peace—even in the case of a multilateral intervention that was not centrally concerned with human rights conditions. But human rights enforcement was clearly subordinated in the Cambodian mission to the short-term imperative to create an electoral democracy and a power-sharing scheme among the warring parties.

Cambodia's recent history is even more overtly one of foreign intervention than that of Central America. A U.S.-supported coup led by General Lon Nol ousted the government of Prince Norodom Sihanouk in March 1970. With China's backing, an alliance of Sihanouk and the Communist Party of Kampuchea, or Khmer Rouge, overturned the ensuing authoritarian republic in April 1975. The Khmer Rouge leader, Pol Pot, unleashed a reign of terror that forced Sihanouk to flee the country, leaving the Khmer Rouge in control. After repeated border raids and provocation, and in response to the humanitarian crisis that sent hundreds of thousands of Cambodian refugees across the border, Vietnam invaded Cambodia on December 25, 1978. In January 1979, a Vietnamese puppet government, the People's Republic of Kampuchea (after 1989, renamed the State of Cambodia, SOC) replaced the Khmer Rouge. Led by the United States, the United Nations refused to recognize the new government, and the Khmer Rouge retained Cambodia's seat at the United Nations.

The invasion by Vietnamese forces in 1978 terminated the Khmer Rouge's reign of violence but created an untenable political situation—an externally imposed government opposed by three armed factions operating from the Thai border. The result was more than a decade of civil war, economic disruption, and the exodus of 400,000 Cambodian refugees. Each faction enjoyed the support of a major power, giving the situation the potential to destabilize the region. The Khmer Rouge continued to enjoy economic and military support from China, which sought to prevent Vietnamese control of the region. The USSR backed the Kampuchean government as part of a Soviet-Vietnamese security alliance. The United States joined China in supporting the Khmer Rouge, to counter the Soviet Union. The United States, with the ASEAN nations, also sponsored the two noncommunist resistance factions, the National United Front for an Independent, Neutral, Peaceful and Cooperative Cambodia (FUNCINPEC, led by Sihanouk) and the Khmer People's National Liberation Front (KPNLF, a conservative movement led by Son Sann).

In 1982 the three opposition factions in exile formed the Coalition Government of Democratic Kampuchea (CGDK, headed by Sihanouk). Britain and France joined the United States and China in supporting it but expressed their disapproval of the U.S.-Sino support for the Khmer Rouge.[1] When cold war hostilities subsided in the late 1980s, during the *glasnost* period, the threat of destabilization in the region outweighed any interests the major powers had in prolonging the conflict. In late 1989, Vietnam withdrew its military presence from Cambodia, and internationally mediated negotiations began in earnest.[2]

International Political Context: A Microcosm of Cold War Hostilities

Cambodia's civil conflict was carried out as a proxy war involving China, the Soviet Union, and the United States. Subsiding confrontation between the United States and the Soviet Union, the Soviet Union and China, and China and Vietnam meant that there was no need to continue the proxy conflict in Cambodia, and the major powers pressured their clients to negotiate.[3] As early as 1980, in the wake of the Vietnamese invasion, the United Nations had begun to seek an internationally brokered solution to the conflict. The General Assembly resolved in 1980 to convene a conference with the goal of designing a political settlement. The conference, which met in July 1981 in New York, was boycotted by Vietnam and Soviet bloc countries on the grounds that its focus on a Vietnamese withdrawal ignored the subject of Khmer Rouge atrocities and made almost no mention of restitution for past human rights abuses. (Again, the Khmer Rouge still occupied Cambodia's seat at the United Nations.)

By 1989 the Cambodian conflict was an obstacle to détente between the Soviet Union and China, while Soviet support for the Kampuchean government left the USSR isolated by the US–China–ASEAN alliance in the region. From China's perspective, continued support for the Khmer Rouge was an unnecessary burden when Beijing's attention was turning to rapid economic development and access to global markets, and Vietnam was still too depleted to pose a significant threat on its own. The United States was interested in preventing either Vietnam or China from gaining hegemonic control of Southeast Asia. As with El Salvador, the Bush administration was eager to hand responsibility for Cambodia to the United Nations in order to remove it from the U.S. foreign policy agenda and eliminate the possibility of having openly to declare support for either the Vietnamese-supported government or the Khmer Rouge, should the fighting escalate.[4]

The regional context for the peace process from 1988 on was similarly conducive to a settlement. Thailand, whose economy was strong and growing, was interested in opening new markets in Cambodia and Vietnam, while the strategic threat these countries posed to Thailand appeared to be diminishing. The high costs of occupying Cambodia were draining Vietnam's coffers, worsening its isolation from global markets, and exacerbating its dependence on the USSR and tensions with China. In addition, Khmer Rouge victories in western Cambodia had convinced Vietnam that a military solution was not possible.[5]

The five permanent members of the Security Council ("P5") took over mediation of the process in September 1989. This was a very different type of international intervention in internal conflict than was the United Nations' role in the Central American dialogue. In this case, the major powers initiated negotiations rather than the process being conducted through the office of the Secretary-General. The Australian representative Gareth Evans and the U.S. Congressman Steven Solarz presented a joint proposal to overcome a deadlock over power-sharing by having the United Nations assume direct control of Cambodia's civil administration during the transitional period leading up to elections.[6] The Security Council adopted the proposal. The final agreements signed on October 23, 1991, in Paris created a semi-sovereign Supreme National Council (SNC), to be administered by the UN Transitional Authority in Cambodia (UNTAC).

The international community remained directly involved in the Cambodian process during UNTAC's operation. A core group of major powers and troop contributors, including Japan, Thailand, Indonesia, Australia, Malaysia, and the Permanent Five, actively promoted cooperation with the mission on the part of neighboring governments. Their representatives advised Yasushi Akashi, UNTAC's chief of mission in Phnom Penh, and lent financial, material, and diplomatic support from the New York headquaters. All states who had participated in the Paris agreements intervened as necessary to overcome crises in implementation.

Unfortunately, outside intervention was not always successful. UNTAC had no mandate to take coercive enforcement action when the Khmer Rouge defected in June 1992 from its commitment to demobilize.[7] Sanctions against the Khmer Rouge therefore depended on diplomatic and economic measures. The mission maintained close relations with the Chinese and Thai governments, hoping that these "past allies" of the Khmer Rouge would exert their influence to return the renegade faction to the peace process.[8] Diplomatic efforts proved futile, and the Khmer Rouge's intransigence led the Security Council to blockade petroleum shipments to areas the Khmer Rouge controlled and threaten to freeze Khmer Rouge assets.[9]

Overall, international intervention in Cambodia to resolve the civil conflict and establish democratic institutions was determined almost entirely by the changing geostrategic interests of regional and global powers. As in the case of El Salvador, international pressure, combined with the parties' perception of military stalemate, led to a mediated peace process and a multilateral peacebuilding operation with extensive powers to intervene in the state's institutional development. Unlike the international responses in Central America, human rights held a far less central position on the peace agenda, for reasons I discuss next.

Muted Transnational Network Activism, Few Leverage Points, Weak Pressure

Cambodia differs most markedly from the Central American cases with respect to transnational human rights activism. Internationally based human rights monitors had no access to the interior or to Khmer Rouge-controlled territory during the 1980s. They had to base what information they had on the reports of refugees and on practices found in the border camps under the control of non-Khmer Rouge opposition factions.[10] For this reason, information communicated by NGOs or in U.S. State Department country reports was scarce and greatly delayed in reaching the outside world. There were no local human rights organizations prior to the signing of the Paris agreement and, therefore, no possibility for anything like the dynamic transnational exchange of resources and information found in the other cases.

During the Khmer Rouge massacres of 1975–78, the weakness of transnational human rights mobilization resulted in virtual inaction on the part of international organizations and other states (described in the Introduction). The dramatic symbolic images necessary for mass public mobilization filtered out of Cambodia too late to be of use for lobbying. Without widespread public protest, the network could not overcome governments' reluctance to openly criticize other governments. Amnesty International was able to include some information on Hun Sen's political prisoners in its annual reports beginning in 1980, based on the accounts of refugees in camps on the Thai border. However, Cambodia remained closed to any outside investigation until the arrival of UN peacekeepers in 1992, leaving the human rights community in the frustrating position of having to cite "unconfirmed reports" and reiterate the government's continued refusal to reply to queries. Son Sann of the opposition CGDK met with Amnesty International representatives in 1986 and promised cooperation with monitors in the camps controlled by the coalition factions, but the Khmer Rouge failed to comply.[11] Asia Watch was finally able to publish a report on conditions in Khmer Rouge camps in 1989, based on information gleaned from interviews with refugees and aid workers outside of Khmer Rouge territory.[12]

The atrocities of the 1970s and reports throughout the 1980s of Khmer Rouge and Kampuchean government violations of human rights were sufficiently well known that participants to the Paris conferences considered it necessary to include sections on rights in the text of the accords.[13] However, the process was not influenced by international and domestic rights experts, as it was in El Salvador and would be in Guatemala. Amnesty International issued a recommendation to all participants in the negotiations that outlined "ways in which effective human rights protection mechanisms could be included in a political settlement."[14] The recommendations were ignored and the following year Amnesty complained that the human rights provisions developed by the P5 were woefully inadequate. Unlike the detailed mandates given to ONUSAL, MINUGUA, and MICIVIH in Haiti, human rights language in the Paris agreements is more in the manner of broad exhortations to comply with international instruments. The UN operation was specifically tasked to promote educational programs, but powers to investigate or take corrective action, while granted in the text, were deliberately left vague to avoid alienating the parties, particularly the Khmer Rouge.

Elite Sensitivity to Regime Pressure

As was the case in El Salvador, all four Cambodian factions were exhausted by the civil war, which had reached a military stalemate with one of the opposition factions controlling a significant amount of territory. Another similarity is that the government's consent to a negotiated settlement and to UN intervention was motivated by the withdrawal of foreign military support and an anxiety to improve its legitimacy with the international community. Sensitivity of any party to its international reputation for human rights violations appears to have been nill in the 1980s. Neither government nor Khmer Rouge leaders ever responded to human rights queries, indicating that no key element among these elites entertained any concerns for reputation. By 1988, both sides to the conflict were accusing the other of human rights abuses.[15] With their major power supporters losing interest in prolonging the conflict, the factions were seeking international legitimation by coopting human rights discourse.

The State of Cambodia and the Khmer Rouge were reluctant participants in the accords process, having consented to a negotiated settlement because their external allies had cut off financial support. Subsequent events would indicate that neither party had negotiated in good faith, for both ultimately defected from agreements.[16] After the Khmer Rouge refused to demobilize in June 1992, the other factions likewise abandoned their commitments, and the demilitarization element of the accords failed. Imbalances in the coalition government that was established following the elections produced ongoing political instability. Continued Khmer Rouge resistance (up until its anticlimactic implosion in 1997–98) threatened the peace itself.[17]

The topic of human rights became deadlocked in the Jakarta meetings of 1988 and 1989. Hun Sen would only permit government practices to be monitored on condition that the Khmer Rouge cooperate with investigations of its past practices. The necessity to keep the Khmer Rouge at the negotiation table resulted in a mandate on human rights that was weak and underspecified. The Khmer Rouge refused to compromise beyond the inclusion of a clause prohibiting a return to past practices. The accords drafters carefully avoided direct reference to past abuses or to mechanisms for bringing their perpetrators to justice. The death of Pol Pot and the subsequent surrender or arrest of the remaining Khmer Rouge leadership has since forced the international judicial community, and the Cambodian government, to confront these issues head on, in an unfortunately politicized manner.

Following the Paris settlement, UNTAC encountered cheating by all parties. The parties were willing to comply with those measures that benefited them individually and sought to hinder those that might benefit their opponents. Among the contenders for control of the state, FUNCINPEC and the KPNLF were generally supportive of the mission, hoping that their popularity would gain them in the national election what they could not win in armed combat. The State of Cambodia, which controlled 80 percent of the country, cooperated insofar as it ensured UNTAC access to its territory; but it subverted the mission's administrative control and conducted a pre-election campaign of intimidation and violence against FUNCINPEC candidates.

SOC consent for an on-site observer mission was presumably motivated by the desire to demobilize the Khmer Rouge and by the need for international legitimacy and diplomatic recognition.[18] In this sense, Hun Sen, the domestic elite capable of exerting authority over the largest military force, was also sensitive to the repercussions of a damaged international reputation. However, the Khmer Rouge controlled an army of ten thousand troops and evidently had very little concern for its international reputation. When material support from China diminished, Thai generals quickly substituted an active trade in lumber, gems, and weapons. With a supply source from a non-cooperating outside state (or part of the state apparatus), the Khmer Rouge was able to undermine the Security Council's economic sanctions.

International Regime Mechanisms for Changing the Behavior of Cambodian Elites

Earlier, I examined bilateral as well as multilateral human rights sanctioning instruments. By contrast, there appears to have been no bilateral human rights pressure on either the Kampuchean government or the opposition coalition. The Khmer Rouge massacres occurred during the post-Watergate period, when U.S. human rights legislation was being enacted, but Cambodia fell into the loophole of national security interests. During the 1980s, the State Department reported violations committed by both sides, but the United States had no diplomatic or trade relations with Phnom Penh and therefore no leverage.

The U.S. embassy in Thailand prepared detailed country reports on the People's Republic of Kampuchea despite the lack of access for outside monitors. Because the United States officially recognized the opposition CGDK as the legitimate government of Cambodia, the State Department had a political incentive to criticize the Hun Sen government.[19] State Department country reports of the period reveal an attempt at balance in that they also reported violations by U.S.-supported factions, but neither the United States nor any other allied state appears to have exerted pressure to curtail these practices.

Multilateral mechanisms invoked to sanction the Khmer Rouge during the 1975–78 massacres were minimal. The British representative to the UN Human Rights Commission brought the case to the attention of the Subcommission on the Prevention of Discrimination and Protection of Minorities in 1978. The subcommission considered the Khmer Rouge's record and sent the case on to the commission, which requested a response from the Khmer Rouge leadership at its spring 1978 meeting. The Khmer Rouge responded in April by refusing to comply, so the subcommission chairman was requested to prepare an analysis of the information and materials that had been submitted. The analysis was to be taken up at the following commission meeting in early 1979, but the examination was postponed because by that time the Khmer Rouge had been ousted.[20]

The United Nations was involved through the 1980s in attempting to mediate an end to the civil war. The Human Rights Commission passed annual, obviously politically motivated, and unintentionally ironic condemnations of "the continued illegal occupation of Kampuchea by foreign forces [which] deprived Kampucheans of their right to self-determination and constituted the primary human rights violation in that country."[21] Commission resolutions did not condemn the serious violations of personal integrity that were being committed by both the Hun Sen government and the opposition forces. Cambodia also remained on the General Assembly agenda during this time; the assembly passed annual resolutions, over Soviet objections, calling for foreign invaders to leave the country, for a return to national autonomy and self-determination, and for Prince Sihanouk (after 1982 the nominal leader of the coalition government in exile) to be restored as head of state. In 1988 an additional clause was added to the annual resolution calling for "non-return to universally condemned practices." This response addressed many states' concerns that a negotiated peace would enable the Khmer Rouge to return to power and the growing conviction that human rights provisions should be included in any settlement.[22]

Despite the weakness of international condemnation during the preceding decade, some elements of human rights intervention were included in the peace settlement. Lacking a legitimate central government to implement the accords, the Security Council undertook the highly intrusive act of establishing an interim sovereign national legislative body, the Supreme National Council (SNC), to be administered by the peacekeeping operation. Creation of the SNC was the most innovative measure of the Cambodian peace process, although UNTAC failed to exert the administrative control it was empowered to exercise. The SNC promoted several institutional reforms to ensure long-term human rights observance, either mandated by the Paris agreements or, in the case of the penal code and electoral legislation, designed and implemented by the UNTAC administration. These included a civil/political and human rights bill fully consistent with the provisions of the Universal Declaration of Human Rights, to be enforceable in national courts, and the bases for an independent judiciary.[23] The accords established the institutions of a pluralist political democracy: regularly held free and fair elections, universal and equal suffrage, a secret ballot, the right to form parties and organize for electoral participation. In the area of internal security, all civil police operated under UNTAC supervision or control for the duration of the transition.

UNTAC's mandate required it to develop and implement a human rights educational program, to monitor and investigate complaints, and to take corrective action as appropriate (left open to interpretation by the chief of mission). UNTAC personnel worked with the ICRC to investigate prison conditions, systematically visiting SOC prisons without prior notice. They obtained the release of a significant number of political prisoners and, at least temporarily, curtailed shackling, food shortages, and physical abuse. The mission instituted a criminal law code and trained around two hundred judges, prosecutors, and police officials.[24]

Under UNTAC's influence, the government acceded to several international human rights treaties, including the two covenants and the conventions on torture, discrimination against women, and status of refugees. The human rights division's education program, facilitated by $1.85 million donated by several governments, encouraged the development of six permanent and effective local nongovernmental human rights organizations. Funds were also used for an international NGO task force to assist in training local organizations. The Ford Foundation underwrote two international conferences in Phnom Penh designed to connect the new Cambodian NGOs with the transnational network.[25] Newly established local human rights NGOs, with UNTAC support, assisted in the Bangkok regional meeting in preparation for the Vienna World Conference on Human Rights. A delegation of Cambodian activists, accompanied by UNTAC human rights personnel, visited Geneva to lobby for the establishment of a permanent human rights field mission.[26] International and local rights organizations were vital to UNTAC's education program and judicial training, as well as to the repatriation of 370,000 refugees.[27] Since UNTAC's withdrawal, there has been a proliferation of domestic human rights organizations. Finally, the mission left behind it a permanent office of the UN Human Rights Center.

Although institutional reforms were generally more successful than the demobilization effort, on-site human rights enforcement for the duration of the mission was severely limited. The rights division was understaffed and under-resourced, whether compared to other missions or to other components of UNTAC. It had little independent capacity to control abuses during its eighteen-month tenure and, therefore, focused its limited resources on monitoring prisons and on investigating allegations of political and ethnic violence. With the cooperation of the civilian police unit, observers investigated approximately 1,300 killings, attacks, and disappearances, but were unable to convince the parties to act on their reports.[28]

Three areas of weakness explain UNTAC's relative lack of success in enforcing compliance. First, the topic of human rights was subordinated to geopolitical interests on the negotiating agenda, resulting in a flawed mandate. The direct participation of the Security Council in the negotiations resulted in a "peace by committee." Russia negotiated terms to shield the State of Cambodia from UNTAC control; China negotiated for greater UN control of the state apparatus to provide political space for the Khmer Rouge. The United States supported Sihanouk in the hopes that he would choose to head a pluralist democracy and sought to avoid giving either of the other two major factions an advantage.[29] The negotiations thus focused on regional security issues, leaving human rights as a side issue of lesser priority. This scenario was very different from the Salvadoran and Guatemalan peace processes, in which human rights accords preceded negotiations on military topics.

The second cause of UNTAC's mixed outcome was that the paucity of resources allocated to the human rights component at the planning stage made on-site verification impossible. From its establishment, the Secretary-General had decided that UNTAC's human rights component would be modest and stationed only in Phnom Penh. Mission planning was not coordinated with the human rights staff, and information from the preliminary assessment team was not made available to them.[30] While pragmatic, the decision to focus resources on the May 1993 election and to limit the mission's presence to the election period was short-sighted. More careful preparation of follow-through procedures for monitoring the strength of the institutions being established might have mitigated the extreme factionalism and eventual collapse of the post-election coalition government and, certainly, would have ensured that the institutions left behind would weather the transition better.

Third, the chief of mission was unwilling to challenge violations, because of his concern that such action might jeopardize the parties' cooperation. This led to vacillation and delay in responding to abuses.[31] The tension between the United Nations' dual purpose—the diplomatic imperative to make peace and the observers' mandate to ensure compliance with human rights principles—was even sharper than it was in El Salvador or Guatemala, and officials were less successful in making the two aspects of peacebuilding complement each other.

Cambodian Responses to International Regime Pressure

Viewing Cambodia through the framework for compliance, we see how the range of human rights sanctioning mechanisms has extended since the mid-1970s. At the time of the Khmer Rouge killing fields, members of the international human rights network who were aware of the situation could do little about it from a lack of mobilizing information; moreover, Cambodia occupied a sensitive geostrategic position in the cold war and was politically protected from the UN's reporting system. When international monitor reports gained more substance in the mid- to late 1980s, violators refused consistently to acknowledge NGO requests for information or contact, certain of continued support by their major power allies. By the time peace negotiations had become serious and external support for the factions was eroding, human rights obligations were considered an appropriate part of a peacekeeping mandate, even where human rights were not an issue central to the peace process itself.

UNTAC was certainly not a complete failure in promoting compliance with rights norms. Despite the limitations on the human rights component, and despite the ongoing armed conflict, important reforms were made to state institutions, especially to the judiciary. Now, for the first time, Cambodia has an active human rights community.[32] The UN Commission on Human Rights is committed to long-term monitoring of the situation, and the Human Rights Center has a permanent office in the country. Although the Khmer Rouge's intransigence and cheating by the State of Cambodia caused the failure of one of the operation's principal objectives—an end to armed conflict and the demobilization of forces—the institution-building aspects of the mission were more successful. While still imperiled by the ongoing political instability (Hun Sen overturned the coalition government in 1997 by ousting First Prime Minister Prince Norodom Ranariddh and assassinating several members of his party), the international peacebuilding mission left behind it an independent press, an active domestic human rights community, a trained judiciary, and an independent parliament.[33]

INSTITUTIONAL LEARNING AND THE FUTURE OF MULTILATERAL HUMAN RIGHTS ENFORCEMENT

In an endeavor to pass on some of his and other officials' observations concerning the variables that affect a human rights mission's efficacy, the former MINUGUA director, Leonardo Franco, offered the following "keys to success" in design and deployment:[34]

1. adequate planning, based on the recommendations of a preparatory assessment mission;
2. clear mandates and uniform guidelines;
3. careful integration of civilian and uniformed personnel, with clear civilian-led lines of authority;
4. clear and forceful reporting;
5. attention to national institutions, and care not to appear to usurp their functions;
6. good working relations with local NGOs;
7. autonomy of human rights verification from political or tactical considerations;
8. interagency cooperation and coordination, and recognition of the mission's complementary relationship with other UN human rights bodies, particularly the UN Human Rights Center and the High Commissioner for Human Rights;
9. adequate backup from the Secretariat.

Based on my own observation of ONUSAL and MINUGUA, I would offer some further procedural recommendations. First, accords should include careful consideration of post-mission follow through. Procedures for any uncompleted implementation and long-term verification of continued compliance should be worked out early in the operation, to take effect after the mission's final withdrawal. Next, human rights experts, both international and local, should be included in the design, verification, and follow up phases. ONUSAL and MINUGUA benefitted tremendously from the involvement of UN independent experts Drs. Christian Tomuschat, Pedro Nikken, and Mónica Pinto. Finally, working closely with international financial institutions and donor states, the parties and the United Nations should negotiate a schedule for incentives that would best encourage post-mission compliance.

Although changes in global norms of sovereignty and nonintervention point the way to an increase in the international community's ability to protect and promote human rights standards, obstacles to human rights enforcement remain. They will be particularly difficult to overcome where a multilateral human rights operation is not called for as part of a negotiated peace package. For example, in the case of a failed or ungovernable state, the mission director would have to enlist the cooperation of any domestic leaders who can credibly commit those sectors of the population they claim to represent. Especially where political authority is extremely fragmented or where the civilian leadership fails to exercise control over the military, the problem is to decide whose consent is binding, and how likely it is that factional leadership will not be able to control their followers. In cases where state institutions and apparatus remain intact, operation designers might work out agreements with the government and opposition leaders, or between opposing governments, but actual power may reside with the armed forces rather than with the civilian authorities. The government may agree in good faith to human rights intervention but be structurally incapable of implementing reforms or enforcing cooperation. The residual political authority retained by a military opposed to reforms that threaten its institutional prerogatives will always be a risk factor.

This is especially true where the military is factionalized, with some parts of the officer corps conditionally willing to cooperate with a human rights mission and others opposed. Militia killings of human rights personnel in Rwanda demonstrate this point. There was broad international support for the UN human rights field operation in Rwanda (governments pledged approximately $18 million to support this mission, although not all of the funds were received in a timely manner),[35] transnational and domestic human rights organizations were active in the country, and the government cooperated with its establishment, yet the operation became imperiled by paramilitary forces. It may not be advisable to deploy a mission under these circumstances. Particularly if the operation were small, underfunded, and understaffed, it would absorb scarce resources and potentially undermine the United Nations' credibility with little payoff. On the other hand, the UN human rights mission in Colombia is small and understaffed, and also threatened by paramilitary violence, but has quite effectively focused its resources on drafting and assisting in the implementation of legal/judicial reforms.

International intervention to protect human rights is considerably more problematic where it is not the product of a mediated peace process. This is, to an extent, an organizational problem for the UN system—the human rights bureaucracy lacks the Security Council's institutional authority (and its resources), and the Security Council only intervenes in a state's domestic affairs where requested to under Chapter VI, "pacific settlement of disputes" provisions, or under Chapter VII, as (coercive) "action with respect to threats to the peace." To date, given permissive political conditions, the UN human rights system has intervened most effectively when the organization is already involved in resolving the target state's internal conflict. Where the United Nations is not already implicated in such a conflict resolution process, a major state or states would have to change from a permissive position (not inhibiting enforcement) to a more assertive one (actively promoting action by arguing that the conflict is "likely to endanger the maintenance of international peace and security")[36] before the United Nations could expend significant resources on such an operation.

In a few cases (Burundi, Rwanda, Cambodia, Colombia), the Office of the UN High Commissioner for Human Rights maintains permanent field offices to support an independent expert or special rapporteur. These are all very limited operations, not comparable in mandate or in resources to the human rights divisions operated under the Department of Peacekeeping Operations or, in the case of Guatemala, the General Assembly. The Human Rights Centre lacks the expertise, operational capacity, and the resources to conduct large scale peacebuilding operations.[37]

Unless the Security Council undertakes such an operation, a violator could still subvert the UN mechanisms that would lead to enforcement action, despite the growing legitimacy of human rights intervention. The existing hortatory instruments of the Human Rights Commission are still subject to political manipulation. Commission members may be reluctant to condemn violators to protect their allies, as a quid pro quo to prevent their own governments from facing condemnation, because they are members of a regional coalition or simply out of diplomatic cautiousness. This is as much the case in 2000, with China still able to exert enough diplomatic pressure to prevent the passage of a condemnatory resolution, as it was in the late 1970s, when Argentina was maneuvering to evade condemnation. Even meeting the conditions proposed in this book, international human rights advocates might be hard pressed to generate the necessary interest among member states to invoke enforcement measures where these measures are not part of a conflict resolution process.

Moving from obstacles to deployment to ensuring cooperation with a human rights mission once there is one on the ground, these cases demonstrate that the cooperation of domestic actors requires a careful balancing of diplomacy, threat of sanctions, and material incentives. The continued cooperation of international donors is therefore crucial. Reforms can be mandated by an internationally guaranteed accord, but their implementation depends upon the political will of domestic parties, especially armed parties. The United Nations is pushing at the edges of sovereignty, but diplomatically and with a lot of backup. Compliance with agreements in El Salvador and Guatemala was not a matter of direct imposition, coercion, or even of public criticism, but often of extensive cooperative ventures (such as the UNDP/MINUGUA Joint Unit working with the Guatemalan Public Prosecutor's office), relationships built over time between nationals and international advisers, that lend credibility and long-term guarantees to the implementation process.

Officials in charge of implementing the agreements drew on an established network of diplomatic ties and ongoing relations with intergovernmental organizations. MINUGUA projects were coordinated with UNDP, USAID, European foundations and governments, and U.S. and European private donor groups—agencies on whom most developing states depend for assistance. As a result of this direct linkage, although the governments are not technically forced to comply with mission recommendations, noncompliance has much higher costs than it did formerly under the UN human rights reporting system.

CONCLUSION: WHERE DO WE GO FROM HERE?

Was the phenomenon of multilateral human rights operations limited to a moment, a particular time and place? The brief overview of Cambodia demonstrates that the analytical framework for compliance can travel to another region altogether. A much briefer glance at how international human rights politics played out in Argentina during the late 1970s will show how this argument applies in a different historical context—a much earlier stage of human rights institutionalization—and a different political context—no civil war, no negotiated peace.

The Argentine military overthrew the civilian government on March 24, 1976. Following the coup, the armed forces formed a joint ruling junta and proceeded to build an authoritarian system aimed at restructuring the wayward economy and eliminating political opposition. Between 1976 and 1980, the junta government engaged in a systematic policy of state terror, targeting any real or symbolic opposition, including "potentially subversive" groups such as students, attorneys, journalists, organized labor, and Jews.[38]

The human rights regime at this time had only weak implementation mechanisms (on-site investigatory visits and condemnatory declarations)— nothing like the multilateral enforcement measures of the 1990s. The U.S. government targeted Argentina for bilateral human rights sanctions under the Foreign Assistance Act, Section 502(b), in 1977.[39] Following the 1979 Soviet invasion of Afghanistan, Argentina's geostrategic significance changed so that it qualified for the national-security exemption from foreign assistance conditionality. Argentina and the USSR had arranged a trade agreement in 1977, and between 1978 and 1980 Argentine grain exports to the Soviet Union grew from 1.4 million to 7.6 million tons. The United States called for a global grain embargo to protest the Soviet invasion of Afghanistan and sought Argentina's cooperation. Furthermore, U.S. businesses with commercial interests in Argentina had been lobbying since mid-1978 against economic sanctions that threatened financing for joint ventures and exports. Congressional support for human rights sanctions against Argentina eroded under pressure from the commerce lobby and with the changed geostrategic climate.

Almost from the start, military rule was resisted by a domestic human rights movement, which developed extensive links to international actors during the period of terror. The transnational network was very effective in mobilizing international pressure and helping to delegitimize the government. International human rights activists mobilized diplomatic pressure from the United States and from European governments which, when exerted, elicited at least a limited response from the Argentine military. For example, the government permitted the International Committee of the Red Cross to visit prisons and invited the Inter-American Commission on Human Rights to make an investigatory visit in late 1978, in response to diplomatic pressure.[40]

Those in the ruling junta who were sensitive to human rights criticism and its effect on Argentina's international reputation carried out intensive diplomatic and public relations campaigns to quell such criticism. During the height of the terror, 1976–77, competing factions within the armed forces were held together by a mutual consensus on the national security strategy. The strategic consensus began to break down in 1978. A comparatively pragmatic faction represented by Army General Videla was maneuvering for gradual liberalization under continued military rule. By late 1978 the Videla faction had gained sufficient autonomy from hardliners to be able to credibly commit the military to cooperate in the Inter-American Commission inspection, which Videla invited in order to improve Argentina's international image.[41] This visit was the only one by an intergovernmental organization and is widely considered to have been more effective than either UN condemnation or bilateral pressure in clearing out clandestine prisons and torture centers (although many allege that prisoners were simply hidden or murdered).[42]

By the end of 1979, mass killings had ended and disappearances were rapidly diminishing. The number of official prisoners detained under executive order peaked in 1977, with 5,018 reported political prisoners in May 1977, dropping to 3,472 in January 1978, and down to 1,438 by the time of the IACHR visit (which finally took place in September 1979). Did international human rights pressure cause the Argentine military to change its behavior? Transnational activism was certainly effective in protecting the local human rights community, and the publicity campaign that damaged the junta's reputation helped to delegitimize it in international circles and in Argentine civil society.[43] The government issued public statements proclaiming human rights to be a national goal and paid for public relations campaigns to improve its image abroad. Advocates' efforts were undermined by the internal problems of a politicized and overly cautious human rights bureaucracy in Geneva, by the inherent contradictions of the U.S. bilateral human rights policy, and overall by the regime's lack enforcement machinery. But the regime did matter, because its carriers— the moral entrepreneurs of the human rights network—were, in the end, able to raise the costs of repression for the Argentine military dictatorship.

Other focused case studies would enable policymakers to evaluate an array of conditions so as to ascertain what human rights enforcement mechanisms, if any, would be feasible. Further research should also assist human rights advocates in designing and adapting mobilization strategies based on the level of development achieved by domestic organizations and on the nature of the ruling coalition. Even where government elites are impervious to human rights pressure, or where the country is closed to human rights monitors, focusing international attention on a situation and publicizing any confirmable report is worth the candle. The reports on Cambodia published by international NGOs in the 1980s undoubtedly influenced major power representatives in their decision to include human rights provisions in the Cambodian peace agreements.

With peace talks between the government and the major guerrilla factions now underway, Colombia has emerged as an interesting case for comparison. A number of factors peculiar to the Colombian situation make it more complicated than El Salvador and Guatemala (although not more complicated than Cambodia): the greater size and strength of the armed opposition, the strength and relative autonomy of paramilitary organizations, the resources available to both the guerrillas and the paramilitaries through drug traffic and kidnapping, and the intervening interest of the U.S. government in narcotics eradication. But for the sake of comparison, I will isolate the factors examined in this book to discover what light they may shed on prospects for human rights enforcement and peacebuilding in Colombia.

First, this is another case of a state apparatus often criticized by the international community for human rights violations. Colombia is under scrutiny by the UN Human Rights Commission, which established a permanent field office in Bogotá in May 1997. Representatives of the Colombian government met with UN, Salvadoran, and Guatemalan officials in 1994 to discuss the possibility of a peace process following the model developed in El Salvador.[44] President Andrés Pastrana (elected in June 1998), like Alfredo Cristiani in El Salvador and Alvaro Arzú in Guatemala, campaigned heavily on his intention to negotiate an end to the civil war and gained in the polls by meeting with FARC leadership shortly before the election. Pastrana expressed his interest in UN mediation from the earliest round of negotiations (May 1999), proposing early deployment of a verification mission. The largest guerrilla organization, the FARC (Fuerzas Armadas de la Revolución Colombiana), made it clear that it was adamantly opposed to international verification on its territory (a zone in the south of the country from which government personnel were withdrawn in November 1998).[45] A year later, however, the second largest guerrilla organization (Ejército de Liberación Nacional, ELN) negotiated its own demilitarized zone and accepted the establishment of an international observer mission on its territory as part of the agreement.[46] In January 2000, the UN Secretary-General indicated his willingness to play a mediating role in the Colombian negotiations when he appointed a seasoned negotiator, Jan Egeland, as his special envoy to the country.

Regarding regional strategic interests, the United States has placed restrictions on assistance to military units implicated in human rights abuses, and recent State Department reports have been uncharacteristically critical of the Colombian military. However, the United States is increasing its support for the armed forces by linking counterinsurgency to prosecution of the drug war. In some cases, the U.S. government has protected military and paramilitary violators from inspection by the Colombian government, even while rhetorically backing Pastrana's peace initiatives.[47] An emergency counternarcotics aid package proposed by the Clinton administration was approved by the Senate on June 21, 2000, allocating $1.3 billion in military assistance to Colombia over two years. The example of El Salvador is a warning that increased lethal aid is likely to prolong the conflict and delay the moment at which the parties perceive a mutually hurting stalemate. On the other hand, this bonanza for the military may have the opposite effect, by convincing the FARC to negotiate in good faith in the face of a vastly improved military force.[48]

The domestic factors I have examined are the level of concern for international reputation among core members of the ruling elite, their ability to control and commit the armed forces, and the extent of the local human rights community and its links to the transnational network. The Colombian government, both former and current, has expressed a strong interest in improving its international human rights image. The Samper administration did so by signing the Geneva Conventions Second Protocol, which regulates the behavior of combatants in internal conflict, and by establishing a presidential human rights counsel and public defender for human rights. Colombian officials have expressed publicly their concern that critical human rights reports might damage their international prestige and apprehension about efforts by members of the U.S. Congress to place human rights conditions on trade ties.[49] Pastrana dismissed four generals associated with the paramilitaries in 1999, although others in the high command and half of the active-duty brigades remain closely associated with paramilitary organizations as of mid-2000.[50] The Colombian government is demonstrably less timid about exerting its authority over the military than were either the Salvadoran or the Guatemalan governments during their periods of conflict. The government is clearly ready for a negotiated peace, although the FARC appears to be somewhat less committed to the process—and it controls significant territory and resources.

Perhaps the clearest influence of the Salvadoran and Guatemalan peace processes is found in the widespread assumption that civil sectors will be involved in some fashion in the Colombian negotiations. The Colombian human rights community is dynamic and active in regional and international human rights organizations, but in this case the private sector—the target of guerrilla kidnapping activities—appears to be taking the initiative in promoting peace talks. Finally, institutional reforms designed to promote human rights are priority items on the Colombian negotiating agenda. If and when such reforms are implemented, conditions for human rights in Colombia will have gained immeasurably from the achievements of the mediated peace processes in El Salvador and Guatemala.

To return to the question posed at the beginning of this book, how can we explain the innovations in human rights enforcement of the 1990s?

Following decades of glacial expansion of the international community's capacity to criticize or monitor its members, how do we account for those recent instances in which member states have rented their police and military advisers to the United Nations, to oversee compliance with human rights agreements? The first part of the answer is the trend in the postwar international system to recognize human rights as a legitimizing principle. In this sense, the institutionalization of the human rights regime and the prevalence of human rights in elite discourse is the meta-narrative of this story. But the evolution of the regime's enforcement capacity has been neither steady, nor linear, nor predetermined. States are constrained by human rights principles, *under certain circumstances*.

The international political context is critical, in that a major state (a regional hegemon or permanent member of the Security Council, or a major trading partner) can essentially veto enforcement action by the international community if perceived to be detrimental to that state's economic or security interests. At the domestic level, some key element in the ruling coalition, one with the authority to control and commit other and especially military elites, must perceive damage to the state's international reputation to be sufficiently costly to warrant a change in practice or policy. Within civil society, local human rights activists play an essential role in providing allies abroad with information about domestic conditions, in establishing a base of operations at home, and in keeping the issue on the international agenda. Finally, to mobilize the international human rights protection machinery, the transnational network of human rights activists must be engaged. It is these individuals and organizations who apply pressure at appropriate leverage points, provide decision makers with the incentives to cooperate, and elevate moral concerns to the level of a renewed understanding of our identity and purpose as members of an international society.

APPENDIX A
GLOSSARY OF ACRONYMS

INTERNATIONAL OR UNITED STATES

AIFLD	American Institute for Free Labor Development
ALDH	Latin American Association for Human Rights
CALDH	Center for Legal Action and Human Rights
CAWG	Central America Working Group
CEJIL	Center for Justice and International Law
CIIR	Catholic Institute for International Relations
CODEHUCA	Central American Human Rights Commission
FEDEFAM	Federation of Families of Those Disappeared and Detained for Political Reasons
ICRC	International Committee of the Red Cross
IIDH	Inter-American Institute of Human Rights
LAWG	Latin America Working Group
LCHR	Lawyers' Committee for Human Rights
LWF	Lutheran World Federation
MINUGUA	United Nations Mission in Guatemala
NCC	National Council of Churches
ONUCA	United Nations Observer Group in Central America
ONUSAL	United Nations Observer Mission in El Salvador
PBI	Peace Brigades International
UNTAC	United Nations Transitional Authority in Cambodia
UNV	United Nations Volunteer Program
USCC	United States Catholic Conference
WCC	World Council of Churches
WOLA	Washington Office on Latin America

El Salvador

ARENA	National Republican Alliance
CD	Democratic Convergence
CDH	Nongovernmental Human Rights Commission
COPAZ	National Commission for the Consolidation of the Peace
ERP	People's Revolutionary Army
FAL	Armed Forces of Liberation
FDR	Democratic Revolutionary Front
FENASTRAS	National Federation of Salvadoran Union Workers
FMLN	Farabundo Martí National Liberation Front
FPL	Popular Liberation Forces
PCS	Salvadoran Communist Party
PDC	Christian Democratic Party
PDH	Office of the National Counsel for the Defense of Human Rights
PNC	National Civil Police
PRTC	Central American Revolutionary Workers Party
RN	National Resistance

Guatemala

ASC	Assembly of Civil Society
CACIF	Chamber of Agricultural, Commercial, Industrial, and Financial Associations
CDHG	Guatemalan Human Rights Commission
CERJ	Council of Ethnic Communities Runuel Junam
CIEPRODH	Center for Investigation, Study, and Promotion of Human Rights in Guatemala
CII	Inter-Institutional Coordinating Councils
CNR	National Reconciliation Commission
COCIPAZ	Civil Coordination for Peace
CONAVIGUA	National Coordination of Guatemalan Widows
COPAZ	Government Peace Commission
COPREDEH	President's Commission for Human Rights
CPR	Communities of Population in Resistance
CSC	Coordination of Civil Sectors
DCG	Christian Democratic Party
DIT	National Police Technical Investigations Directorate
EGP	Guerrilla Army of the Poor
EMP	Presidential General Staff
FAR	Rebel Armed Forces
FDNG	New Guatemala Democratic Front
FUR	United Revolutionary Front

G-2	Army High Command Intelligence Directorate
GAM	Mutual Support Group
MAS	Movement for Solidarity Action
MLN	National Liberation Movement
ODHA	Archbishop's Office for Human Rights
ORPA	Organization of the People in Arms
PAC	Civil Defense Patrols
PAN	National Action Party
PDH	Office of the Human Rights Counsel
PGT	Guatemalan Communist Party
PID	Institutional Democratic Party
PSD	Socialist Democratic Party
RUOG	Representation of the Guatemalan Opposition
SIPROCI	Citizen Protection System
URNG	Guatemalan National Revolutionary Unity

Cambodia

CGDK	Coalition Government of Democratic Kampuchea
FUNCINPEC	National United Front for an Independent, Neutral, Peaceful and Cooperative Cambodia
KPNLF	Khmer People's National Liberation Front
PRK	People's Republic of Kampuchea
SOC	State of Cambodia
SNC	Supreme National Council

APPENDIX B
LIST OF INTERVIEW SUBJECTS

Formal interviews in New York and Washington were conducted in 1996 and 1997. Formal interviews in El Salvador and Guatemala were conducted from May 1994 to September 1995. I have done some informal followups since those dates.

New York, N.Y.

Juan Méndez, Americas Watch
Denise Cook, UN Department of Political Affairs
Paul Wee, Lutheran World Federation
Ambassador Alvaro de Soto, UN Department of Political Affairs
Michael Posner, Lawyers Committee for Human Rights
Mireille Hector, Lawyers Committee for Human Rights

Washington, D.C.

Cynthia Arnson, Woodrow Wilson Center
George Vickers, WOLA
Geoff Thale, WOLA
Thomas Quigley, Policy Adviser, U.S. Catholic Conference
George Biddle, President, Institute for Central American Studies
Leonel Gómez, Consultant Centro DEMOS

El Salvador

United Nations Personnel

Blanca Antonini, ONUSAL Chief Political Affairs Officer
Reed Brody, ONUSAL Director of Human Rights

Colleen Duggan, UNDP Program Officer
Leila Lima, ONUSAL Regional Coordinator San Salvador
Renzo Pomi, ONUSAL Legal Adviser Chalatenango
Jan Perlin, ONUSAL Legal Adviser San Miguel
Juan Faroppa Fontana, ONUSAL Human Rights Legal Officer

NGO Staff, Academics, Political Analysts

David Holiday, Consultant, Americas Watch
Dean Brackley, University of Central America Pastoral Center
Benjamin Cuéllar, Director, University of Central America Institute for Human Rights
Rodolfo Cardenal, Vice-Rector, University of Central America
Linda Garrett, Consultant, El Rescate
Francisco Díaz, Director, CESPAD
Ricardo Córdova M., Fundación Guillermo Ungo
Héctor Dada, FLACSO
Roberto Turcios, Editor-in-Chief, *Tendencias*
Rafael Nieto Loaiza, IIDH (San José)
Maria Julia Hernández, Tutela Legal
Bishop Medardo Gómez, Lutheran Church of El Salvador

Negotiators and Government Officials

Ana Guadalupe Martínez, FMLN delegation
Salvador Samayoa, FMLN delegation
Oscar Santamaría, government delegation
David Escobar Galindo, government delegation
General Mauricio Vargas, government delegation
Rodolfo Parker, COPAZ

GUATEMALA

United Nations Personnel

Gerald Plantegenest, MINUGUA Deputy Director
Alejandro Artucio, MINUGUA Chief Human Rights Adviser
Hugo Lorenzo, MINUGUA Director FORIN
Alfredo Forti, MINUGUA Director Documentation and Analysis
Leila Lima, MINUGUA Regional Coordinator Guatemala
Renzo Pomi, MINUGUA Subregional Coordinator Cantabal
Goran Fejic, MINUGUA Regional Coordinator Cobán
Vladimir Huaroc, MINUGUA Regional Coordinator Huehuetenango
Marie Cervetti, MINUGUA Regional Coordinator Zacapa
Major Bjorn Fogstam, MINUGUA Military Liaison Cobán

Ditas Amry, MINUGUA/UNV Cantabal
Michael Gort, MINUGUA/UNV Cantabal
Lee Tucker, MINUGUA Legal Officer Cantabal
Susana Gularte Estrada, UNDP/ACOBIDH Projects and Education Assistant

NGO Staff, Academics, Political Analysts

Frank LaRue, Director CALDH
Rolando Cabrera, Director FUNDAPAZD/Secretary-General ASC
Gabriel Aguilera Peralta, FLACSO
Luis Alberto Padilla, IRIPAZ
Fernando López, Instituto de Estudios Comparados de Ciencias Penales
Fáctor Méndez, CIEPRODH
Edgar Gutierrez, Fundación Myrna Mack
Liam Mahoney, Consultant, MacArthur Foundation
Justina Tzoc, CERJ
Fermina López-Castro, CONAVIGUA
Marcie Merskey, ODHA
Nineth Montenegro, GAM
Mario Polanco, GAM
Will Harrell, CALDH Legal Assistant
Amanda Rodas, Coordinación de ONG y Cooperativas/ASC delegate

Negotiators and Government Officials

Héctor Rosada, COPAZ
Antonio Arenales Forno, COPAZ
Alfonso Castillo, Director COPREDEH Huehuetenango office
Ricardo Alvarado Ortigoza, Deputy Human Rights Counsel (PDH)

NOTES

Why Do States Cooperate?

1. On transnational advocacy networks see Kathryn Sikkink, "Human Rights, Principled Issue-networks, and Sovereignty in Latin America," *International Organization* vol. 47, no. 3 (Summer 1993), and Margaret E. Keck and Kathryn Sikkink, *Activists beyond Borders: Advocacy Networks in International Politics* (Ithaca: Cornell University Press, 1998). For lengthier discussion, see Susan Burgerman, "The Evolution of Compliance: The Human Rights Regime, Transnational Networks, and United Nations Peacebuilding," Ph.D. diss., Columbia University, 1997, pp. 56–79.

2. Stephen D. Krasner, ed., *International Regimes* (Ithaca: Cornell University Press, 1983), p. 2. See also Lisa L. Martin and Beth Simmons, "Theories and Empirical Studies of International Institutions," *International Organization* vol. 52, no. 4 (Autumn 1998); Andreas Hansenclever, Peter Mayer, and Volker Rittberger, *Theories of International Regimes* (Cambridge: Cambridge University Press, 1997); Volker Rittberger, ed., *Regime Theory and International Relations* (Oxford: Clarendon Press, 1993); Stephan Haggard and Beth A. Simmons, "Theories of International Regimes," *International Organization* vol. 41, no. 3 (Summer 1987). For a detailed discussion of how this area of theory applies to human rights law, please see Burgerman, "The Evolution of Compliance," pp. 32–56.

3. Audie Klotz, *Norms in International Relations: The Struggle against Apartheid* (Ithaca: Cornell University Press, 1995) gives a concise overview of the debates on international community norms, state preference formation, and reputational constraints. Also see Thomas Risse, Stephen C. Ropp, and Kathryn Sikkink, eds., *The Power of Human Rights: International Norms and Domestic Change* (Cambridge: Cambridge University Press, 1999), and Martha Finnemore and

Kathryn Sikkink, "International Norm Dynamics and Political Change," *International Organization* vol. 52, no. 4 (Autumn 1998). Ann Florini, "The Evolution of International Norms," *International Studies Quarterly* vol. 40, no. 3 (September 1996) develops an evolutionary explanation of why certain norms become institutionalized. On the social construction of national identity, see Martha Finnemore, *National Interests in International Society* (Ithaca: Cornell University Press, 1996).

4. See Ethan A. Nadelman, "Global Prohibition Regimes: The Evolution of Norms in International Society," *International Organization* vol. 44, no. 4 (Autumn 1990).

5. The British reaction to the slaughter of Christians in Turkey in the 1870s is an early example of nonstate actors mobilizing public opinion and government policy on the basis of moral principles (observation by Robert Jervis).

6. See former bureau official Patrick J. Flood's account, "U.S. Human Right Initiatives Concerning Argentina," in *The Diplomacy of Human Rights*, ed. David D. Newsom (Lanham, Md.: University Press of America, 1986), pp. 129–39.

7. Jack Donnelly, *Universal Human Rights in Theory and Practice* (Ithaca: Cornell University Press, 1989), pp. 211–13; see also Donnelly, *International Human Rights* (Boulder, Colo.: Westview Press, 1993), p. 138.

8. David Forsythe refers to this as the "legal empirical approach," in *The Internationalization of Human Rights* (Lexington, Mass.: D. C. Heath, 1991), pp. 10–11.

9. This is not to suggest that international legal scholars have not made an effort to clarify state responsibility for socioeconomic rights, or to establish criteria for evaluating state performance in this area. The United Nations adopted principles for implementing the Covenant on Economic, Social, and Cultural Rights (the "Limburg Principles") in 1986, and in January 1997 the International Commission of Jurists met to elaborate specific guidelines for their implementation.

10. See Patrick E. Tyler, "U.S. and Chinese Seen Near a Deal on Human Rights," *New York Times*, February 24, 1997, A1.

11. Ethan Nadelman coined the expression "transnational moral entrepreneurs" in "Global Prohibition Regimes," p. 482.

12. Kathryn Sikkink, "The Emergence, Evolution, and Effectiveness of the Latin American Human Rights Network," in *Constructing Democracy: Human Rights, Citizenship, and Society in Latin America*, ed. Elizabeth Jelin and Eric Hershberg (Boulder, Colo.: Westview Press, 1996), p. 64. On priority rights in UN missions, see the text of *Agreement on Human Rights*, signed at San José, Costa Rica, on July 26, 1990, between the Government of El Salvador and the FMLN, I(1) (UN Document A/44/971-S/21541).

13. The following is intended as a general account of how the human rights network formed and functioned through the 1980s. It is constructed almost entirely of the personal memories of several individuals who were network activists during this period. I fully acknowledge the methodological drawbacks of relying on oral history. However, since my purpose here is to provide some insight into the operations of the human rights network and its link-

ages, the benefits outweigh the costs, even in terms of the accuracy of historical data.

14. Author's interviews with Thomas Quigley, policy adviser to the Office of International Justice and Peace, U.S. Catholic Conference, March 12, 1996, and George Vickers, executive director, Washington Office on Latin America, March 11, 1996.

15. Author's interview with Cynthia Arnson, resident scholar at the Woodrow Wilson Center, March 13, 1996. Dr. Arnson worked as a congressional staffer during the Carter administration.

16. Author's interview with Frank LaRue, June 6, 1995.

17. Author's interview with Michael Posner, executive director, Lawyers' Committee on Human Rights, April 19, 1996.

18. Central Intelligence Agency, "El Salvador: Controlling Rightwing Terrorism, An Intelligence Assessment," Directorate of Intelligence, February 1985, p. 12.

19. For a detailed analysis of congressional debates over Central America policy, see Cynthia J. Arnson, *Crossroads: Congress, the President, and Central America, 1976–1993* (University Park: Pennsylvania State University Press, 1993).

20. This is the third phase of the spiral model of human rights behavior change developed in Risse et al., eds., *The Power of Human Rights*.

21. Keck and Sikkink, *Activists beyond Borders*, pp. 12–16, describe the strategies used by domestic organizations to appeal to their international allies.

22. In 1978, the commission began publishing a list of countries considered under this procedure at commission meetings. The advantage of the 1503 procedure is that it can be initiated by individuals or NGOs rather than by commission members, who are representatives of states. The disadvantage is that Working Group discussions and decisions remain confidential; the secretiveness of the procedure enables violators to evade public scrutiny for as long as their case remains on the 1503 agenda.

23. Amnesty International, *Political Killings by Governments* (London: Amnesty International Publications, 1983), p. 43.

24. Fernando Tesón develops a roughly similar categorization of action: soft (implementation), hard (nonmilitary enforcement), and forcible (humanitarian intervention requiring use of force); see Tesón, "Collective Humanitarian Intervention," *Michigan Journal of International Law* vol. 17, no. 2 (Winter 1996), and idem, "Changing Perceptions of Domestic Jurisdiction and Intervention," in *Beyond Sovereignty: Collectively Defending Democracy in the Americas*, ed. Tom Farer (Baltimore: Johns Hopkins University Press, 1996). Alternatively, Stephen Marks refers to the UN's authorized promotion of human rights through on-site investigations, public resolutions denouncing abuses, and direct communications with violator states as soft intervention. He refers to the opposite end of the spectrum, coercive measures under Chapter VII, as hard intervention, leaving intrusive but not, strictly speaking, interventionary action under the rubric of consent-based peacebuilding. See Stephen P. Marks, "Preventing Humanitarian Crises through Peace-Building and Democratic Empowerment: Lessons from Cambodia," *Medicine and Global Survival* vol. 1, no. 4 (December 1994). Jack

Donnelly applies the categories of declaratory, promotional, implementation, and enforcement regimes in an earlier typology in *Universal Human Rights in Theory and Practice*, p. 206. It should be noted that Donnelly's work provides a precedent for the broader usage of the term *enforcement*.

25. Ann Kent makes a similar point, arguing that multilateral monitoring has the advantage of collective, consensual, institutionally based moral authority lacking in bilateral pressure; that norms, although selectively applied, are at least consistent; and that multilateral monitoring, by pitting one state against a community of states, necessitates a process of cooperation and coalition-building. Kent, "China and the International Human Rights Regime: A Case Study of Multilateral Monitoring, 1989–1994," *Human Rights Quarterly* vol. 17 no. 1 (1995): 3.

26. Newsom, ed., *The Diplomacy of Human Rights*, p. 134.

27. A detailed description of UN Commission procedures can be found in Philip Alston, ed., *The United Nations and Human Rights: A Critical Appraisal* (Oxford: Clarendon Press, 1992).

28. Donnelly, *International Human Rights*, offers a critical evaluation of Resolution 1503 procedures in general. For a critique of the work of UN experts in Guatemala, see Lawyers' Committee for Human Rights, *Abandoning the Victims: The UN Advisory Services Program in Guatemala* (New York: Lawyers' Committee for Human Rights, 1990).

29. The introductory chapter of Michael Doyle, Ian Johnstone, and Robert Orr, eds., *Keeping the Peace: Multidimensional UN Operations in Cambodia and El Salvador* (Cambridge: Cambridge University Press, 1997), gives an overview of this development in peacekeeping.

30. Author's interview with Reed Brody, October 7, 1994.

31. See especially Alison Brysk, "The Politics of Measurement: The Contested Count of the Disappeared in Argentina," *Human Rights Quarterly* vol. 16, no. 4 (November 1994). Brysk reviews the methodological and ethical concerns in the use of quantitative measures, and concludes that "the measurement of human rights violations is politically-framed, limited, and deployed. Furthermore, the most common indicators of human rights violations—aggregate body counts—may not reflect demographic and qualitative factors which significantly influence public policy" (p. 692).

32. Author's interview with David Holiday, former Americas Watch representative in Central America, August 17, 1994. Kathryn Sikkink also discusses the political ramifications of overlooking international humanitarian law in human rights reporting in "The Emergence, Evolution, and Effectiveness of the Latin American Human Rights Network," pp. 70–71.

33. Interview with Cynthia Arnson, March 13, 1996.

34. Interview with George Vickers, March 11, 1996.

35. Stoll analyzes the implications for human rights activism of bestowing legitimacy on victimhood in "Guatemala, the Dead, and the Homage We Pay Them," unpublished paper, Woodrow Wilson Center, January 1996.

36. See United Nations, *Report of the Preparatory Committee on the Establishment of an International Criminal Court*, A/Conf.183/2/Add.1 (14 April 1998).

1. Arnson, *Crossroads*, pp. 40–43, and observation of Ambassador Robert White, September 23, 1999.
2. William LeoGrande, "From Reagan to Bush: The Transition in US Policy towards Central America," *Journal of Latin American Studies* vol. 22, pt. 3 (October 1990).
3. For an elaboration of U.S. government response to the Jesuit murders, see Martha Doggett, *Death Foretold: The Jesuit Murders in El Salvador* (Washington, D.C.: Lawyers' Committee for Human Rights/Georgetown University Press, 1993), pp. 209–36. For more on the Dodd-Leahy bill (HR 5114), see Teresa Whitfield, *Paying the Price: Ignacio Ellacuría and the Murdered Jesuits of El Salvador* (Philadelphia: Temple University Press, 1995), pp. 174–89.
4. For an analysis of how the economic effects of the Salvadoran civil war caused the agrarian elite to seek a political settlement, see Elizabeth Wood, "Agrarian Social Relations and Democratization: The Negotiated Resolution of the Civil War in El Salvador," Ph.D. dissertation, Stanford University, 1995.
5. George Vickers, "The Political Reality after Eleven Years of War," in *Is There a Transition to Democracy in El Salvador?*, ed. Joseph S. Tulchin and Gary Bland (Boulder, Colo.: Lynne Rienner, 1992), p. 29.
6. Cristina Eguizábal, "Parties, Programs, and Politics in El Salvador," in *Political Parties and Democracy in Central America*, ed. Louis W. Goodman, William M. LeoGrande, and Johanna Mendelson Forman (Boulder, Colo.: Westview Press, 1992), pp. 141–42.
7. Central Intelligence Agency, "Arrest of Rightist Coup Plotters," May 1980.
8. Central Intelligence Agency, "El Salvador: Controlling Rightwing Terrorism," February 1985.
9. Thomas R. Pickering, "Address before the American Chamber of Commerce in San Salvador," November 25, 1983.
10. "Statement by the Minister of Defense of El Salvador, General Carlos Eugenio Vides Casanova, San Salvador," November 2, 1983.
11. Central Intelligence Agency/Department of State, "Briefing Paper on Right-Wing Terrorism," October 27, 1983.
12. Robert S. Leiken, "The Salvadoran Left," in *Central America: Anatomy of Conflict*, ed. Robert S. Leiken (New York: Pergamon Press, 1984), p. 115; also Enrique A. Baloyra, *El Salvador in Transition* (Chapel Hill: University of North Carolina Press, 1982), pp. 36–37.
13. Leiken, "The Salvadoran Left," p. 118.
14. Sam Dillon, "Dateline El Salvador: Crisis Renewed," *Foreign Policy* vol. 73 (Winter 1988–89): 156.
15. Alvaro de Soto, "Ending Violent Conflict in El Salvador," in *Herding Cats: Multiparty Mediation in a Complex World*, ed. Chester A. Crocker, Fen Osler Hampson, and Pamela Aal (Washington, D.C.: U.S. Institute of Peace Press, 1999), p. 371.

16. Salvador Samoyoa, FMLN spokesperson, interviewed by Terry Karl, "El Salvador: Negotiations or Total War," *World Policy Journal* vol. 6, no. 2 (Spring 1989): 342.

17. See Robert G. Kaiser, "White Paper on El Salvador is Faulty," *Washington Post*, June 8, 1981.

18. Max Manwaring and Court Prisk, eds., *El Salvador at War: An Oral History* (Washington, DC: National Defense University Press, 1988), pp. 123–51.

19. Manwaring and Prisk, eds., *El Salvador at War*, pp. 273–319; Tommie Sue Montgomery, *Revolution in El Salvador: From Civil Strife to Civil Peace* (Boulder, Colo.: Westview Press, 1995), pp. 164–71.

20. Montgomery, *Revolution in El Salvador*, pp. 197–98; Americas Watch, *El Salvador's Decade of Terror: Human Rights since the Assassination of Archbishop Romero* (New Haven: Yale University Press, 1991), p. 58.

21. Author's interview with an FDR member who requested anonymity, April 1995.

22. Supplements to the original Americas Watch (with the American Civil Liberties Union) *Report on Human Rights in El Salvador, January 26, 1982* (New York: Vintage Books, 1982). In addition, Americas Watch published reports on specific topics, such as compliance with the Central American Peace Plan, labor rights, use of land mines, methodological and ideological debates in the reporting of violations, administration of justice by FMLN field commanders, and violations of the laws of war.

23. For an account of the formation and operations of one key Salvadoran human rights organization, COMADRES, see Maria Teresa Tula, *Hear My Testimony*, trans. and ed. Lynn Stephen (Boston: South End Press, 1994).

24. A dossier documenting persecution of Salvadoran religious workers had been compiled by Jesuits at the University of Central America, El Salvador in 1977. Two copies of this dossier were smuggled to the United States, marking one of the first occasions on which the government of El Salvador was formally charged with human rights violations. From author's interview with Thomas Quigley, U.S. Catholic Conference, March 12, 1996.

25. Section 502(b) contains an exception clause that enables the executive to override the prohibition on military aid in cases of "extraordinary circumstances." The legislation does not specify what circumstances qualify as extraordinary, but humanitarian need and strategic importance are most commonly referred to in justifying continued assistance to human rights violators. See discussion of the exception clause in Americas Watch and American Civil Liberties Union, *Report on Human Rights in El Salvador, January 26, 1982*, pp. 202–205.

26. Arnson, *Crossroads*, p. 30.

27. See Americas Watch and ACLU, *Report on Human Rights in El Salvador, January 26, 1982*, pp. 54–56.

28. UN General Assembly, *Report of the Economic and Social Council: Situation of Human Rights and Fundamental Freedoms in El Salvador*, A/36/608 (28 October 1981), p. 20.

29. See the Report of the Commission on the Truth for El Salvador, "From Madness to Hope: The Twelve-year War in El Salvador," in *The United Nations and*

El Salvador, 1990–1995, UN Blue Books Series, vol. 4 (New York: United Nations Publications, 1995).

30. State Department memorandum, "Assassinations of Four U.S. Religious Persons December 2, 1980," January 16, 1981.

31. Report of the Truth Commission, "From Madness to Hope," pp. 320–23.

32. State Department cable, "Armed Forces Responds to Mrs. Avila's Charge," October 14, 1982; Central Intelligence Agency, "Responsibility of 'Death Squad' Run by Businessman Ricardo Sol Mesa and National Guard Major Denis Moran for Murders of Rodolfo Viera and U.S. Citizens Michael Hammer and Mark Pearlman," May 30, 1981.

33. For a full account of this incident, see Mark Danner, *The Massacre at El Mozote: A Parable of the Cold War* (New York: Vintage Books, 1994).

34. Public reaction to the certification is the subject of a letter from the assistant secretary of state for congressional relations to Representative Richard Ottinger, dated January 28, 1982. In it, the State Department rejects a request made by several members of Congress, urging the president to withdraw his certification in light of the ACLU–Americas Watch report and the reports on El Mozote.

35. In fact, an FBI investigation was underway of the "Millionaire Murderers," a group of six Salvadoran emigrés living in Miami, suspected of financing and directing death squad operations, including the Sheraton Hotel murders. Department of State, "Millionaires' Murder Inc.?," January 6, 1981; Department of State, "Investigation of Domestic Support for Violence in El Salvador," December 8, 1983.

36. Department of State, "Vice President Bush's Meetings with Salvadoran officials," December 14, 1983.

37. Department of State, "Vice President Bush's Meetings with Salvadoran officials."

38. Department of State, "Early Assessment, Vice President Bush's Visit," December 13, 1983.

39. Central Intelligence Agency, Directorate of Intelligence. "El Salvador: Dealing with Death Squads," January 20, 1984.

40. The Watch Committees and Lawyers' Committee for Human Rights, *Critique: A Review of the Department of State's Country Reports on Human Rights Practices in 1986* (New York: Layers' Committee for Human Rights, 1987), p. 30.

41. Department of State, "Talk with President Magaña, Bush Visit Reaction," December 15, 1983.

42. Central Intelligence Agency, "El Salvador: Dealing with Death Squads."

43. Central Intelligence Agency, "El Salvador: Dealing with Death Squads."

44. Department of State, "Human Rights in El Salvador," June 29, 1988; also UN General Assembly, *Situation of Human Rights in El Salvador,* A/43/736 (21 October 1988), para. 32.

45. See interviews with General Wallace Nutting, U.S. Southern Command, and Colonel John Waghelstein, U.S. Military Group, in Manwaring and Prisk, eds., *El Salvador at War,* pp. 222–23.

46. Americas Watch, *El Salvador's Decade of Terror*, pp. 51–63; Department of State, "Security Force Human Rights Abuses, Part One: Murders," May 2, 1989.
47. William Bollinger and Deirdre A. Hill, "The *Index to Accountability:* Identifying Perpetrators of Human Rights Violations in El Salvador, 1980–1990," unpublished paper presented at the international congress of the Latin American Studies Association, September 1992, pp. 25–26. Bollinger and Hill suggest that this represents an alternation in government policy, which shifted the emphasis from one category of violation (paramilitary killing) to another (armed forces attack).
48. General Assembly Resolution 35/192, passed 15 December 1980. The resolution was co-sponsored by Nicaragua, Angola, Mozambique, Iraq, Yemen, São Tomé and Principe.
49. Department of State, "Cuban Draft Resolution on Human Rights in El Salvador," November 27, 1980.
50. Author's interview with FMLN negotiator who requested anonymity, April 1995.
51. Arnson, *Crossroads*, p. 140.
52. For a discussion of the problems inherent to measuring human rights practices, see Brysk, "The Politics of Measurement."
53. This correlation was implied in a State Department cable, which speculated that a marked increase in death squad killings had been caused by the expiration of a state of siege decree enabling security forces to detain suspects well beyond the constitutional time limit. "The military is convinced that, without the ability to detain people for more than 72 hours, it is useless to arrest people and turn them over to the courts" leaving security forces no option but to kill suspects. U.S. Embassy in San Salvador, "Human Rights in El Salvador," June 29, 1988.
54. See especially Bollinger and Hill, "The *Index to Accountability*," pp. 25–30.
55. Danner, *The Massacre at El Mozote*, pp. 16–20.
56. Under fire from the international human rights community, in July 1984 the U.S. embassy publicly retracted its position that civilian casualties were legitimate because the victims were affiliated with subversives. See Americas Watch, *El Salvador's Decade of Terror*, pp. 53–54.
57. Terry Karl, "Imposing Consent? Electoralism vs. Democratization in El Salvador," in *Elections and Democratization in Latin America, 1980–1985*, ed. Paul Drake and Eduardo Silva (San Diego: University of California, San Diego, 1986).
58. Author's interviews with Rodolfo Cardenal, vice rector of the University of Central America, September 12, 1994; Héctor Dada, FLACSO, January 3, 1995; and Francisco Díaz, Director of CESPAD, September 9, 1994.
59. Americas Watch, *El Salvador's Decade of Terror*, pp. 53–54.
60. See Jack Child, *The Central American Peace Process, 1983–1991: Sheathing Swords, Building Confidence* (Boulder, Colo.: Lynne Rienner, 1992), for an extensive analysis of the Contadora process. Documents relating to the Central American peace process generally are found in Ricardo Córdova and Raul Benítez

Manaut, eds., *La Paz en Centroamérica: Expediente de Documentos Fundamentales, 1979–1989* (Mexico, DF: Centro de Investigaciones).

61. Salvador Samayoa, interviewed by Terry Karl, "El Salvador: Negotiations or Total War," pp. 331–32.

62. For Salvadoran electoral politics of this period, see Tricia Juhn, *Negotiating Peace in El Salvador: Civil-Military Relations and the Conspiracy to End the War* (New York: St. Martin's Press, 1998).

63. Terry Karl, "El Salvador's Negotiated Revolution," *Foreign Affairs* vol. 71, no. 2 (Spring 1992): 148.

64. Enrique Baloyra, "Salvaging El Salvador," *Journal of Democracy* vol. 3, no. 2 (April 1992): 74.

GUATEMALA: INTERNATIONAL PARIAH TO TENTATIVE COMPLIANCE

1. Asociación Centroamericana de Familiares de Detenidos-Desaparecidos, *La Práctica de la Desaparición Forzada de Personas en Guatemala* (San José: Asociación Centroamericana de Familiares de Detenidos-Desaparecidos, 1988), p. 271.

2. These figures are taken from Beatriz Manz, *Refugees of a Hidden War: The Aftermath of Counterinsurgency in Guatemala* (Albany: State University of New York Press, 1988), p. 30; and Susanne Jonas, *The Battle for Guatemala: Rebels, Death Squads, and U.S. Power* (Boulder, Colo.: Westview Press, 1991), p. 149. The numbers of victims vary among sources, and these generally agree with most press and human rights reports. The figures cited for civilian deaths are, however, on the conservative side, and recent reports tend to estimate more than 100,000 dead and disappeared during this period.

3. Héctor Rosada Granados, "Parties, Transitions, and the Political System in Guatemala," in *Political Parties and Democracy in Central America*, ed. Goodman et al., pp. 103–108.

4. Gabriel Aguilera Peralta, "Terror and Violence as Weapons of Counterinsurgency in Guatemala," *Latin American Perspectives* vol. 7, no. 2 (Spring 1980): 111.

5. For a synopsis of EMP's paramilitary activities, see Washington Office on Latin America, *Military Intelligence and Human Rights in Guatemala: The Archivo and the Case for Intelligence Reform* (Washington, DC: Washington Office on Latin America, March 1995).

6. Jim Handy, "Resurgent Democracy and the Guatemalan Military," *Journal of Latin American Studies* vol. 18, no. 2 (November 1986): 400–401.

7. Rachel M. McCleary, *Dictating Democracy: Guatemala and the End of Violent Revolution* (Gainesville: University Press of Florida, 1999), p. 47.

8. Tom Barry, *Central America Inside Out* (New York: Grove Weidenfeld, 1991), pp. 221–22.

9. Jean-Marie Simon, *Guatemala: Eternal Spring, Eternal Tyranny* (New York: W. W. Norton, 1987), p. 118.

10. National Security Archive, *Human Rights Violations in Guatemala: A Chronology by the Staff of the National Security Archive's Guatemalan Documentation Project* (Washington, DC: National Security Archive, October 1995), p. 4.

11. Handy, "Resurgent Democracy," pp. 404–5.

12. These were the Rebel Armed Forces (FAR), the Guatemalan Communist Party (PGT), the Guerrilla Army of the Poor (EGP), and the Organization of the People in Arms (ORPA). The FAR and EGP both split off from the PGT in the late 1960s, to reemerge as guerrilla forces in the 1970s. ORPA originated as a FAR splinter group in 1979. The PGT, its leadership mostly in exile and sharply divided over the question of armed struggle, did not rejoin the armed opposition until the late 1970s. See Marta Harnecker, *Pueblos en Armas* (Managua: Editorial Nueva Nicaragua, 1985); David Stoll, *Between Two Armies in the Ixil Towns of Guatemala* (New York: Columbia University Press, 1993); Jonas, *The Battle for Guatemala*, pp. 135–42; Robert H. Trudeau, *Guatemalan Politics: The Popular Struggle for Democracy* (Boulder, Colo.: Lynne Rienner, 1993), pp. 40–41.

13. Tanya Palencia Prado, *Peace in the Making: Civic Groups in Guatemala*, trans. David Holiday and Matthew Creelman (London: Catholic Institute for International Relations, 1996), p. 6.

14. Author's interview with Frank LaRue, founder of the United Representation of the Guatemalan Opposition (RUOG), June 6, 1995.

15. Author's interview with a former URNG intelligence operative who wished to remain anonymous, July 1995.

16. Amnesty International, *Guatemala: A Government Program of Political Murder* (London: Amnesty International, 1981).

17. Liam Mahony and Luis Enrique Eguren, *International Accompaniment for the Protection of Human Rights: Scenarios, Objectives, and Strategies* (Fairfax, Va.: Institute for Conflict Analysis and Resolution, George Mason University, 1996), p. 21.

18. Founded in 1976, the Parliamentary Human Rights Group is an independent forum within Parliament, comprising 130 members. See Americas Watch and British Parliamentary Human Rights Group, *Human Rights in Guatemala during President Cerezo's First Year* (New York: AW/BPHRG, February 1987).

19. Author's interviews with Mario Polanco, GAM coordinator, March 6, 1995, and Justina Tzoc, CERJ coordinator, July 8, 1994.

20. Author's interview with Juan Méndez, Americas Watch director, August 14, 1996.

21. Author's interview with attorney Will Harrell, CALDH, March 30, 1995.

22. Americas Watch, *Guatemala: A Nation of Prisoners* (New York: Americas Watch Committee, January 1984), pp. 23–25.

23. Interview with Will Harrell, CALDH, March 30, 1995.

24. Interview with Juan Méndez, August 14, 1996.

25. By way of comparison, U.S. military assistance to Guatemala (not including the fungible Economic Support Funds administered by USAID) was $5.5 million in 1987, as compared to $117 million to El Salvador.

26. Department of State, *Country Reports on Human Rights Practices for 1990*, p. 631.

27. From McCleary, *Dictating Democracy*, pp. 88, 214, n. 55.

28. Human Rights Watch, *Human Rights Watch World Report 1993: Events of 1992* (New York: Human Rights Watch, 1993), pp. 117–18.

29. Human Rights Watch, *Human Rights in Guatemala during President de León Carpio's First Year* (New York: Human Rights Watch, June 1994), p. 114.

30. *International Herald Tribune*, "U.S. Cuts Off Remaining Military Aid to Guatemala," March 13, 1995. Ms. Harbury is a U.S. attorney who is an extremely active member of the Guatemala solidarity community. Her protest was aimed at forcing the Clinton administration to release information concerning the fate of her husband, ORPA commander Efraín Bámaca, who was reported to have been captured in battle, tortured, and killed by ranking Guatemalan officers, at least one of whom was at one time on the CIA payroll. The Bámaca case was a cause célèbre for the human rights network.

31. Intelligence Oversight Board, *Report on the Guatemala Review, June 28, 1996*, p. 20. Following the suspension of direct military assistance, overall CIA funding levels decreased from approximately $3.5 million in fiscal year 1989 (a sizeable amount, considering how low the overall level of direct military assistance was) to approximately $1 million in 1995.

32. Investigations into the CIA's use of paid operatives in the Guatemalan army who were allegedly involved in major cases of extrajudicial execution did have a beneficial side effect—they helped unblock the peace negotiations in March 1995.

33. See *Miami Herald*, "Welcome Mat Gone for Guatemalan Linked to Atrocities," April 20, 1995, A18.

34. *Note by the Chairman of the Commission on Human Rights at Its Thirty-eighth Session*, E/CN.4/1983/43 (4 February 1983).

35. Interview with Juan Méndez, August 14, 1996.

36. Lawyers' Committee for Human Rights, *Abandoning the Victims*, p. 9.

37. Mónica Pinto, "Revisión de los Mecanismos Internacionales de Protección," unpublished paper, delivered at the Inter-American Institute for Human Rights, San José, Costa Rica, July 1994, p. 15, explains that Item 12 was conceived to deal with human rights violations perpetrated under dictatorships. Governments that are constitutionally elected but nevertheless oversee grave violations insist on being treated differently and are analyzed under Item 19, advisory services (author's translation).

38. Interview with Frank LaRue, June 6, 1995.

39. Lawyers' Committee for Human Rights, *Abandoning the Victims*, pp. 60–62.

40. *Report by the Independent Expert, Mr. Christian Tomuschat, on the Situation of Human Rights in Guatemala, Prepared in Accordance with Paragraph 11 of Commission Resolution 1991/51*, E/CN.4/1992/5 (21 January 1992), paras. 42, 51, 54–59. Tomuschat was named to head the Guatemalan Commission to Clarify the Past in March 1997.

41. Interview with Frank LaRue, June 6, 1995. RUOG is considered by many analysts to have maintained an unofficial affiliation with the URNG throughout the 1980s.

42. Author's interview with Mario Polanco, GAM co-director, March 6, 1995.
43. Author's interview with Factor Méndez, CIEPRODH director, June 8, 1995.
44. Author's interview with Amanda Rodas, representative of Coordinación de Organizaciones No Gubernamentales y Cooperativas, former Catholic Relief Services coordinator of ODHA, May 30, 1995.
45. It is a sad comment that, eight years and a peace accord later, the church was still unable to guarantee the personal security of its human rights staff. ODHA's founder, director general, and guiding light, Bishop Juan Gerardi, was assassinated in his home on April 27, 1998, two days after he presented the ODHA Project for the Recovery of Historical Memory report on violations committed in the course of the civil war.
46. See Mahony and Eguren, *International Accompaniment for the Protection of Human Rights.*
47. Author's interview with Mario Polanco, GAM, March 6, 1995.
48. This is the conclusion Alison Brysk reaches in "From Above and Below: Social Movements, the International System, and Human Rights in Argentina," *Comparative Political Studies* vol. 26, no. 3 (October 1993).
49. Interview with Mario Polanco, March 6, GAM, 1995 (author's translation).
50. Author's interview with Amanda Rodas, COORDI, May 30, 1995.
51. The International Committee of the Red Cross does require that the state extend its invitation.
52. Washington Office on Latin America, *Military Intelligence and Human Rights in Guatemala*, pp. 3–8.
53. Trudeau, *Guatemalan Politics*, pp. 119–120.
54. McCleary, *Dictating Democracy*, pp. 71–80.
55. For a detailed analysis of the events surrounding the autogolpe, see McCleary, *Dictating Democracy*, pp. 97–187.
56. McCleary, *Dictating Democracy*, pp. 129–30.
57. See *Report of the Independent Expert, Mr. Christian Tomuschat, on the Situation of Human Rights in Guatemala*, E/CN.4/1993/10 (18 December 1992).
58. A murmur of dissent was heard from the military's hardliners following the highly charged negotiations on a Truth Commission agreement. The response from Enriquez was unambiguous: the government and the military signed an accord in good faith; there are no nonconformists in the military, the peace process affects the military as an institution, and no individual has permission to interpose their personal interests. See *Siglo Veintiuno*, June 25, 1994.
59. Some Guatemalan political analysts suggest that de León Carpio was reluctant to confront the military after he took office because he saw a warning in the assassination of his cousin, Jorge Carpio Nicolle (newspaper publisher and a former centrist presidential candidate), by members of a local civil patrol only weeks after de León took office.
60. Lawyers' Committee for Human Rights, *Critique: Review of the Department of State Country Reports on Human Rights Practices for 1994* (New York: LCHR, July 1995).

61. *Siglo Veintiuno,* "No más comisionados militares," July 1, 1995; p. 3; *Report of the Independent Expert, Ms. Mónica Pinto, on the Situation of Human Rights in Guatemala,* E/CN.4/1994/10 (20 January 1994), para. 158; *Report of the Independent Expert, Ms. Mónica Pinto, on the Situation of Human Rights in Guatemala,* E/CN.4/1995/15 (20 December 1994), para. 187.

El Salvador: Negotiated Revolution to ONUSAL

1. For further application of these concepts, see especially I. William Zartman, ed., *Elusive Peace: Negotiating an End to Civil Wars* (Washington, D.C.: Brookings Institution, 1995).
2. This observation from author's interview with Lic. Rodolfo Antonio Parker, formerly the Salvadoran armed forces legal counsel, November 10, 1994.
3. This characterization of military hardliners and moderates is, of course, an oversimplification. For details, see Tom Gibb and Frank Smyth, *El Salvador: Is Peace Possible?* (Washington: Washington Office on Latin America, April 1991); also George Vickers, "The Political Reality after Eleven Years of War," in Tulchin and Bland, eds., *Is There a Transition to Democracy in El Salvador?*, p. 29.
4. Whitfield, *Paying the Price,* p. 176. The importance of the Jesuit murders in maintaining pressure on the military high command was emphasized by nearly every individual I interviewed who had been involved in the process.
5. Bill HR 5114, *Congressional Record,* vol. 136, no. 142, pt. 2, October 19, 1990 (Dodd-Leahy amendment). The bill was intended to provide both sides with incentives to negotiate in good faith. The proviso for the FMLN was that the 50 percent of military aid that was cut would be reinstated if the FMLN were to leave the negotiating table, instigate military action that would threaten the government's survival, or receive foreign military aid. The last condition was in fact met in January 1991, when the FMLN used surface-to-air missiles acquired from the Nicaraguan government to shoot down a military helicopter and summarily execute two U.S. advisers. U.S. aid was restored to the Salvadoran armed forces in March 1991.
6. For a revealing first-person account of the Salvadoran negotiations by the Secretary-General's personal representative, see Alvaro de Soto, "Ending Violent Conflict in El Salvador."
7. Eva Bertram, "Reinventing Governments: The Promise and Perils of United Nations Peacebuilding," *Journal of Conflict Resolution* vol. 39, no. 3 (September 1995): 406–9; also William Stanley and David Holiday, "Under the Best of Circumstances: ONUSAL and Dilemmas of Verification and Institution Building in El Salvador," in *Peacemaking and Democratization in the Western Hemisphere,* ed. Tommie Sue Montgomery (Boulder, Colo.: Lynne Rienner, 2000).
8. An earlier version of certain parts of the following discussion was published in Susan Burgerman, "Building the Peace by Mandating Reform: United Nations-Mediated Human Rights Agreements in El Salvador and Guatemala," *Latin American Perspectives* vol. 27, no. 3 (May 2000).

9. Samayoa (interviewed by Terry Karl), "El Salvador: Negotiations or Total War," pp. 325–26 and n.10; and Dillon, "Dateline El Salvador," p. 165.

10. For an eyewitness account of the November offensive, see Jemera Rone, *Carnage Again: Preliminary Report on Violations of the Laws of War by Both Sides in the November 1989 Offensive in El Salvador, November 24, 1989* (New York: Americas Watch, 1989). The assassination of the UCA Jesuits is a subject deserving of far greater attention than can be given here. See Doggett, *Death Foretold*, and Whitfield, *Paying the Price*.

11. General Maxwell Thurman before the Senate Armed Services Committee, February 1, 1990. It has since become conventional wisdom that the offensive demonstrated to both sides that the military conflict had reached a stalemate. All of those interviewed by this author, with the sole exception of Ret. General Mauricio Vargas, concurred in this analysis, and also in the conclusion that the international attention drawn by the Jesuit case provided the final impetus to proceed with the negotiated settlement.

12. For details of this meeting and its outcome, see de Soto, "Ending Violent Conflict in El Salvador," pp. 356–57.

13. Author's interview with Ambassador Alvaro de Soto, UN assistant secretary-general for political affairs, April 9, 1996.

14. *Agreement on Human Rights Signed at San José, Costa Rica, on 26 July 1990*, A/44/971-S/21541 (16 August 1990).

15. *Report of the ONUSAL Human Rights Division for the Period from 1 February to 30 April 1993*, A/47/968 S/26033 (2 July 1993). The policy shift to press for implemenation of ONUSAL recommendations is discussed in Ian Johnstone, *Rights and Reconciliation: UN Strategies in El Salvador* (Boulder, Colo.: Lynne Rienner, 1995), pp. 26–27.

16. Author's interview with Blanca Antonini, the ONUSAL chief officer for political affairs, November 10, 1994. Ms. Antonini served as Ambassador de Soto's assistant during the negotiation process.

17. Author's interview with Alvaro de Soto, April 9, 1996.

18. Interview with Alvaro de Soto, April 9, 1996.

19. *First Report of the United Nations Observer Mission in El Salvador*, A/45/1055-S/23037 (16 September 1991), paras. 23 and 25.

20. Author's interview with Foreign Minister Oscar Santamaría, November 23, 1994.

21. Author's interview with Francisco Díaz, director, Centro de Estudios para la Aplicación del Derecho (CESPAD), September 9, 1994 (author's translation).

22. Lawyers' Committee for Human Rights, *Improving History: A Critical Evaluation of the United Nations Observer Mission in El Salvador* (New York: Lawyers' Committee for Human Rights, December 1995), pp. 18–28, and Human Rights Watch, *The Lost Agenda: Human Rights and U.N. Field Operations* (New York: HRW, 1993), pp. 24–27. Bertram, "Reinventing Governments," pp. 396–400, argues that this dilemma reveals an essential tension between peace and security, or between human rights and democracy.

23. Author's interview with Alvaro de Soto, April 9, 1996. De Soto emphasized that the United Nation had internalized this lesson from the Salvadoran experience and later made similar efforts in Haiti and Guatemala.

24. Author's interview with Reed Brody, ONUSAL Division of Human Rights Director, October 7, 1994.
25. Author's interview with Alvaro de Soto, April 9, 1996.
26. Lawyers' Committee for Human Rights, *Improvising History*, pp. 9–11.
27. David Holiday and William Stanley, "Building the Peace: Preliminary Lessons from El Salvador," *Journal of International Affairs* vol. 46, no. 2 (Winter 1993).
28. See Latin America Working Group, Legislative Update, February 9, 1996. On the importance of land transfers for reintegrating former combatants, see Alvaro de Soto and Graciana del Castillo, "Implementation of Comprehensive Peace Agreements: Staying the Course in El Salvador," *Global Governance* vol. 1, no. 2 (August 1995): 195–96.
29. See El Salvador Information Project, *Keeping Hope Alive: An International Campaign for El Salvador 1994* (San Salvador: ESIP, January 1994), and Kevin Murray, *Rescuing Reconstruction: The Debate on Post-War Economic Recovery in El Salvador* (Cambridge: Hemisphere Initiatives, May 1994).
30. Author's interview with a member of the FMLN delegation, who requested anonymity.
31. Interview with Alvaro de Soto, April 9, 1996. De Soto also makes a strong case for the need to maintain control of negotiations in "Ending Violent Conflict in El Salvador."
32. Many evaluations of ONUSAL, both detailed and general, have been published since its establishment in 1991 and completion in 1995. See especially Lawyers' Committee for Human Rights, *Improvising History*; Doyle, Johnstone, and Orr, eds., *Keeping the Peace*; the series of reports published by Hemisphere Initiatives in conjunction with Washington Office on Latin America; de Soto and del Castillo, "Implementation of Comprehensive Peace Agreements"; Diego García-Sayán, "The Experience of ONUSAL in El Salvador," in *Honoring Human Rights and Keeping the Peace: Lessons from El Salvador, Cambodia, and Haiti, Recommendations for the United Nations*, ed. Alice H. Henkin (Washington, D.C.: The Aspen Institute, 1995). The topic of the Truth Commission and the debate over the competing demands of justice and reconciliation are too vast to be dealt with in this work and too important to be glossed over. For detailed analyses of the Truth Commission, see Americas Watch, *Accountability and Human Rights: The Report of the United Nations Commission on the Truth for El Salvador* (New York: Human Rights Watch, August 1993); Priscilla B. Hayner, "Fifteen Truth Commissions, 1974 to 1994: A Comparative Study," *Human Rights Quarterly* vol. 16, no. 4 (November 1994), and José Zalaquett, "Truth, Justice, and Reconciliation: Lessons for the International Community," in *Comparative Peace Processes in Latin America*, ed. Cynthia Arnson (Stanford: Stanford University Press, 1999). For analysis of the Electoral Division, see Jack Spence, David Dye, and George Vickers, *El Salvador: Elections of the Century, Results, Recommendations, Analysis* (Cambridge: Hemisphere Initiatives, July 1994); Tommie Sue Montgomery, "The Good, the Bad, and the Ugly: Observing Elections in El Salvador," in *Peacemaking and Democratization in the Western Hemisphere*, ed. Tommie Sue Montgomery (Boulder, Colo.: Lynne Rienner, 2000).

33. James Boyce et al., *Adjustment toward Peace: Economic Policy and Post-war Recon-struction in El Salvador* (San Salvador: UN Development Programme, 1995), p. 77. The amounts cited were drawn from the UNDP study and reflect an over-all commitment of funds, including aid not specifically related to the accords.

34. As of mid-2000; see Ricardo Córdova Macias, "A Balance of the Process of Peace of El Salvador," unpublished paper, prepared for U.S. Institute of Peace conference, Washington, D.C., December 8, 1999.

35. See especially Pedro Nikken's report to the General Assembly, *Situation of Human Rights in El Salvador*, A/47/596 (13 November 1992).

36. García-Sayán, "The Experience of ONUSAL in El Salvador," pp. 37–38.

37. For a thorough critique, see the "Recruitment and Deployment" chapter in Lawyers' Committee for Human Rights, *Improvising History*, pp. 44–49.

38. Rodolfo Cardenal and Martha Doggett, p. 5 of an untitled document produced for The Aspen Institute Meeting on Human Rights and UN Peacekeeping, Sep-tember 1994.

39. See especially Lawyers' Committee for Human Rights, *Improvising History*, pp. 93–102.

40. Author's interview with Leila Lima, Coordinator of ONUSAL's San Salvador regional office, October 18, 1994.

41. Author's interview with Blanca Antonini, November 10, 1994.

42. *Report of the ONUSAL Human Rights Division for the Period from 1 January to 30 April 1992*, A/46/935 s/24066 (5 June 1992).

43. Author's interview with Colleen Duggan, UNDP program officer in charge of human rights, September 1, 1994.

44. Boyce et al., *Adjustment toward Peace*, p. 55.

45. See Margaret Popkin, *Justice Delayed: The Slow Pace of Judicial Reform in El Sal-vador* (Washington, D.C.: WOLA/Hemisphere Initiatives, December 1994).

46. See *Proceso* 715, 26 June 1996.

47. This important topic is given only brief attention here. See Gino Costa, "The United Nations and Reform of the Police in El Salvador," *International Peace-keeping* (Autumn 1995); William Stanley, *Protectors or Perpetrators?: The Institu-tional Crisis of the Salvadoran Civilian Police* (Washington, D.C.: Hemisphere Ini-tiatives and the Washington Office on Latin America, 1996); William Stanley and Charles T. Call, "Building a New Civilian Police Force in El Salvador," in Krishna Kumar, ed., *Rebuilding Societies after Civil War: Critical Roles for Interna-tional Assistance* (Boulder, Colo.: Lynne Rienner, 1997).

48. See Stanley and Call, "Building a New Civilian Police Force."

49. See *Proceso* 766, 24 July 1997. For a political analysis of the implementation of legislative reforms, see Jack Spence, George Vickers, and David Dye, *The Sal-vadoran Peace Accords and Democratization: A Three-Year Progress Report and Rec-ommendations* (Cambridge: Hemisphere Initiatives, March 1995).

50. The government and the organization representing the demobilized ex-com-batants, with ONUSAL mediation, negotiated new terms for compensation in January 1995, following a series of government building takeovers. See *Proceso* 647, 1 February 1995.

51. Boyce et al., *Adjustment toward Peace*, p. 59.
52. From Stanley and Holiday, "Under the Best of Circumstances," and private interviews with UN representatives.

Guatemala: National Dialogue to MINUGUA

1. An earlier version of parts of the following was published in Burgerman, "Building the Peace by Mandating Reform."
2. Estimated size of guerrilla forces from Herbert Ortega Pinto, "Negociaciones de paz en Guatemala: Análisis de los actores políticos y de las incompatibilidades básicas," *Estudios Internacionales* vol. 5, no. 9 (January–June 1994), p. 51. Armed forces troop size from Julia Preston, "Guatemala and Guerrillas Sign Accord to End 35-Year Conflict," *New York Times*, September 20, 1996, A1. Number of civil patrols as reported for 1993 by the government to the UN independent expert; *Report of the Independent Expert, Ms. Mónica Pinto, on the Situation of Human Rights in Guatemala*, E/CN.4/1995/15 (20 December 1994), p. 32. It should be noted that these figures are all from the mid-1990s but reflect the relative balance of forces that obtained in the late 1980s.
3. Gabriel Aguilera Peralta and Karen Ponciano, *El Espejo Sin Reflejo: La negociación de paz en 1993* (Guatemala: Facultad Latinoamericano de Ciencias Sociales, 1994), p. 17.
4. One of Alvaro Arzú's first acts in office was to purge the high command, dismissing eight of the sixteen generals and several colonels, eliminating ranking officers accused of human rights abuses and corruption, and fully consolidating the position of the pro-negotiation faction. Among those cashiered were Col. Julio Roberto Alpírez, the G-2 officer named by the Intelligence Oversight Board as a CIA operative and accused of obstructing the investigation of the Michael Devine case and of murder in the Efraín Bámaca case, and Col. Mario García Catalán, also implicated in the Devine case. The new interior minister, Rodolfo Mendoza, immediately announced the dismissal of 118 police officers, including eighty commanders, who had been implicated in human rights violations or corrupt practices. Responding to a rapid increase in kidnappings for ransom, Mendoza openly stated that kidnapping gangs operated with armed forces protection. Soon thereafter, Congress passed a military code reform under which common criminal offenses committed by military officers were to be tried in civilian rather than in military courts. An even more ambitious purge of the so-called "Guatemalan mafia," a network of ranking officers and government officials, was announced on September 18, 1996. Nine army officers, including two generals (one of whom was Viceminister of Defense), were dismissed on corruption and contraband charges.
5. Author's interview with Rolando Cabrera, director of FUNDAPAZD and secretary general of the Asamblea de la Sociedad Civil, August 2, 1995. Cabrera was Bishop Quezada's secretary at the time.
6. Palencia, *Peace in the Making*, p. 9.

7. Author's interview with Frank LaRue, July 13, 1995.

8. Interview with Rolando Cabrera, August 2, 1995 (author's translation).

9. Author's interview with Dr. Paul Wee, then assistant general secretary for international affairs and human rights, Lutheran World Federation, March 18, 1994.

10. *Acuerdo Básico para la Búsqueda de la Paz por Medios Políticos (Acuerdo de Oslo)*, May 30, 1990, in FUNDAPAZD, *Acuerdos Sustantivos entre el Gobierno de Guatemala y la URNG, Comentados (Julio 1991–Marzo 1995)* (Guatemala: FUNDAPAZD, 1995).

11. IRIPAZ, *Cronologías de los Procesos de Paz: Guatemala y El Salvador* (Guatemala: IRIPAZ, 1991), pp. 60, 64.

12. September 1, 1990, *Comunicado de la Comandancia General de la URNG, al Término de la Reunión Realizada en Ottowa, Canada con el CACIF; Comunicado del CACIF*, in Inforpress Centroamericana, *Guatemala 1986–1994: Compendio del Proceso de Paz, Cronologías, análisis, documentos, acuerdos* (Guatemala: Inforpress Centroamericana, 1995), pp. 66, 67. Following the Ottawa round, the URNG decided that the agricultural sector would never be sufficiently concerned about the ongoing bloodshed as long as the war did not impinge upon their properties. In order to "bring the war home" to plantation owners, the comandancia decided to impose war taxes. Statement by Pablo Monsanto (FAR), *Prensa Libre*, April 1, 1996. The collection—or extortion—of funds from landowners became one of the United Nation's chief criticisms of the URNG.

13. Interview with Dr. Gabriel Aguilera Peralta, Facultad Latinoamericana de Ciencias Sociales (FLACSO), July 13, 1995.

14. *Inforpress* #932, "Negociaciones de México Señalan Dificultoso Camino para la Paz," May 2, 1991.

15. I am using "logics of appropriateness" as conceptualized by Finnemore in *National Interests in International Society*.

16. *Acuerdo Marco Sobre Democratización para la Búsqueda de la Paz por Medios Políticos* (Acuerdo de Querétaro), July 25, 1991, in FUNDAPAZD, *Acuerdos Sustantivos*.

17. Naturally, a great deal of informal discussion on the topic took place during this time. This is a necessarily abbreviated account of a rich and byzantine story. See Burgerman, "The Evolution of Compliance" for a more detailed narrative.

18. *Inforpress* #971, "Negociaciones de Paz con Pálidos Acuerdos," February 20, 1992. The commitments were to strengthen the institutions that protect human rights, to eradicate impunity, not to bring cases of human rights violations before special military tribunals, to purge and professionalize the security forces, to protect human rights activists, to end discriminatory and forced recruitment, and to request UN verification of the human rights agreements.

19. Interview with Rolando Cabrera, August 2, 1995.

20. Inforpress Centroamericana, *Guatemala, 1986–1994: Compendio*, pp. 93–94.

21. Frank LaRue emphasized this factor to explain the increased level of participation by the United States and Norway. Interview, July 13, 1995.

22. Interview with Dr. Héctor Rosada, then director of the government's delegation to the negotiations (COPAZ), June 28, 1995.

23. This observation was made by Héctor Rosada, interviewed on June 28, 1995.
24. Interview with Antonio Arenales Forno, member of government delegation to the negotiations (COPAZ), July 4, 1995 (author's translation).
25. *Acuerdo para el Reasentamiento de las Poblaciones Desarraigadas por el Enfrentamiento Armado*, June 17, 1994, in FUNDAPAZD, *Acuerdos Sustantivos*.
26. *Prensa Libre*, May 12, 1994, and May 13, 1994.
27. *Acuerdo sobre el Establecimiento de la Comisión para el Esclarecimiento de la Violaciones a los Derechos Humanos y los Hechos de Violencia Que Han Causado Sufrimientos a la Población Guatemalateca*, June 23, 1994, in FUNDAPAZD, *Acuerdos Sustantivos*.
28. On background, from a source in the Department of Political Affairs.
29. Unidad Revolucionaria Nacional Guatemalteca, Comandancia General, "Memorandum de la CG de la URNG," unpublished mimeo, July 12, 1994 (author's translation).
30. Although observers would face threatening incidents despite these precautions. For example, a MINUGUA military liaison in Cantabal was fired upon by an EGP contingent on March 27, 1995. The same military officer and a UN Volunteer observer from the Cantabal office, along with a UNHCR representative, a World Council of Churches negotiator, and a nurse from Medecins du Monde were captured by the head of a local civil patrol on June 28, 1995, and held hostage for twenty-six hours.
31. Author's interview with Alvaro de Soto, April 9, 1996. Boutros-Ghali himself stated that his initial intention had been to follow the ONUSAL model by creating a multidisciplinary mission under Security Council authorization, with the human rights division to be deployed immediately. His plan was sidelined, however, by "strong representations from some of the Member States who constitute the friends of the Guatemalan peace process to the effect that, as international verification will, in its initial phase, be concerned only with human rights, its establishment is a matter for the General Assembly rather than the Security Council. I have also been informed by the Government of Guatemala that, although it wishes the mission to be approved rapidly, it cannot for that reason favour a matter related to a specific mechanism for human rights being submitted to the Security Council." In General Assembly, *Establishment of a Human Rights Verification Mission in Guatemala: Report of the Secretary-General*, A/48/985 (18 August 1994), p. 11.
32. Approximately 60% of the population is indigenous. These are primarily of Mayan descent, plus smaller populations of Garífuna and Xinca. The Maya have evolved over several centuries into culturally and linguistically distinct subgroups, speaking twenty-one separate languages, five of which (Kaqchikel, Kiche, Mam, Q'eqchi, and Tz'utujil) are spoken most widely.
33. *Siglo Veintiuno*, July 8, 1994; July 9, 1994; July 10, 1994.
34. For an examination of how women's rights became an issue in human rights mobilization, see the chapter on "Transnational Networks on Violence Against Women," in Keck and Sikkink, *Activists beyond Borders*.
35. Alison Brysk, "Acting Globally: Indian Rights and International Politics in Latin America," in *Indigenous Peoples and Democracy in Latin America*, ed. Donna

Lee Van Cott (New York: St. Martin's Press, 1994), offers an analysis of how Latin American indigenous groups came to establish network ties to environmental organizations, largely because they were disaffected with the human rights network.

36. Tim Weiner, "In Furor over Killings, President Warns of Shake-Up in the C.I.A.," *New York Times*, March 25, 1995, A1.

37. *Acuerdo Sobre Identidad y Derechos de los Pueblos Indígenas*, March 31, 1995, in FUNDAPAZD, *Acuerdos Sustantivos*.

38. Although representatives of the Mayan sectors did travel to Mexico to voice their opinion that, while they considered that the accord represented significant progress, the reforms it mandated were minimal

39. Interview with Rolando Cabrera, August 2, 1995.

40. *Acuerdo Sobre Aspectos Socioeconómicos y Situación Agraria*, May 6, 1996.

41. The brevity was later explained by General Julio Balconi, who was defense minister at the time. The army had been holding informal second-track meetings with the URNG since 1991, and had "achieved a high level of trust" by 1996. Julio Balconi, "Reflections," in *Comparative Peace Processes in Latin America*, ed. Arnson, pp. 127–28.

42. Unlike the majority of the agreements, the provisions for police reform in Guatemala are much less extensive and carefully detailed than those in the Salvadoran peace accords. For a critical evaluation, highlighting deficiencies in screening and training of agents and government compliance with the accord, see Rachel Garst, "The New Guatemalan National Civilian Police: A Problematic Beginning," *WOLA Briefing Series* (Washington, DC: Washington Office on Latin America, November 1997). Also see William Stanley, "Building New Police Forces in El Salvador and Guatemala: Learning and Counter-Learning," unpublished paper, presented at the annual meeting of the Latin American Studies Association in Miami, March 2000.

43. For analysis of the problematic implementation of this accord, see Jack Spence et al., *Promise and Reality: Implementation of the Guatemalan Peace Accords* (Cambridge: Hemisphere Initiatives, August 1998), pp. 22–34, and Susanne Jonas, *Of Centaurs and Doves: Guatemala's Peace Process* (Boulder, Colo.: Westview Press, 2000), pp. 137–65.

44. *Prensa Libre*, "Congreso aprobará hoy ley de reconciliación nacional," December 18, 1996. Debate over the constitutionality of the National Reconciliation Law began immediately upon its passage; see Margaret Popkin, "Update on the Guatemalan Amnesty," unpublished memorandum, Robert F. Kennedy Memorial Center for Human Rights, March 5, 1997.

45. *Agreement on the Implementation, Compliance and Verification Timetable for the Peace Agreements*, A/51/796 (7 February 1997).

46. See especially Spence et al., *Promise and Reality*, and William Stanley and David Holiday, "Everyone Participates, No One Is Responsible: Peace Implementation in Guatemala," unpublished paper, Stanford CISAC/International Peace Academy, August 1999.

47. On problems of interagency coordination, see Patricia Weiss Fagen, "El Salvador: Lessons in Peace Consolidation," in *Beyond Sovereignty: Collectively De-*

fending Democracy in the Americas, ed. Tom Farer (Baltimore: Johns Hopkins University Press, 1996).

48. Author's interview with Ms. Denise Cook, Guatemala Desk Officer, UN Department of Political Affairs, March 5, 1997.

49. Interview with Leila Lima, May 3, 1995.

50. Discussion with Auxiliatora, Procuraduría de Derechos Humanos, Cobán, Alta Verapaz, August 16, 1995.

51. Interview with Frank LaRue, June 6, 1995. The subject of human rights until this time had been politicized by both sides and was almost universally associated with "communist subversion."

52. *First Report of the Director of MINUGUA,* A/49/856 (1 March 1995), paras. 142–50.

53. *Convenio de Cooperación Técnica entre el Ministerio Público de la Republica de Guatemala y la MINUGUA y el PNUD,* unpublished document, January 1995.

54. MINUGUA, Unidad de Fortalecimiento Institucional, "Proyecto de Fortalecimiento del Estado Democrático de Derecho en Guatemala (Sumario Ejecutivo)," unpublished document, 1995.

55. Author's interview with Hugo Lorenzo, then director of Institutional Building/Education-Promotion office, MINUGUA, June 1, 1995.

56. Author's interview with Gerald Plantegenest, deputy director of mission, MINUGUA, April 17, 1995. As of March 1997, the Trust Fund held a total of US$3.8 million. Donations came from the governments of Norway, Sweden, the United States, and the Netherlands, in that order.

57. It should be noted that ONUSAL was not the only precedent for MINUGUA. The experience accumulated in Haiti by MICIVIH observers—who also worked for many months without a procedures manual, suffered from insufficient preparatory work and had weak communications between regional offices and mission headquarters—contributed to MINUGUA's relative professionalism. From author's interview with Marie Cervetti, regional coordinator, Zacapa, March 19, 1995.

How Do Institutions Matter?

1. Frederick Z. Brown, ed., *Rebuilding Cambodia: Human Resources, Human Rights, and Law* (Baltimore: Foreign Policy Institute, Nitze School of Advanced International Studies, Johns Hopkins University, 1993), p. 3.

2. Gareth Evans, *Cooperating for Peace: the Global Agenda for the 1990s and Beyond* (New South Wales, Australia: Allen & Unwin, 1993), p. 107.

3. Yasushi Akashi, "UNTAC in Cambodia: Lessons for U.N. Peace-Keeping," Rostov Lecture on Asian Affairs, Paul Nitze School of Advanced International Studies, Johns Hopkins University, 14 October 1993, p. 18.

4. Michael W. Doyle, *UN Peacekeeping in Cambodia: UNTAC's Civil Mandate* (Boulder, Colo.: Lynne Rienner, 1995), p. 24.

5. Brown, ed., *Rebuilding Cambodia,* pp. 3–4.

6. Evans, *Cooperating for Peace,* p. 107.

7. Michael Doyle argues that one of the reasons for UNTAC's partial success was the "discrete, impartial, but non-neutral, use of force" employed by the mission when it subcontracted coercive enforcement to the armies of the three cooperating factions during the elections. Doyle, "War in Peace in Cambodia," unpublished paper, January 1997, pp. 40–41.

8. Akashi, "UNTAC in Cambodia," pp. 16–20.

9. See Stephen John Stedman, "Spoiler Problems in Peace Processes," *International Security* vol. 22, no. 2 (Fall 1997): 30–31.

10. Human Rights Watch, *The Lost Agenda*, p. 44.

11. Amnesty International, *Amnesty International Report 1986* (London: Amnesty International, 1987).

12. Asia Watch Committee, *Khmer Rouge Abuses Along the Thai-Cambodian Border* (New York: Asia Watch, 1989).

13. Steven R. Ratner, "The Cambodian Settlements," *American Journal of International Law* vol. 87, no. 1 (1993): 25.

14. Amnesty International, *Amnesty International Report 1989*, p. 181.

15. See Amnesty International, *Amnesty International Report 1988*.

16. Stephen Marks, who was chief of UNTAC's Education, Information and Training Unit, pointed out that although the Khmer Rouge's defection was more blatant, SOC also gave its consent to the mission only under pressure and sought throughout the operation to exploit the terms and to cheat wherever possible. SOC's refusal to compromise on any real sharing of state power, and the mission directorship's appearance of partiality in not insisting on SOC cooperation, furnished Khmer Rouge with a pretext for its defection (private conversation, April 1997).

17. See Seth Mydans, "Cambodia's Real Boss Rules from the No. 2 Post," *New York Times*, March 25, 1996, A3.

18. Michael W. Doyle and Nishkala Suntharalingam, "The UN in Cambodia: Lessons for Multidimensional Peacekeeping," *International Peacekeeping* vol. 1, no. 2 (Summer 1994): 129–30, and Michael Doyle, "Authority and Elections in Cambodia," in ed. *Keeping the Peace,* Doyle et al., pp. 157–58.

19. The Watch Committees and Lawyers' Committee for Human Rights, *Critique: A Review of the Department of State's Country Reports on Human Rights Practices for 1985* (New York: HRW, 1986), p. 10.

20. Ratner, "The Cambodia Settlement Agreements," pp. 3–5, and Amnesty International, *Political Killings by Governments*.

21. For example, UN Economic and Social Council decisions 1981/154, 1982/143, 1983/155, 1984/148, 1985/155, 1986/146, 1987/155 were all rejected by the USSR.

22. Ratner, "The Cambodia Settlement Agreements," p. 4.

23. On the establishment of the Constitution, see Stephen P. Marks, "The New Cambodian Constitution: From Civil War to a Fragile Democracy," *Columbia Human Rights Law Review* vol. 26, no. 1 (Fall 1994).

24. Human Rights Watch, *The Lost Agenda*, p. 53.

25. Dennis McNamara, "UN Human Rights Activities in Cambodia: An Evaluation," in *Honoring Human Rights and Keeping the Peace*, ed. Henkin pp. 72–76.

See also Terence Duffy, "Towards a Culture of Human Rights in Cambodia," *Human Rights Quarterly* vol. 16, no. 1 (February 1994).

26. My thanks to Stephen Marks for this information.

27. Doyle, *UN Peacekeeping in Cambodia*, p. 62.

28. McNamara, "UN Human Rights Activities in Cambodia," pp. 64–66.

29. See Nishkala Suntharalingam, "The Cambodian Settlement Agreements," in *Keeping the Peace*, ed. Doyle et al., pp. 96–99.

30. McNamara, "UN Human Rights Activities in Cambodia," p. 61.

31. Human Rights Watch, *The Lost Agenda*, pp. 53–54, and Doyle and Suntharalingam, "The UN in Cambodia," p. 128.

32. See Seth Mydans, "Fragile Stability Slowly Emerges in Cambodia," *New York Times*, June 25, 2000, A1. Also Mydans, "New in Cambodia: Justice Without Torture," *New York Times*, February 10, 1997, A1.

33. Human Rights Watch/Asia, *Cambodia at War* (New York: Human Rights Watch, 1995), p. 10.

34. Franco, "Human Rights Verification in the Context of Peace."

35. Stephen Marks, "Social and Humanitarian Issues: Human Rights," in *A Global Agenda: Issues before the 51st General Assembly of the United Nations*, ed. John Tessitore and Susan Woolfson (Lanham, Md.: Rowman & Littlefield, 1996), pp. 195–97.

36. *Charter of the United Nations*, Chapter VI, Article 37, para. 2.

37. For a discussion of this problem, see Marks, "Social and Humanitarian Issues," pp. 191–94.

38. See John Simpson and Jana Bennett, *The Disappeared: Voices from a Secret War* (London: Robson Books, 1985), pp. 249–67; and Jacobo Timerman, *Prisoner Without a Name, Cell Without a Number*, trans. Toby Talbot (New York: Alfred A. Knopf, 1981).

39. *Foreign Assistance Authorizations: Hearings before the Senate Committee on Foreign Relations and the Subcommittee on Foreign Assistance of the Senate Committee on Foreign Relations*, 95th Congress, 1st sess. (1977), cited in Gracia Berg, "Human Rights Sanctions as Leverage: Argentina, A Case Study," *Journal of Legislation* vol. 7 (1980): 102.

40. The significance of the IACHR on-site visit as a sanctioning mechanism is elaborated by Lisa L. Martin and Kathryn Sikkink, "U.S. Policy and Human Rights in Argentina and Guatemala, 1973–1980," in *Double-Edged Diplomacy: International Bargaining and Domestic Politics*, ed. Peter B. Evans, Harold K. Jacobson, and Robert D. Putnam (Berkeley: University of California Press, 1993).

41. From Martin and Sikkink, "U.S. Policy and Human Rights in Argentina and Guatemala," pp. 342–44.

42. See Iain Guest, *Behind the Disappearances: Argentina's Dirty War against Human Rights and the United Nations* (Philadelphia: University of Pennsylvania Press, 1990), pp. 175–76; and Alison Brysk, *The Politics of Human Rights in Argentina: Protest, Change, and Democratization* (Stanford: Stanford University Press, 1994), p. 55.

43. This is the principal argument made by Brysk in "From Above and Below."

44. *Diario Latino,* October 3, 1995. The Colombian high commissioner for peace, Carlos Holmes Trujillo, met in San Salvador with negotiators from both delegations to discuss how the lessons of the Salvadoran peace process could be applied to Colombia. He also visited Guatemala and met with government negotiators.

45. Larry Rohter, "Like Carrot, Stick Fails with Rebels in Colombia," *New York Times,* September 27, 1999, A9.

46. Larry Rohter, "Colombia Agrees to Turn over Territory to Another Rebel Group," *New York Times,* April 26, 2000, A5.

47. Diana Jean Schemo, "Report Says Colombia Misused U.S. Aid on Rebel War," *New York Times,* November 26, 1996, A10; Diana Jean Schemo and Tim Golden, "Bogotá Aid: To Fight Drugs or Rebels?," *New York Times,* June 2, 1998, A1; Marc Chernick, "Negotiating Peace amid Multiple Forms of Violence: The Protracted Search for Settlement to the Armed Conflicts in Colombia," in *Comparative Peace Processes in Latin America,* ed. Arnson.

48. I have heard this argument expressed in private conversations and public forums by such distinguished Colombian political analysts as Eduardo Pizarro Leongómez (former director of the Instituto de Estudios Políticos y Relaciones Internacionales de la Universidad Nacional de Colombia) and Andelfo Garcia (director, Center for Research and Special Projects, Universidad Externado de Colombia and former deputy permanent representative of Colombia to the UN).

49. See "Rights Groups Stepping Up Pressure on Colombian Officials," *New York Times* April 26, 1994, A12, and Lawyers' Committee for Human Rights, *Comments Relating to the Fourth Periodic Report on Colombia before the U.N. Human Rights Committee* (New York: Lawyers' Committee for Human Rights, March 1997).

50. See Human Rights Watch, *The Ties That Bind: Colombia and Military-Paramilitary Links* (New York: Human Rights Watch, February 2000), and Larry Rohter, "Colombians Tell of Massacre, as Army Stood By," *New York Times,* July 14, 2000, A1.

DOCUMENTS CITED

Nongovernmental Organizations

Americas Watch. *Accountability and Human Rights: The Report of the United Nations Commission on the Truth for El Salvador.* New York: Human Rights Watch, August 1993.

Americas Watch. *Peace and Human Rights: Successes and Shortcomings of the United Nations Observer Mission in El Salvador (ONUSAL).* New York: Americas Watch, September 1992.

Americas Watch. *El Salvador's Decade of Terror: Human Rights since the Assassination of Archbishop Romero.* New Haven: Yale University Press, 1991.

Americas Watch. *Guatemala: A Nation of Prisoners.* New York: The Americas Watch Committee, January 1984.

Americas Watch. *Human Rights in Guatemala: No Neutrals Allowed.* New York: The Americas Watch Committee, 1982.

Americas Watch and the American Civil Liberties Union. *Report on Human Rights in El Salvador, January 26, 1982.* New York: Vintage Books, 1982.

Americas Watch and British Parliamentary Human Rights Group. *Human Rights in Guatemala during President Cerezo's First Year.* New York: Americas Watch/BPHRG, February 1987.

Americas Watch and Physicians for Human Rights. *Guatemala: Getting Away with Murder.* New York: Human Rights Watch, August 1991.

Amnesty International. *Peace-keeping and Human Rights.* AI Index IOR 40/01/94 (January 1994).

Amnesty International. *El Salvador: Peace without Justice.* AI Index AMR 29/12/93 (June 1993).

Amnesty International. *Political Killings by Governments.* London: Amnesty International, 1983.

Amnesty International. *Guatemala: Massive Extrajudicial Executions in Rural Areas under the Government of General Efraín Ríos Montt.* London: Amnesty International, July 1982.

Amnesty International. *Guatemala: A Government Program of Political Murder.* London: Amnesty International, 1981.

Amnesty International. *Report of an Amnesty International Mission to Argentina, 6–15 November 1976.* London: Amnesty International Publications, 1977.

Amnesty International. *Amnesty International Report (. . .).* London: Amnesty International Publications, annual.

Asia Watch Committee. *Khmer Rouge Abuses along the Thai Cambodia Border.* New York: Asia Watch, 1989.

Associación Centroamericana de Familiares de Detenidos Desaparecidos. *La Práctica de la Desaparición Forzada de Personas en Guatemala.* San José: ACAFADE, 1988.

British Parliamentary Human Rights Group. *Bitter and Cruel: Report of a Mission to Guatemala.* London: BPHRG, 1985.

CIEPRODH (Centro de Investigación, Estudio y Promoción de los Derechos Humanos en Guatemala). *Guatemala: La Búsqueda de la Verdad.* Guatemala: CIEPRODH, 1994.

CIEPRODH (Centro de Investigación, Estudio y Promoción de los Derechos Humanos en Guatemala). *Guatemala: Situación de los Derechos Humanos, Informe Anual.* Guatemala: CIEPRODH, annual.

El Salvador Information Project. *Keeping Hope Alive: An International Campaign for El Salvador 1994.* San Salvador: ESIP, January 1994.

FUNDAPAZD (Fundación para la Paz, la Democracia y el Desarrollo). *Documentos de la Asamblea de la Sociedad Civil—ASC—(Mayo–octubre 1994).* Guatemala: FUNDAPAZD, 1994.

FUNDAPAZD (Fundación para la Paz, la Democracia y el Desarrollo). *Acuerdos Sustantivos entre el Gobierno de Guatemala y la URNG, Comentados (Julio 1991–Marzo 1995).* Guatemala: FUNDAPAZD, 1995.

Human Rights Watch. *The Ties That Bind: Colombia and Military Paramilitary Links.* New York: Human Rights Watch, February 2000.

Human Rights Watch. *Human Rights in Guatemala During President de León Carpio's First Year.* New York: Human Rights Watch, June 1994.

Human Rights Watch. *The Lost Agenda: Human Rights and UN Field Operations.* New York: Human Rights Watch, 1993.

Human Rights Watch. *Human Rights Watch World Report: Events of (. . .).* New York: Human Rights Watch, annual.

Human Rights Watch/Asia. *Cambodia at War.* New York: Human Rights Watch, 1995.

IDHUCA (Instituto de Derechos Humanos de la Universidad Centroamericana José Simeón Cañas). "Los ataques contra el último informe de Pedro Nikken." *Estudios Centroamericanos* (January/February 1994).

IRIPAZ (Instituto de Relaciones Internacionales y de Investigaciones Para la Paz). *Cronologías de los Procesos de Paz: Guatemala y El Salvador.* Guatemala: IRIPAZ, 1991.

Lawyers' Committee for Human Rights. *Comments Relating to the Fourth Periodic Report on Colombia before the U.N. Human Rights Committee.* New York: Lawyers Committee for Human Rights, March 1997.

Lawyers Committee for Human Rights. *Improving History: A Critical Evaluation of the United Nations Observer Mission in El Salvador.* New York: Lawyers Committee for Human Rights, December 1995.

Lawyers Committee for Human Rights. *Abandoning the Victims: The UN Advisory Services Program in Guatemala.* New York: Lawyers Committee for Human Rights, 1990.

Lawyers Committee for Human Rights. *Critique: Review of the Department of State Country Reports on Human Rights Practices for (...).* New York: Lawyers Committee for Human Rights.

National Security Archive. *Human Rights Violations in Guatemala: A Chronology by the Staff of the National Security Archive's Guatemalan Documentation Project.* Washington, D.C.: National Security Archive, October 1995.

Oficina de Derechos Humanos Arzobispado de Guatemala. *Informe Anual.* Guatemala: ODHA, annual.

Procurador de los Derechos Humanos. *Informe Circunstanciado de Actividades sobre la Situación de los Derechos Humanos durante (...).* Guatemala: Procuraduría de Derechos Humanos, annual.

The Watch Committees and Lawyers' Committee for Human Rights. *Critique: A Review of the Department of State's Country Reports on Human Rights Practices.* New York: Lawyers Committee for Human Rights and the Fund for Free Expression for the Watch Committees, annual.

Washington Office on Latin America. *Military Intelligence and Human Rights in Guatemala: The Archivo and the Case for Intelligence Reform.* Washington, D.C.: Washington Office on Latin America, March 1995.

GOVERNMENT AND INTERGOVERNMENTAL ORGANIZATIONS

Organization of American States

Organization of American States. Inter-American Commission on Human Rights. *Annual Report of the Inter-American Commission on Human Rights, 1993.* OEA/Ser.L/V/II.85, Doc. 9 rev. (11 February 1994).

Organization of American States. Inter-American Commission on Human Rights. *Report on the Situation of Human Rights in Argentina.* OEA/Ser.L/V/II.49 (11 April 1980).

United Nations

Economic and Social Council. *Report of the Independent Expert, Ms. Mónica Pinto, on the Situation of Human Rights in Guatemala.* E/CN.4/1995/15 (20 December 1994).

Economic and Social Council. Commission on Human Rights, Fiftieth Session. *Report of the Independent Expert, Mr. Pedro Nikken, on Developments in the Human Rights Situation in El Salvador.* E/CN.4/1994/11 (3 February 1994).

Economic and Social Council. Commission on Human Rights, Fiftieth Session. *Report of the Independent Expert, Ms. Mónica Pinto, on the Situation of Human Rights in Guatemala.* E/Cn.4/1994/10 (20 January 1994).

Economic and Social Council. Commission on Human Rights, Forty-ninth Session. *Report of the Independent Expert, Mr. Christian Tomuschat, on the Situation of Human Rights in Guatemala.* E/CN.4/1993/10 (18 December 1992).

Economic and Social Council. *Report by the Independent Expert, Mr. Christian Tomuschat, on the Situation of Human Rights in Guatemala, Prepared in Accordance with paragraph 11 of Commission Resolution 1991/51.* E/CN.4/1992/5 (21 January 1992).

Economic and Social Council. *Note by the Chairman of the Commission on Human Rights at Its Thirty-eighth Session.* E/CN.4/1983/43 (4 February 1983).

General Assembly. *Agreement on the Implementation, Compliance and Verification Timetable for the Peace Agreements.* A/51/796 (7 February 1997).

General Assembly. *Fifth Report of the Director of the United Nations Mission for the Verification of Human Rights and of Compliance with the Commitments of the Comprehensive Agreement on Human Rights in Guatemala.* A/50/1006 (19 July 1996).

General Assembly. *Fourth Report of the Director of the United Nations Mission for the Verification of Human Rights and of Compliance with the Commitments of the Comprehensive Agreement on Human Rights in Guatemala.* A/50/878 (24 February 1996).

General Assembly. *Third Report of the Director of the United Nations Mission for the Verification of Human Rights and of Compliance with the Commitments of the Comprehensive Agreement on Human Rights in Guatemala.* A/50/482 (12 October 1995).

General Assembly. *Second Report of the Director of the United Nations Mission for the Verification of Human Rights and of Compliance with the Commitments of the Comprehensive Agreement on Human Rights in Guatemala.* A/49/929 (29 June 1995).

General Assembly. *Report of the Director of the United Nations Mission for the Verification of Human Rights and of Compliance with the Commitments of the Comprehensive Agreement on Human Rights in Guatemala.* A/49/856 (1 March 1995).

General Assembly. *Establishment of a Human Rights Verification Mission in Guatemala: Report of the Secretary-General.* A/48/985 (18 August 1994).

General Assembly. *Report of the ONUSAL Human Rights Division for the period from 1 February to 30 April 1993.* A/47/968-S/26033 (2 July 1993).

General Assembly. *Proposal for the Immediate Signing of the Agreement on a Firm and Lasting Peace in Guatemala.* A/47/873 (19 January 1993).

General Assembly. *Situation of Human Rights in El Salvador.* A/47/596 (13 November 1992).

General Assembly. *Report of the ONUSAL Human Rights Division for the period from 1 January to 30 April 1992.* A/46/935-s/24066 (5 June 1992).

General Assembly. *The Compressed Negotiations.* A/46/502/Add.1-S/23082/ Add.1 (7 October 1991).

General Assembly. *First Report of the United Nations Observer Mission in El Salvador.* A/45/1055-S/23037 (16 September 1991).

General Assembly. *Agreement on Human Rights Signed at San José, Costa Rica, on 26 July 1990.* A/44/971-S/21541 (16 August 1990).

General Assembly. *Report of the Economic and Social Council: Situation of Human Rights and Fundamental Freedoms in El Salvador.* A/36/608 (28 October 1981).

MINUGUA. *Convenio de Cooperación Técnica entre el Ministerio Público de la Republica de Guatemala y la MINUGUA y el PNUD.* Unpublished document, 1995.

MINUGUA. Unidad de Fortalecimiento Institucional. "Proyecto de Fortalecimiento del Estado Democrático de Derecho en Guatemala (Sumario Ejecutivo)." Unpublished document, 1995.

ONUSAL. *Informe del Grupo Conjunto para la Investigación de Grupos Armados Ilegales con Motivación Política en El Salvador.* San Salvador: ONUSAL, 28 July 1994.

ONUSAL. División de Derechos Humanos. *ONUSAL Como Mecanismo de Verificación Activa en Materia de Derechos Humanos.* San Salvador: ONUSAL, April 1993.

Security Council. *Report of the Secretary-General Containing an Analysis of the Recommendations of the Commission on the Truth.* S/25812/Add.3 (25 May 1993).

Security Council. *Security Council Resolution Concerning the Situation in Central America and the Esquipulas II Agreement.* S/RES/637 (27 July 1989).

The United Nations and El Salvador, 1990–1995. UN Blue Books Series. vol. 4. New York: United Nations Publications, 1995.

Blue Helmets: A Review of United Nations Peace-keeping. New York: United Nations Publications, 1990.

U.S. Government

Department of State. *Country Reports on Human Rights Practices for (. . .).* Washington, D.C. Department of State, annual.

Intelligence Oversight Board. *Report on the Guatemala Review, June 28, 1996.* Washington, D.C.: U.S. Government Printing Office, 1996.

Unpublished Documents, Declassified and Available through the National Security Archive

Central Intelligence Agency. "Arrest of Rightist Coup Plotters." May 1980.

Central Intelligence Agency. "Responsibility of 'Death Squad' Run by Businessman Ricardo Sol Mesa and National Guard Major Denis Moran for Murders of Rodolfo Viera and U.S. citizens Michael Hammer and Mark Pearlman." May 30, 1981.

Central Intelligence Agency. Directorate of Intelligence. "El Salvador: Dealing with Death Squads." January 20, 1984.

Central Intelligence Agency. "El Salvador: Controlling Rightwing Terrorism."
February 1985.

Central Intelligence Agency and Department of State. "Briefing Paper on Right-
Wing Terrorism." October 27, 1983.

Congressional Arms Control and Foreign Policy Caucus Report. "Barriers to
Reform: A Profile of El Salvador's Military Leaders." May 21, 1990.

Department of State. "Cuban Draft Resolution on Human Rights in El Salvador." November 27, 1980.

Department of State. "Millionaires' Murder Inc.?" January 6, 1981.

Department of State. "Assassinations of Four U.S. Religious Persons December
2, 1980." January 16, 1981.

Department of State (cable). "Senate Foreign Relations Committee Questions
on Human Rights Related Topics." September 24, 1982.

Department of State (cable). "Armed Forces Responds to Mrs. Avila's Charge."
October 14, 1982.

Department of State. "Statement by the Minister of Defense of El Salvador,
General Carlos Eugenio Vides Casanova, San Salvador." November 2, 1983.

Department of State. "Thomas R. Pickering, Address before the American
Chamber of Commerce in San Salvador." November 25, 1983.

Department of State. "Investigation of Domestic Support for Violence in El Salvador." December 8, 1983.

Department of State (cable). "Early assessment, Vice President Bush's visit."
December 13, 1983.

Department of State (cable). "Vice President Bush's meetings with Salvadoran
officials." December 14, 1983.

Department of State (cable). "Talk with President Magaña, Bush visit reaction."
December 15, 1983.

Department of State (cable). "Human Rights in El Salvador." June 29, 1988.

Department of State. "Security Force Human Rights Abuses, Part One: Murders." May 2, 1989.

INDEX

China: and Cambodia, 126–28, 132, 135; and human rights pressure, 9–10, 17, 19, 139

Civil Defense Patrols (PAC), 55–57, 63, 69, 106, 114, 119

civil sectors, and peace talks: in El Salvador, 90–91; in Guatemala, 103–5, 107–16, 121–22 (*see also* Assembly of Civil Society)

Clinton, William Jefferson, regional policy, 64, 102, 113, 143

Coalition Government of Democratic Kampuchea (CGDK), 126, 129–30, 132. *See also* Sihanouk, Prince Norodom

Colombia: and human rights system, 9, 138; and peace process, 142–44

Colville of Culross, Viscount, 66–67

Contadora peace process. *See* Esquipulas II

Cristiani, Alfredo, 32, 49–50, 80, 83–84, 90, 99

Cuba: and El Salvador, 36, 43–44, 82, 84; and Guatemala, 58–59; and human rights system, 19

D

D'Aubuisson, Roberto, 34, 39, 43, 49

De León Carpio, Ramiro, 55, 73–75, 107, 109

De Soto, Alvaro, 83–85, 88–91, 96

Death squads. *See* paramilitary organizations

Dodd-Leahy amendment (Bill HR 5114), 32, 82

Duarte, José Napoleón, 29, 31–32, 47–49, 83

E

El Mozote, massacre at, 40, 46–47

Esquipulas II, and Contadora regional peace process, 48, 103–4, 106

F

Farabundo Martí National Liberation Front (FMLN), 25, 35–37, 47–49, 58, 80–92, 99

FUNCINPEC (National United Front for an Independent, Neutral, Peaceful and Cooperative Cambodia), 126, 131. *See also* Sihanouk, Prince Norodom

G

GAM (Mutual Support Group), 68–72

Geneva Conventions. *See* international humanitarian law

Gramajo, Héctor, 65, 104

"group of friends" mechanism: in Cambodian talks, 128; in Guatemalan talks, 107–8, 110, 171; in Salvadoran talks, 83–84, 90

Guatemalan National Revolutionary Unity (URNG), 58–59, 102–16, 121

H

Haiti, and the human rights system, 9, 16, 173

Harkin Amendment. *See* U.S. Department of State: Foreign Assistance Act

human rights ombudsman: in El Salvador, 95–96; in Guatemala, 73–75, 118–19

Hun Sen, 129, 131–33, 136. *See also* Peoples Republic of Kampuchea/State of Cambodia

I

indigenous rights, 69, 112–13

inter-American human rights system, 11, 13, 20; and Argentina, 7, 141–42; and El Salvador, 30, 39, 96; and Guatemala, 52, 57, 61–62

International Committee of the Red Cross, 9, 20, 23; and Argentina,141; and Cambodia, 134; and El Salvador, 48, 86–87; and Guatemala, 60, 64,

International human rights regime, 4–23, 123–24, 137–40, 145; and Argentina, 140, 142; and Cambodia, 132–35; and El Salvador, 30, 43–45, 80, 98–99; and Guatemala, 52, 60–62, 66–67, 121

international humanitarian law, 23–24, 45, 60, 85–87

international reputation, elites' concern for, 8, 15–16, 144, 145; Argentine, 141–42; Cambodian, 125, 130–32; Guatemalan, 52–54, 102, 122; Salvadoran, 29–30, 50, 80, 92

J

Jesuits, assassinations of, 31, 81–83, 92